En~ / + Share

One Footstep at a Time

Tony + Cat

One Footstep at a Time: Our Race Against Early-Onset Alzheimer's Continues © Copyright 2024 by Anthony L. Copeland-Parker

First Printing: June 2024
First Edition

Paperback ISBN: 978-1-955541-46-6
eBook ISBN: 978-1-955541-47-3
Hardcover ISBN: 978-1-955541-48-0
LCCN: 2024911775

Interior and cover design by Ann Aubitz
Photos are the collection of Anthony L. Copeland-Parker, unless otherwise noted.

Published by FuzionPress
1250 E 115th Street
Burnsville, MN 55337
kirkhousepublishers.com
612-781-2815

One Footstep at a time

Our Race Against Early-Onset Alzheimer's Continues

Anthony L. Copeland-Parker

DEDICATION

To Susie Singer Carter and Don Priess with the podcast Love Conquers ALZ. Their goal is to let others know they are not on their own and to help them find the JOY in the journey and that's what they do in their Podcast "Love Conquers Alz". That has been Catherine and I's mantra through the 10-plus years with Early Onset Alzheimer's. They both encouraged me to write this second book since they stressed that I still had vast insights into this disease progression from a male's caregiving perspective.

To ALZ.Authors.com, a global community of authors writing about Alzheimer's and dementia. They strive to raise awareness, reduce stigma, and encourage those whose lives have been touched by dementia through sharing Alzheimer's disease and dementia books, blogs, and stories. They also encouraged me to write this book. A portion of the proceeds from selling both books will be donated to Alzheimer's charities such as ALZ.Authors.com.

TABLE OF CONTENTS

ACKNOWLEDGMENTS

I want to thank Susie Singer Carter, who has tirelessly dedicated her life to Alzheimer's awareness for those of all ages who struggle on this winding and tumultuous road. As an actress, producer, director, and writer, she has allowed millions to see this disease through various lenses.

FOREWORD

By
Susie Singer Carter

Alzheimer's is a stealthy disease. Similar to the villain in a horror film, Alzheimer's makes its presence long before anyone is aware. And like the antagonist's next victim who hears a strange bump in the night but chalks it up to a mischievous cat, we ignore the subtle signs. We brush them off with oh-so-logical excuses. "Everybody forgets!" (That's true.) "She's always been forgetful." (She has.) "I'm just juggling a lot right." (You are.) But deep down inside, we know this time is different.

Ultimately, we turn a corner and are face to face with the ugly truth. We, or someone we love, have fallen prey to a relentless, cruel monster. Although our initial instinct is to run or fight like hell, sooner or later we are forced to accept the fact that we are not going to defeat this enemy.

Our story will not have a happy ending.

Given that fact, what can we do? Turns out… a lot. I mean, truth be told, despite all efforts, everyone's story ends. As a filmmaker, if I was asked to produce a story with these parameters, I would focus on the parts of the story I could control. I would ascertain everything my protagonist can do and lean into those strengths to develop a story that represents a life well lived. A journey that showcases the best life has to offer which would include love, purpose, consistency, and new adventures. One that embraces each and every new normal like we would a new friend.

It's what I did in my short film, My Mom and The Girl, which starred the irrepressibly talented Valerie Harper in her final performance. The film reflected a day in the life of my mother who lived with Alzheimer's for 16 years. The film showcases what it looked like once I learned to lean into my mother's world as opposed to constantly trying to bring her back into the one where she once belonged. I describe the film as a "joyous look at Alzheimer's."

It's also how I describe this book, "One Footstep at a Time, Our Race Against Early-Onset Alzheimer's Continues", written by Anthony L. Copeland-Parker, as well as his first book, "Running All Over the World: Our Race Against Early-Onset Alzheimer's." The first book covers the initial five years of Tony's journey in his new role as caregiver for his Lifetime Partner, Catherine, who was diagnosed with early-onset Alzheimer's at the age of 53. This book proffers the next five years.

I first met Tony when he was a guest on my podcast, Love Conquers Alz. As he described how he was honoring his commitment to support, Cat, in sickness and in health, not only did he debunk the idea that there are no male caregivers, but I also realized he was the living, breathing poster child for the title of our show.

While there is nothing inherently joyous about Alzheimer's, our perspective and approach to the disease can forge some of the most remarkable, rewarding, and, ironically, memorable moments of our lives. That's what Tony has achieved and what he explicitly shares in this inspiring, easy-to-read, and highly informative book. He also imparts step by step how he has remained fluid by leaning into Cat's ever-changing abilities throughout her Alzheimer's Journey. The result is a story that represents a life—make that two—well lived. And that's really all anyone can hope for.

Through their mutual love of running—and each other—Tony holds Cat's hand throughout the Alzheimer's marathon, as they traditionally do every single finish line they cross.

~ Susie Singer Carter, Award-winning filmmaker, actor, podcast producer/ host, and Alzheimer's/caregiver advocate

Projects include: "No Country for Old People", a 2018 Oscar-qualified short film, "My Mom and The Girl", "Bratz the Movie", "Soul Surfer", as well as award-winning podcasts "Love Conquers Alz" and "I Love Lucifer".

CHAPTER 1
I Can't Help Myself
♦ ♦ ♦

"Travel makes one modest. You see what a tiny place
you occupy in the world." ~Gustave Flaubert

I had decided that I would not write to my blog anymore. As always, I could not help myself, so here we are. The writings from my blog made up the first book, Running All Over the World, Our Race Against Early Onset Alzheimer's, and the same will happen once again.

This chapter will be written about what we have been up to since the book ended, with Catherine getting her 50th state done in Rhode Island. She always wanted her last state to be Maine, but with COVID-19, you must be flexible and go with the flow. Timing-wise and finding races that were still being held, it was decided to do Rhode Island last. Two friends with whom we have made several trips with Marathon Tours in the past drove over from Boston to meet us at the finish.

I have to admit that completing a marathon in all 50 states is quite a feat. I thought about doing it myself, but since I still have 8 states left to complete, I decided to let Catherine have that achievement to herself. That will now mean that she has 15 more marathons than me. Her fastest marathon time is 8 minutes faster than mine, and she qualified for the Boston Marathon. You will have to read my first book to find out how I was able to run it myself.

To celebrate this accomplishment, we went to Puerto Vallarta, Mexico, for two weeks and planned to get a half marathon in all 50 states. We have done 23 of them already. After that, we were off to Aruba, where the infection rate is very low, but they still allow tourists on their small island. I must say they do it right. It is quite obvious that during the downtime, they came up with a great plan of action to protect their citizens and all tourists who come for fun in the sun.

I will give a few examples. You can get tested for COVID-19 72 hours before arrival or at the airport. We chose to get tested upon arrival since we did not have enough time between Mexico and Aruba to get tested and get our results back within the time period required. With that said, I was concerned that we would spend hours waiting to get tested. That was further from the truth.

The process was very streamlined, and we were out of the airport door and in the cab 30 minutes after arrival. You were required to download their health application, which helped greatly. It took exactly 6 hours after we arrived for our negative results to be posted. We were quarantined in our room during that period of time, so, when we woke up the next morning, we were free to roam the island.

You also had to buy health insurance for 30 bucks that covered if you got sick while there, with specific instructions on what to do at the first sign of illness. In turn, after answering questions on their site and buying the insurance plus the COVID test, you then get a large green check mark, which means you are allowed on the plane and also once again out the door at the airport and lastly in the hotel.

We stayed at the Marriott Surf Club resort, and they, too, had their act together. Signage and arrows everywhere letting you know exactly what to do while on the property, and I could see they take this virus very seriously. They opened back up in July and kept most staff on the payroll so they could make the modifications needed to open back up safely.

One day, we made our way to the Super Foods grocery store, and they took the virus extremely seriously and required everyone entering to have a cart. The thought there was to limit the number of people in the store to actual shoppers. They also had monitors to ensure everyone followed the store's flow patterns, including wearing masks while there. I liked that grocery store for one very important reason. Since I no longer drink alcohol but love the taste of cold beer, they had at least a dozen varieties of non-alcoholic beer. What made it so special was that they were sold as singles, which meant I could get a great sampling of what they had to offer.

I was wondering why most grocery stores on the island were owned by the Chinese, and with the help of the web, I learned that the first Chinese family came to Aruba when the Lago oil refinery opened in the late 20s. Most of them came from Trinidad and Tobago at that time and started with grocery stores. The tourism development in the 80s brought new Chinese to the island, and most of them have been involved in Supermarkets, Chinese restaurants, and, for the past couple of years, even in hardware. However, other than Columbians, the Chinese are not Aruba's biggest group of immigrants.

The two official languages are Dutch and the predominant national language, Papiamento, which is classified as a Creole language. This Creole language is formed primarily from 16th-century Portuguese and several other languages. Spanish and English are also spoken. Islanders can often speak four or more languages.

Most of the restaurants had outdoor dining options. Temperature checks were taken before seating, and you had to give them information about where you were staying, including room number, for contact tracing. As Catherine and I have traveled the USA during these unprecedented times, it was nice to see constant messaging on controlling the virus.

We rented a car for several days and noticed that the only stop light on the island was being replaced with another of the hundreds of roundabouts. It sure keeps traffic flowing, but you must be on your toes while driving here. We went to the island's other, very rocky side, and visited Airlock Natural Park. I was drawn to the windmill farm. We could walk right up to the 10 windmills, which was my first.

We have spent Thanksgiving in various ways and places during our travels. The traditional family get-together is at Catherine's mom's house, Barb's, with 20 of us crowded around the dinner tables. One year, we went to Boston Market for takeout and ate the scrumptious meal back in the Motor Home while we were in Florida. This year, we went up to the California Lighthouse, named after the ship, that came aground in the area. The Italian restaurant, Faro Blanco, had great food offerings but a lack of luster sunset. I hate when clouds come out of nowhere right as the sun says goodbye for the day.

It was not so easy getting off the island. Maybe because we did not want to go. On one of the local channels, it talked about being at the airport 3 hours prior. I have been doing two hours recently but decided I did not want to be one of those people they mentioned that get left. But at the same time, we had to take one more walk along the snow-white sand of Baby Beach, so I split the difference and got to the airport two hours and 30-ish minutes before departure.

You cleared US customs in Aruba, and the last time I had that happen in Canada, we had to run to the gate to make the flight. After immigration, the security line was unbelievable. It turns out they are shoes, belts, hats, computers, and gels out-of-your-bags type people—no TSA pre-check or Clear there. Every time we got close to the one X-ray machine, they had four available. They would call passengers for one of the flights that was about to leave, and a dozen folks jumped ahead of everyone. I carry many supplements in my carry-on, which they go through each baggie with a fine-tooth comb. The security team kept asking each other if it was okay to have so many. This happened once in Puerto Rico with the agricultural folks, and after 15 minutes, they let me go through.

It was security, so they kept checking them for a bomb substance. Next, you had to claim and carry your checked bags through US customs. We had global entry, so we went to the kiosk to do our thing. I helped Catherine first and then myself. By then, the customs agent from afar commented that something must be wrong. I replied that it was working fine, and she replied, "It must not since it has been taking you 10 minutes." I am very good at this; it took 30 seconds a piece at most. I got my slip and walked up to her when she said. "You realize that global entry is a privilege, not a right." I replied, "Yes, ma'am." She then told me that when she tells me something to do, I am to do it right away without the back talk of it is working fine. She continued, "We are using new face recognition, and with the mask and hat, it probably was not working." However, it worked fine, and we handed her our slips. She reminded me I should pay her more respect next time, and I apologized. She asked if I had any of the prohibited items; she rattled off one by one, and I answered no to each. She then told me to go through the lane, where I dragged our bags to a belt to drop them off.

I saw others getting the full bag search, so I was glad I kept my mouth shut, and the lady did not send us that way. Now, on to US security, so once again, everything is off and out. Catherine is pretty good at airports but needs constant direction, so by then, I was a bit frazzled, to say the least. When we reached the gate after Catherine went to the bathroom, they boarded our flight, and we taxied out 15 minutes early.

I have been through a lot of airports, but this was screwed up. They call this place the happy island. Not so much outbound. It would pay dividends if they had all four security lanes open so we could have spent some more money on the island at some of the shops and restaurants in the gate area.

After two weeks there, we were back in Atlanta for a few days with a 4-month follow-up appointment with the Integrated Memory Center for Catherine. Speaking of which, she is doing well. I have referred to her illness as a sine wave. Some days are better than others, but unfortunately, she is still slightly declining overall.

After Atlanta, to find someplace warmish to hide out from COVID-19, we went to Myrtle Beach, SC, for three weeks, which took us to right after Christmas, then on to our first half marathon for 2021 outside of Houston. While in Myrtle Beach, we got in some great runs or walks along the beach since the weather was mostly in the high 50s to mid-60s.

We stayed once again at another Marriott Vacation Club villa called Ocean Watch at Grand Dunes. It turns out they were practically giving away weeks there due to COVID-19 and the off-season. They also took extra care with their COVID precautions. Catherine and I decided to get tested for COVID once a month, as a local TV commercial suggested. The nearby CVS had you swab your noses at the drive-thru lane and were once again able to get our negative results 3 days later. I must admit it was a bit un-nerving to stick a swab that far up your nose for 15 seconds per nostril.

We got a lot of miles in while in South Carolina, and the mid-50s temps made it very enjoyable. I love to do something I have never done before. Since I have slowed down over the years, you have to find those first-time events when it comes to running when you can. The beach here is not as slanted as you will find elsewhere, so we went for a 6-mile out-and-back run along the beach; the previous longest distance on a beach was 4 miles. Since it was later in the day, the sand was well-packed, and it overall felt great, the crashing waves made it an outstanding experience.

In the time column, it sounded like a good idea. We ran the 9.5 miles from our villa to the airport to pick up a car for a few days. All was going well as we ran along Ocean Boulevard when a clump of concrete grabbed my foot, and I took a spill around mile 8. Of course, I dusted myself off and continued with the run, but I must say I am still sore and healing up a scuffed-up right knee three days later. All that does not kill you makes you stronger.

We found a nearby track and were able to do some quarter-mile track repeats, which I have not done in many years. I could run each quarter mile a bit faster over the 4 miles. That was a really good mental boost since I was still healing from my spill.

We are off to Texas to start our new goal of running a half marathon in all 50 states on January 1, 2021. I think that will be a great way to start the year. This will take me back to a race we often ran in Louisville, Kentucky. We would do the New Year's Day 10 miler each year, where many would dress up, which we did again for this race.

Puerto Vallarta, Mexico
November 5, 2020

CHAPTER 2
Women's Running Magazine Article
♦ ♦ ♦

"This Couple Races Around the World, Fighting Alzheimer's Along the Way." ~Julianne Mcshane

When Catherine Popp was diagnosed with Alzheimer's at age 53, her partner quit his job so they could make the most of their time together by traveling and running.

Earlier this November 2021, Christie Popp, 42, went on a four-mile run with her mother, Catherine Popp, 60, and Popp's partner, Anthony "Tony" Copeland-Parker, 66. It was on a trail near her Bloomington, Indiana, home, and the weather was perfect: 50 degrees, no wind, no clouds in the sky. It was the first time the mother and daughter had run together in six years. It was also the first time in a long time that Catherine could recall memories of running with Christie when she was in college.

In 2014, Catherine was diagnosed with early-onset Alzheimer's, a less common form of memory loss that affects people younger than age 65, according to the Mayo Clinic; it affects about five to six percent of people with Alzheimer's overall. An estimated 6.2 million Americans age 65 or older live with Alzheimer's, and almost two-thirds are women, according to the Alzheimer's Association.

During their recent run, the mother and daughter reminisced about how Christie would wake up at 4 a.m., just as her mother would arrive home from her night shift as a scheduler at UPS, and the pair would head out together for marathon training. "It was kind of nice to have a real conversation with her again," Christie says. "We don't get to talk like that much anymore."

Tony has to help Catherine get dressed and undressed, take showers, and find her way around, he says. She struggles to answer questions and engage in conversation. But running "seems to be one of those things that is so deeply ingrained in who she is that it's like second nature to her," says Christie.

"She has such trouble functioning in so many ways, but she can still run, which is amazing," she says. Over the course of her decades spent running, Catherine has completed 83 marathons. Tony has run 68—including 16 since he had open-heart surgery in June 2014, just a few months after Catherine received her diagnosis.

Since then, the couple has sought to make the most of the time they have by running and traveling the globe: they've completed 60 marathons and half marathons and visited 82 countries, running at least a half marathon in 35 of those countries. They're constantly traveling, making pit stops at a storage unit in Atlanta every few months to leave their marathon medals and grab new clothes. They fill their calendar with plane rides to races ranging from 5Ks to half marathons. Tony chronicles the couples' adventures on a blog, which served as inspiration for his book, *Running All Over The World: Our Race Against Early-Onset Alzheimer's*.

Their lifestyle "takes us away from the day-to-day tasks and trials and tribulations of Catherine's disease and takes my mind off thinking whether my heart's going to stop," Tony says.

They prefer to focus on the challenges that they can control, he adds, rather than the ones they can't.

The couple met in 2000 at a 5K race in Louisville, Kentucky, Tony says. Before the race began, Tony overheard Catherine "talking about the fact that she had already run several marathons and that her goal was to run a marathon in all 50 states." (She completed this goal last October, with the Ocean State Rhode Race Marathon in Narragansett, Rhode Island, Tony says.)

Having run track and cross-country in high school, Catherine became a marathoner, using training in part to cope with the loss of her husband, Rick, who had died of lung cancer after only one year of marriage.

That day at the race, Tony approached Catherine with a request: would she help him train for the New York City Marathon? She agreed—with the caveat that once he finished his first marathon, he'd want to keep going. "I just thought I was going to do one marathon and be done with it, but Catherine explained to me that's not the way it works," he says.

They ran New York City together that fall, finishing in about four and a half hours. When Tony hit the wall around mile 18, Catherine helped him push through. "What will your kids think if you don't finish?" he recalls her asking. "She ended up using that as motivation to keep me going."

After they crossed the finish line, Catherine's prediction proved true: Tony wanted to run another marathon, but not for the reason she expected.

"I had become enamored by Catherine during our training," he says. "I started thinking, 'OK, I guess I could manage to do another one if that means I get to see you.'"

Their relationship developed slowly, during training runs and races, as Tony juggled a separation and parenting his three kids.

"We were kind of using running and races to kindle the relationship," he says. "She used running as a way for her to cope with the loss of her husband, and she instilled that in me to use running to cope with my separation."

She still has that grit, he says. "She refuses to give up. I see it now with her Alzheimer's."

"We'll keep doing it." Tony started noticing changes in Catherine's cognitive functioning in 2013, when she would repeat herself, ask questions about something he had just explained, and take far longer than usual to complete basic tasks, like balancing her checkbook.

The diagnosis of early-onset Alzheimer's or "a like condition" followed in April 2014. (An Alzheimer's diagnosis can only be confirmed through an autopsy.) The diagnosis "gave her some peace of mind," Tony says, by offering an explanation for what she was going through and, therefore, a path forward. For her family, though, it came as a blow.

"It was just a shock to learn that Cathy had started to experience the loss of memory at such an early age," says her sister, Teri Popp, 64. For Christie, the diagnosis meant that her adult relationship with her mother would no longer unfold as she had imagined it would. "I always assumed that she would be there and be a young grandma, so it was a really sad shock to have her taken away in a way that she's physically there but not mentally there," she says.

Tony, for his part, worried about whether he'd be able to fully recover from his June 2014 open heart surgery, which followed doctors' 2012 discovery that he had a leaky aortic valve, to be able to resume running with Catherine—and taking care of her. "My concern was, I'm not going to be able to [run] anymore, and we're not going to have that bond we've had all these years," he says.

To say he recovered would be an understatement: he ran the Berlin Marathon, his 53rd, 108 days after his surgery. In December of that year, he resigned from his job as a commercial management pilot at UPS, and they sold their Indiana condo.

Given their love for both running and travel, their plan seemed like the perfect way to live the fullest lives they could, Tony says. And studies show that consistent exercise (and running in particular) can reduce the risk of dying from Alzheimer's disease. Among the highlights of their travels have included half marathons in Antarctica, Bhutan, and Madagascar. Many of their trips have been with Marathon Tours, a company that hosts expeditions to international races. Its president, Jeff Adams, calls their relationship "an amazing love story," he says. "His patience just never wavers," Adams says of Tony.

Tony's book chronicles their travels and runs and tells of how he developed a sense of patience on their travels (in part, by running the Berlin Marathon following his surgery) as a former self-described "type 'A' personality," along with tender moments the pair have shared—including finishing 55 marathons hand-in-hand, and lessons they've learned along the way. "I wanted to have something to refer back to to say, 'Look where we were last week," Tony says of the book.

But he's also planning for the future. In January, the couple plans to run several races in Costa Rica. And Tony's setting new goals for the pair to tackle together, including running half marathons in all 50 states (they have eight to go) and 50 countries (they've already checked off 35).

In other words, they don't plan to settle down anytime soon. "As long as she's able to enjoy what's going on," he says of Catherine, "we'll keep doing it."

CHAPTER 3

The Road to Recovery

♦ ♦ ♦

Recovery-noun
A return to a normal state of health, mind, or strength.

Our favorite commercial is a straightforward advertisement for ALZ.org. They talk about their belief that the first person who will be cured of this dreaded disease is alive today. We both feel Catherine is that person. For that to be the case, though, we must preserve what she can do as long as possible. I'm sure the initial cure will be for a specific subset of sufferers. We want to make sure she is part of that subset.

Finding a cure has been my relentless quest over the last seven years. My personality type prevents me from giving up. It might have to do with my struggles in life. I have never been tested, but I have all the markers for someone with dyslexia or a similar learning disability. As a child, I had tutors and was asked to leave the University of Pennsylvania because of poor grades. That is a nice way to say I flunked out.

I found my passion in aviation and excelled in that field because it fits my brain. You go to class in the morning and then get on a plane in the afternoon and apply what you previously learned in the morning prior. I taped my classes and listened to them repeatedly while I worked the night shift cleaning parking lots around Tulsa, Oklahoma.

I found because of my learning disability, I had to hear and apply the knowledge for it to remain in my brain. A known fact is that pilots are well-suited for those who have dyslexia. I must admit reading back complex instructions from air traffic control was not easy. For example, UPS 1273 turn left to heading 360, climb and maintain flight Level 230, and contact New York center on 123.45. Good day.

The pilot not flying would have to repeat word and number for word and number. When it got really busy at some high-density airports, instructions were coming in rapid fire. As the captain, I learned it was best to say to my first officer that I got the airplane; you get the radios. I found it was easier for me to do rather than read back the instructions. That was my workaround.

My point here is threefold. I never gave up, I always figured out a solution to a problem and I probably understand brain problems better than most. Over time, I have devised many workarounds for Catherine. As time went on during her decline, I would always modify what would work best for her.

Our nomadic lifestyle is an example. Instead of living a routine lifestyle, we instead exercise her brain in various ways daily. As she puts it. "I keep moving her cheese." She also gets intensive exercise, which exercises her brain. We see something new and exciting as often as possible. I also ensure she gets plenty of sleep, which removes the deposits of beta-amyloid protein fragments (plaques) and tau protein strands (tangles) that form in her brain, causing nerve cell damage.

I have often said to others that her decline is not a straight line but more of a sine wave in decline. Some days or weeks are either better or worse than previous days or weeks. Another way to look at it is like a dimmer switch being turned to the left slowly as the lights in her brain dim. Back to the sine wave example, there would be periods when it would brighten for a short period of time.

Unfortunately, in March 2020, while in St. Kitts, some of the very negative aspects of Alzheimer's started to take hold. The ones I will reference here are delusions, sundowning, uncooperative, and aggressive behaviors. Repetitive tasks were also a very real problem. Lastly, she was not sure who I was and how I fit into her life.

Covid was in full swing, so isolation was also a factor in her accelerated decline. At this point, I was considering getting a place to live and closing down our running all over the world attributes of our lifestyle, thus giving up on her getting her final marathon for all 50 states.

As time went on, it got worse, and the decline accelerated. Over the years, I have tried many different supplements and was now contemplating giving her a prescribed psychotic medication to help her possibly. I had promised her I would not do that, but my options were becoming limited. It is a known fact that these psychotic medications accelerate the progression of the disease.

I had scheduled a trip to the West Coast in June, so now I was thinking maybe I should cancel that trip and stay put. With Covid, cancellation fees were all being waived, so I was back to thinking we should just settle down.

I had researched everything I could get my hands on. Years earlier, I even watched a 7-day, 2-hour-a-day presentation that talked about curing those with Alzheimer's. It is a recode protocol developed by Dale E. Bredesen, M.D., in his book The End of Alzheimer's. The premise is that the amyloid beta plaques and tau tangles that develop in the brains of Alzheimer's patients are a perfectly normal response to an attack on the brain, so his protocol involves finding the underlying cause of those attacks.

Once the harmful identities are determined, a doctor develops a diet and prescribes appropriate vitamins and minerals. Bredesen's book had gotten mixed reviews. I was rapidly concluding that this disease would not be defeated with a single pill.

Sometime in May, I ran across another 1-hour presentation from Doctor Julia Lundstrom with Simple Smart Science. She talked in great detail about brain inflammation, which I had heard about previously, so I was now very curious about what she thought would help. She did have a few supplements that her company was selling, but near the end, she mentioned something called Mind Restore by Awakened Alchemy.

The name itself got me very interested, and after looking into what they wrote about its benefits, I figured out what did I have to lose. Mind Restore is a nighttime nootropic that nourishes your brain while you sleep, so you wake up better rested and with a stronger and healthier brain. It blends 9 clinically studied all-natural premium nootropic compounds, amino acids, neuro-vitamins, and adaptogenic herbs to promote restorative sleep, improve memory, improve mood, boost neuroplasticity, and support brain and nerve health.

It has a combination of supplements that I have tried in the past but not in combination. You take it at night, and it aids sleep, which I have discussed previously, and nourishes the brain while you sleep. With any new drug or supplement, I phased it into her routine, with me also taking it for any side effects. 3 times a week, half the dosage for the first week. 4 days a week, the second week, then 7 days a week, still at half the dosage, then back to three days at the recommended dosage, and so on.

Catherine has a brother, Larry, who was on temporary assignment in San Fransisco, so maybe seeing him and his family would help. So off we went to the West Coast, and the road to recovery, in my mind, began. It was just like flipping a switch. After a month, her delusions were gone. She stopped doing repetitive actions, no sundowning and started to tell me she loved me regularly.

Right after that, we had an Integrated Memory Center appointment, and I told them about her improvement and showed them what was in the supplement. Our nurse practitioner recognized the components but, like me, had not heard of a supplement with all the components in one pill.

Nootropics: smart drugs and cognitive enhancers are drugs, supplements, and other substances that are claimed to improve cognitive function, particularly executive functions, memory, creativity, or motivation, in healthy individuals. While many substances are purported to improve cognition, research is at a preliminary stage as of 2021, and the effects of most of these agents are not fully determined.

They also have a downloadable PDF that details the science of this product's various components. The one that caught my eye was what they had to say about Acetylcholine. That takes me back to our Mind Set clinical trial days in 2015. The thought was to find a way to increase acetylcholine. Acetylcholine is a vital chemical in the brain that helps with cognition and performing daily tasks.

This product has supplements that naturally increase levels of Acetylcholine. We had much success with the clinical trial, but that drug RVT 101, Intepirdine, did not go to market because it did not get the levels of improvement it had hoped.

I have been in discussions with a representative of Awakened Alchemy, and he stated that they could not make any claims about their products and improvements for those with Alzheimer's because they decided not to spend the millions necessary to satisfy

FDA requirements. 42% of their products are sold to those 65 plus, which is understandable since most diagnosed with Alzheimer's are in that age group. However, it is never too early for you younger folks in the majority group to get the edge. You might need to hold off those senior moments.

I figure it took many years for her to decline. She was diagnosed 7 years ago this April; however, I noticed something was wrong at least one year prior. Some studies suggest that it could be 10 years or more before a person could first be affected, but they can compensate so that no one knows about their ailment. So, going back to my dimmer switch analogy, it might take just that long for the brightness in her brain to be turned up to full brightness.

Only time will tell, but that is okay with us. Yes, I do have to help her with everyday tasks, but as long as she appreciates everything I do for her. She Cooperates when I try to help and tells me that she loves me regularly. I can live like this for the rest of my life. It reminds me of something the doctor who developed both RVT 101 and Donepezil, which she has been taking for 7 years, once said. I paraphrase: In about 5 years, we will find a drug that will eliminate Alzheimer's, and people will simply die from something else.

In the meantime, Catherine and I are listening to an audible book called 100 Days to a Younger Brain, Maximize Your Memory, Boost Your Brain Health, and Defy Dementia by Sabina Brennan, Ph.D. Catherine found this book in paperback while we were in a bookstore in Bloomington. This was the first time she had asked to read a book in several years. Unfortunately, she still cannot read it herself, so I got the audible version. It does talk about dementia-related diseases and how to keep them at bay. It also gives some helpful advice that anyone can use.

It confirmed that our lifestyle has given Catherine many years of quality life. It hit all the points concerning sleep, exercise, diet, and seeing and doing new and exciting activities. She talks about the importance of journaling your day and has exercises to do daily. Catherine cannot do so by herself, but our workaround is for her to tell me how she feels each day, and I put that word for word in the memo section of her phone.

I also found a Phase 2 Clinical Trial in Atlanta called ACT-AD. This trial is evaluating if a new investigational drug (ATH-1017) is safe and effective in improving symptoms of mild to moderate Alzheimer's disease. ATH-1017 is designed to boost and repair regenerative pathways for brain cells, promoting brain health and function. ATH-1017 represents a new approach to treating Alzheimer's disease, potentially targeting the root cause of memory decline by repairing brain cells and rebuilding brain networks.

We had our 4-month follow-up exam at the Integrated Memory Center, and our nurse practitioner, which Catherine loves, suggested that we try a speech therapist to increase her abilities. Also, she gave us the names of several adult day programs. We did find an organization called Fox Rehabilitation that does in-home or hotel services in the areas of memory, cognition, and speech therapy. They have offices both in Atlanta and parts of Indiana.

Returning to my opening paragraph, I aim to have Catherine be one of those folks. As of yet, I can not declare I have found a cure, but at least the road to recovery seems much brighter than it was 8 months ago, and for us, that is okay.

CHAPTER 4
In Pursuit of a Half Marathon in All Fifty States
♦ ♦ ♦

"The most important thing in life is to stop saying 'I wish' and start saying 'I will.' Consider nothing impossible, then treat possibilities as probabilities." ~Charles Dickens

With our new goal of running a half marathon in all fifty states, the only thing left is to do it. We started 2021 with our 24th state in Kingwood, Texas. The first thing that comes to mind about this race is the phrase, helter-skelter. Don't get me wrong, the organizers of this event did a great job. It turns out this was their 22nd year, and they were determined not to let COVID-19 stop them from having another great race.

One of the founders of the 50-state Marathon Club, Steven Boone, was there. I got a picture of him with Catherine as he congratulated her. for completing a marathon in all 50 states. He is a running icon in his own right. We have seen him many times during our running adventures all over the world.

Since we were only doing the half, we only had to run through Greentree Park twice on concrete trails, which were only about 6 feet wide in most places. It rained like all get out the entire day prior so there were some water hazards to contend with. Now throw in 500 people passing you and coming in the opposite direction, which we had to dodge just about the entire 13.1 miles. That all made it very hectic, to say the least.

Rick and Lisa, from Catherine's 50th state race in Rhode Island last year, were also there, with Lisa running the marathon. We drove to nearby Houston to meet up with James and Lois from several Marathon and Tours trips for an outdoor socially distant lunch. It turns out Mary, who we know from several Marathon Expeditions trips, also lives nearby. We met up with her and took a tour around her impressive property, dog Buddy and all.

We are now relaxing and, at the same time, training back in South Carolina. This time, it was on Hilton Head Island in another Marriott Vacation Club Villa called Barony Beach Club. I use the term, training, rather loosely since we are not necessarily trying to improve our times for upcoming races. More to stay upright and on our feet as the scenery goes by ever so slowly. When you tour on foot, you can run across the hidden gems you would miss if you were doing so by car.

Surprisingly enough, my right knee and groin injury are doing well after my trip and fall on Christmas day as we ran 9 miles to pick up a car at the airport in Myrtle Beach. They both did hurt a bit during the first part of the race. Who would think that it would be a good idea to run a half marathon that close after the two injuries? For some strange reason, my body seems to respond better when I stay active. I also think being Alcohol Free for the last nine months has something to do with me bouncing back so quickly.

The mid-50s here make it very enjoyable. I plan to do an uncertified, nonvirtual half marathon all along the beach next week or the week after. We will be here till the end of the month. I like doing a few laps in the outdoor heated saltwater pool after running along the beach or on the asphalt paths that connect the many parks in the area. That would include the stationary bike in the extremely sanitized fitness center. The indoor hot tub is the icing on the cake.

The planning continues for the upcoming spring racing season as we prepare for a race in Tennessee in the latter part of February, New Mexico and Louisiana in March, and Utah in June. I am sure we will find a few more races, thus states, for April and May.

We will mostly do small races in out-of-the-way cities, which is good since we have done all the major city races as marathons. As an example, the one we did in Maine last year and New Mexico this year the races are held by Mainly Marathons. They have various length races as a series. In other words, you can run several races in different states over a week. So far, we are not in that good of a shape, so we only do one of the races in their series at this point.

Speaking of Marathons, I am thinking of doing two more before I turn 70 in 3.5 years. That would be 70 marathons by 70. That will also give Catherine 85 marathons. It would be great to find two outrageous marathons between now and then.

Some people might wonder how we feed ourselves since we have not had a home and, most times, a kitchen in over 6 years. The simple answer is that you have to be flexible. When we first started, most meals were either in a Marriott Executive lounge or a nearby restaurant. Some were on cruise ships or provided by various tours we have been on.

With us moving every 3 to 4 days, it is difficult for us to cook even in a hotel with kitchen facilities. How does one buy all the supplies needed when cooking? Right after Covid hit, we did stay put for several weeks at a time. We then had to shift to folks like Grub Hub to have dinners delivered and, at the same time, go to the grocery store for breakfast items.

Even when staying at a Marriott hotel, we have not found any that have opened back up their executive lounges. Now we have to buy all of our meals. We typically only eat two meals daily unless on a tour or cruise. Now, there are no tours or cruises on the horizon. As time passed, we started to order food on Grub Hub, but we would go pick it up ourselves. I got tired of watching our meals go to several other stops before coming to us.

We also transitioned to a meal delivery service called Freshly. They can send you as many days of dinners as you desire. They only required a microwave for 3 minutes for each meal. The other service that I like somewhat better is Sun Basket. The change there is that you can order prepared meals like Freshly. You can also order a few meals, for which they send all the ingredients and cooking-for-dummies instructions.

Luke Lobster also does a great job sending flash frozen lobster, and there is also the reliable frozen pizza or rotisserie chicken. The chicken makes for two great meals. We often grab a side for the first day, then a chicken noodle soup, adding the leftover chicken.

I have to laugh because when my kids were growing up, they knew dinner was nearly done. They would hear the microwave ding going off every few minutes as I heated leftovers on Fridays. Back then, my go-to cooked meal was either on the grill or Stouffer's baked lasagna. I now do a pretty good tin foiled grilled salmon with mushrooms and peppers.

I got a text from our friend about a delivery service called GoldBelly. They will ship some of America's greatest iconic foods. We still have not eaten inside a restaurant since COVID-19. I am not sure when I will feel comfortable enough to do so.

We did it, which I often do when I put my mind to it. In this case, it was to run a half marathon distance all along the beach. While here, I charted out the course we would use, and today was the day to do it. It was our first time running that long all along a beach. We have run on a beach before, all over the world. This was by far the furthest simply because the beaches here are very level, and if you start in the morning, there is plenty of hard-packed sand to run on.

It went off without a hitch. We went right first out and back for a total of 3 miles. Then, left for a total of another 6 miles. Then, go back to the right 3 miles and another 1.1 miles to the left. We felt great the entire way with temps in the low 50s with little wind. We finished it with a dip into the indoor hot tub to soothe the few sore spots. I like doing things I have never done before. I have noticed that the list is getting shorter and shorter as I get older.

I often have a New Year's resolution, but most of them have to do with improving my body. This year, I picked one that will improve my mind. They say you can only control your attitude, so I settled on PMA, Positive Mental Attitude. This is what it means to me.

I will always have a Positive Mental Attitude through Gratitude. All self-destructive tendencies – pity, anger, selfishness, & resentment will not be tolerated. All negativity, hurt, and discouragement will be avoided. I will always maintain my Positive Mental Attitude under pressure. I will keep Charles Dickens's quote above close to my heart if I should ever struggle.

Since we did a half marathon without getting a medal, I figured, why not do a Tony-style Triathlon? We first started with 12 miles on a stationary bike in the fitness center. The second leg was on the beach for a rather windy 4-mile run. The last leg was somewhere around a 1/4-mile swim in the outdoor heated pool. Once again, there was no medal or T-shirt. We are enjoying the rather moderate temperatures here on HHI, as the locals call it.

In years past, we have spent the winters in the hot, steamy Caribbean. It is much easier to run in these temperatures. In the heat, I have convinced myself that you do not have to run as fast or as far to stay in shape. Here, we must wear a few extra layers of clothes instead of just a T-shirt and shorts like in the Caribbean.

We leave here in a few days and will be getting back to our usual 3-4 days per stop routine. It has been fun to take a breather for the last 26 days. From here, we are returning to ATL for our first COVID-19 vaccine shot. While there, we will catch up with my daughter, Mariah. She just announced that she is expecting her first child. I am so very excited to give her and Dad a big hug.

Kingwood, Texas
January 1, 2021

CHAPTER 5
Finishing Together

♦ ♦ ♦

"When you run alone, you run fast, but when you run together, you run far." ~Zambian Proverb

This picture was taken back in May 2016 in Prague, Czech Republic. We were on one of the many Marathon Tours and Travel trips. Catherine and I now always run together and finish hand in hand. We have done at least 55 marathons where we have crossed the finish line hand in hand. Hundreds of other length races, we have done the same.

Early on, Catherine was much faster and in better shape than me, so she would hang back with the old man to make sure I would make it to the finish. One of her famous sayings is that you should never leave your wingman. Now that she somewhat struggles to stay on course while running our races, it is my turn not to leave my wing woman.

Over the years, we have met many couples who are both runners; however, they do not run races or even train, let alone finish together. I suggest all of you out there give it a try one day. Some say it would drive them crazy to run as slow as their partner. Or there was no way they could keep up with their jackrabbit. Still, there are some couples where only one of the two still runs, and the other one plays the support role. Sadly, even a few are out there on their own since running is not their partner's passion.

To each their own. I must say it gives me great joy each time we cross the finish line hand in hand. I remember one race in Colorado where the announcer said that all couples finishing together had to hug their mate and kiss at the finish. We were more than happy to do so. In Las Vegas, I witnessed one man kneel at the finish and ask his partner to marry him.

Not only do we run together, but we have been joined at the hip 24/7 ever since we began running all over the world 8-plus years ago. I would not change anything. It has been a joy to help her along in her journey. I always tell Catherine that she is one lucky lady since I am the perfect partner in this situation. My mother, whom I cared for in the last nine years of her life, taught me the golden rule well. Do on to others as you would want them to do on to you. I am sure if the tables were turned, she would be right by my side, helping me to achieve my goals.

We decided early on to tackle Early-onset Alzheimer's as a team effort. As we all know, no one will win this race in particular or life in general. No one knows how and when it will end, but we will go down swinging for the fence. We are always looking for opportunities to do things we enjoy doing together.

Here are stories from two couples we have met during our many group trips. Each came about running with their partner a bit differently than Catherine and I, but as you will read, they each have come to enjoy the miles they have done together.

Though Paul and I, (Susan), have been running for thirty-plus years, we haven't always run together because of family constraints. When we made the decision to travel and run destination races, we started running with people from all over the world including Tony and Catherine. It was during this period that we realized it was more enjoyable and meaningful to share the experience "running together" rather than race to the finish line alone. We love to capture scenery along our runs by taking photos and fondly sharing our memories as well as others.

After years of running destination races, we made running together a priority in our daily runs as well. This just made sense to us because we do most things together and have for the 45 years of our marriage. The end result was that it is much easier to stay motivated and committed when you have your best friend and soulmate as your running partner.

Running fast, achieving PRs, and winning races isn't important to us, but finishing upright and "together" is our goal.

Tom and I, (Fran), have been running the marathon distance or longer for over 20 years but it is rare that we run "together". Initially, Tom ran so much faster than me which would result in some very impressive times. I, on the other hand, embraced a run/walk strategy, which would result in some very nice photos of the racecourse. One exception was my first marathon, NYC, in 2001, when Tom ran by my side, stride for stride. I believe that generous gesture helped me to enjoy the race and inspired me to do another and another and over 300 more!

Eventually, we crossed over into the ultra-world and I became obsessed with a race called The Last Annual Vol State 500k. In 2018 I ran that race "screwed", with no crew or support, and after I finished, I rambled on and on about the incredible experiences I had during the 9+ day event. I guess my stories inspired Tom, so in 2019 and 2021, we completed the race together. Step by step for 314 miles! It made the experience even richer than the previous year. We could encourage each other and help one another avoid the "dark" times that occur in these races.

In late July 2022, we experienced a real gut punch. Tom was diagnosed with colon cancer. The operation was successful at removing all traces of the cancer, and his rehabilitation began. We had been planning to run the Loch Ness Marathon in October 2022. There was no question that we would do it together. It was now my turn to run by Tom's side, step by step, in his return to marathoning. We covered the 26.2 miles together and crossed the finish line hand in hand full of joy and gratefulness.

CHAPTER 6

Younger Next Year

♦ ♦ ♦

"Exercise six days a week for the rest of your life."
~Doctor Henry S. Lodge

This chapter is partially about a book, Younger Next Year, which I am presently listening to on Audible. It is the second time I am listening to it, which I usually don't do. This philosophy is something Catherine and I have been living by ever since she was diagnosed with Early Onset Alzheimer's and my recovery from Open Heart Surgery, both back in 2014.

On our last cruise in February 2020, we met a couple on the Windstar Cruise Line in the Caribbean. David recommended the book since he and his wife, Sue, who were also in great shape, thought we could benefit from the thought process behind the book. We usually exercise any day we can and only take travel days off. Even then, we get our 10,000 steps in while waiting for our flights.

Dr. Henry Lodge provides the science. Chris Crowley provides the motivation. Through their New York Times bestselling program, you'll discover how to put off 70 percent of the normal problems of aging—weakness, sore joints, bad balance—and eliminate 50 percent of serious illness and injury. Plus, prominent neurologist Allan Hamilton now explains how following "Harry's Rules" for diet, exercise, and staying emotionally connected directly affects your brain—all the way down to the cellular level. The message is simple: Learn to train for the next third of your life, and you'll have a ball.

We listen to parts of it several times a day and really enjoy their irreverent sense of humor. I highly recommend this book for those of you who are still trying to figure out how to get the best out of the last third of your life.

As we were running all over the world, dealing with physical, logistical, and financial issues, sometimes I couldn't help asking myself, "Is this really helping Catherine?"

Before I answer that question, here's some context. According to the Alzheimer's Association, more than 6 million people over the age of 65 in the United States live with Alzheimer's disease, a figure that is expected to balloon to almost 13 million by 2050. Alzheimer's doesn't just cause dementia: It kills more Americans than breast cancer and prostate cancer combined. Since 2000, deaths from the biggest killer, heart disease, have gone down 7.8 percent, while deaths from Alzheimer's have gone up 146 percent.

One in three seniors dies from Alzheimer's disease and other forms of dementia. Experts have been looking for ways to prevent all forms of dementia, including Alzheimer's. Currently, there is no cure. Research into this subject has become more pressing as America's population is aging rapidly. More than 10,000 people turn 65 years old each day. The risk of developing dementia rises with age. About 5 to 8 percent of people over age 60 have a form of dementia, says the World Health Organization. During the pandemic, Alzheimer's disease and other dementia-related deaths rose 16 percent. The risk of developing dementia rises with age.

Many people think of Alzheimer's as genetic bad luck, but scientists have also been studying associations between Alzheimer's and a variety of lifestyle choices. In the report, "Dementia and Risk Reduction: An Analysis of Protective and Modifiable Factors," Alzheimer's Disease International identified four categories of risk factors: developmental, psychological, lifestyle, and cardiovascular—all of which have been repeatedly linked to Alzheimer's.

Most doctors and nurses who treat Alzheimer's patients now believe that common-sense lifestyle adjustments can help people avoid the disease or slow its progression. As Robert Roca, Vice President of Medical Affairs at Baltimore's Sheppard Pratt Health System, said in an interview with the Woman's Brain Health Initiative, "The good news is that if you take simple steps that are beneficial for your overall health, you can reduce your risk."

We've all seen the PSAs about quitting smoking and the ads telling us to eat this or that "heart-healthy" food. Partly because we know less about it, there has been less public education about Alzheimer's. As it turns out, some of the same choices and habits that protect against heart disease (including regular exercise) also protect against Alzheimer's.

When it comes to treating the symptoms of Alzheimer's, there are five FDA-approved drugs. Unfortunately, according to Robert Stern, director of the clinical core at Boston University's Alzheimer Center, "Medications can bring about some improvement for some people some of the time, but they don't modify the course of the disease." In fact, according to David Bennett, director of the Alzheimer's Disease Center at the Rush University Medical School, "The best current tool involves not taking medication but building up resilience."

Bennett said that people who get more education early in life have a greater amount of "cognitive reserve"—a technical term for various cognitive skills—which can help them compensate for the damage to their brains. No matter how educated someone is, they can improve their resilience by learning new skills. In an article for Scientific American Mind called "Banking Against Alzheimer's," Bennett wrote steps that we can all take to age-proof our brains to make them more resistant to dementia: remaining socially and intellectually active, achieving goals that we set for ourselves, and even helping others. I would say that our nomadic lifestyle forces us to do all those things.

It's hard to say exactly how much benefit Catherine got from our constant flow of new experiences, but Yaakov Stern, a professor of neuropsychology at Columbia University's Taub Institute for Research on Alzheimer's Disease and the Aging Brain, who has published several papers on cognitive reserve, has said that "…experiences acquired over a lifetime can stave off dementia—often for several years."

What's easier to say is the benefit she got from regular cardiovascular exercise. Aerobic exercise protects against Alzheimer's through its impact on the heart, but it can also slow down the deterioration of the brain. In a neuro-imaging study published in the Annals of the New York Academy of Sciences in 2007, Bonita L. Marks, a professor in the Department of Exercise and Sport Science at the University of North Carolina at Chapel Hill, showed that greater aerobic fitness was associated with more white matter integrity in several regions of the brain. A 2016 paper published in Alzheimer's Dementia, by Dane Cook, professor of kinesiology at the University of Wisconsin at Madison showed that regular physical activity can protect against temporal lobe atrophy.

What does "regular physical activity" mean? One book I read called Cured has an entire section on Alzheimer's and exercise. It turns out that merely exercising several times a week is not enough. It's great to get your ten thousand steps a day but to reap the true benefits; you need to participate in intensive exercise for at least thirty minutes at least four times a week. Other articles I have read recommended an hour at least six days a week.

The science behind the need for this much exercise is complicated, but the bottom line is that you need to get your heart rate up, sweat, and be worn out when you're finished. They say that it reduces the inflammation in the brain, which they feel is the root of the problem. As time passed, I read more and more about inflammation, and I adjusted Catherine's supplements to help with that issue.

Your brain isn't actually a muscle. It's an organ that plays a huge role in controlling muscles throughout your body. Even though the brain is not a muscle, we all know the effects of inflammation on our joints and muscles.

Physical activity is very important for several reasons – including that it helps protect the structure and function of our brain as we age. This may be key in reducing the risk of developing certain neurodegenerative conditions, such as Alzheimer's disease.

Though researchers have known about the protective effect of exercise for many years, exactly why it has this effect on the brain has remained a mystery. However, a recent study published in the Journal of Neuroscience might shed some light on this puzzle. According to its findings, physical activity alters the activity of the brain's immune cells, which lowers inflammation in the brain.

The brain contains a class of special immune cells known as microglia, which constantly survey the brain tissue for damage or infection and clear away debris or dying cells. Microglia also help direct the production of new neurons (nerve cells in the brain that communicate and send messages to other cells) via a process called neurogenesis, which is linked with learning and memory.

But in order for microglia to step up and do their job, they need to switch from a resting state to an activated state. Signals from pathogens (such as a virus) or from damaged cells will activate the microglia. This changes their shape and causes them to produce pro-inflammatory molecules – allowing them to resolve and repair damage or infection.

However, microglia can also be inappropriately activated as we age, causing chronic brain inflammation and impairing neurogenesis. This inflammation has been suggested as a reason why brain function often declines with age, and these changes can be even worse in the case of neurodegenerative conditions such as Alzheimer's.

But recently, we've shown that exercise can reprogram these microglia in the aged brain. Exercise was shown to make the microglia more energy efficient and capable of counteracting neuro-inflammatory changes that impair brain function. Exercise can also modulate neuro-inflammation in degenerative conditions like Alzheimer's disease and multiple sclerosis. This shows us the effects of physical activity on immune function may be an important target for therapy and disease prevention.

Studies in laboratory mice and rats have shown that exercise can counteract some of the damaging effects of microglial activation. But this latest study has revealed for the first time a link between physical activity, reduced microglial activation, and better cognitive function in the human brain.

The study's researchers looked at 167 men and women who participated in the Rush Memory and Aging Project. This is a long-term project at Rush University in Chicago that seeks to identify factors that contribute to brain health in older people. Participants completed annual assessments of their physical activity, which was monitored by a wearable activity tracker, alongside assessments of their cognitive function and motor performance (such as muscle strength and walking speed).

Participants also donated their brains for post-mortem analysis as part of the study. This allowed the researchers to analyze the brain tissue for evidence of activated microglia, and for signs of disease in the brain — such as unhealthy blood vessels, or the presence of plaques containing the protein beta-amyloid (a hallmark of Alzheimer's disease). The researchers also looked at the levels of synaptic proteins in participants' brains. Synapses are the tiny junctions between nerve cells where information is transmitted, so the levels of these give a broad indication of healthy brain function.

On average, the participants were 86 years old when their physical activity began to be monitored and around 90 years old when they died. About a third of the participants had no cognitive impairment, a third had mild cognitive impairment, and a third had been diagnosed with dementia.

However, post-mortem analysis revealed that around 60% of participants had signs of Alzheimer's disease in the brain (such as amyloid plaques). This shows that the presence of typical signs of Alzheimer's disease doesn't necessarily mean a person will show major symptoms of cognitive impairment while they're alive.

More than half of participants showed signs of Alzheimer's in the brain, such as amyloid plaques. Unsurprisingly, the younger the participants, the more physically active they were and the better their motor function. Overall, being more physically active was associated with lower microglial activation in certain brain regions (such as the inferior temporal gyrus, which is involved in memory and recall), which are typically affected early on when Alzheimer's begins developing.

This was true even when signs of Alzheimer's were present in the brain. This suggests that physical activity can reduce the damaging effects of inflammation in the brain — even when a disease has already started to develop. The study also showed that more microglial activation was linked with greater cognitive decline and lower synaptic protein levels.

Not only do these findings indicate that inflammation in the brain can significantly affect cognitive function, and maybe a risk factor in developing Alzheimer's disease, but they also show that physical activity may help us to develop resilience in the brain to effects that would otherwise be damaging.

While these findings are promising, there are some limitations to the study. Post-mortem analysis can only reveal one single snapshot in time of the status of the brain. This means that we can't tell exactly when signs of disease developed in participants' brains – and at what point physical activity could have made a difference.

The study was also only observational, meaning it observed changes in participants going about their lives – as opposed to an interventional study in which different people would be randomly assigned to two different groups where some exercised, and some did not. We therefore cannot conclude with certainty that physical activity directly caused the observed changes in brain tissue and cognitive function. These findings also don't explain the mechanism by which exercise induces these effects.

But this study still adds weight to the growing body of evidence that physical activity can protect brain health and function – even into old age. Being active throughout our lives is likely to give us the best chance of preventing Alzheimer's and other neurodegenerative conditions from developing, helping us to live long, healthy, and independent lives.

Researchers are investigating ways to help improve cognitive function and potentially decrease dementia risk. Now a new study, published in the Journal of Applied Physiology, has found evidence that one year of aerobic exercise training improved cardiorespiratory fitness, cerebral blood flow regulation, and memory function in people with mild cognitive impairment.

Moderate to vigorous-intensity aerobic exercise may benefit adults with mild cognitive impairment, according to a new study by researchers at the University of Texas Southwestern Medical Center. Finding ways to help people with mild cognition is important to potentially combat rising cases of Alzheimer's disease and other forms of dementia.

"Aerobic exercise is essential for improving both vascular function and brain function," said Rong Zhang, Ph.D., a professor of neurology at the University of Texas Southwestern Medical Center, a research scientist at Texas Health Presbyterian Hospital in Dallas, and the study's principal investigator. "The brain is a unique organ. It needs constant blood flow and oxygen supply."

While this study didn't look at combating Alzheimer's disease directly, it looked at helping people with mild cognitive impairment. Mild cognitive impairment has been shown to increase the risk of developing dementia caused by Alzheimer's disease or other neurological conditions.

For this study, researchers observed 37 people ages 55 to 80 with mild cognitive impairment. These adults were observed over a 12-month period. For the first 10 weeks of the study, these subjects participated in three exercise sessions a week that included brisk walking for 25 to 30 minutes, according to Tsubasa Tomoto, Ph.D., the paper's lead author and a post-doctoral fellow at the Institute for Exercise and Environmental Medicine at Texas Health Presbyterian and the University of Texas Southwestern.

At the beginning of the study, the subjects participated in three brisk walking exercise sessions each week for 25 to 30 minutes. Beginning in week 11, they exercised 4 times a week, walking briskly uphill for 30 to 35 minutes per session. After week 26, exercise sessions increased to 4 to 5 times a week for 30 to 40 minutes.

Researchers found that vigorous exercise was associated

with a host of benefits for people with mild cognitive impairment. They not only improved their cerebral blood flow regulation and cardiorespiratory fitness but they also their memory and executive function.

"While we don't have any effective treatment for Alzheimer's yet, prevention is the most important key," at this time, said Tomoto. "We are focused on mild cognitive dysfunction. There is some research that suggests that if you do intervention, you could have some hope in reducing Alzheimer's. That's why we focused on this population. If you could exercise, it could improve vascular function and may lead to cognitive improvement."

Dr. Santosh Kesari, Ph.D., a neurologist, neuroscientist, and neuro-oncologist, said there has been some evidence suggesting a connection between exercise and reducing the risk of Alzheimer's. "It's an interesting study," said Kesari, director of neuro-oncology at Providence Saint John's Health Center in Santa Monica, California. "It validates the fact that exercise can improve cardiovascular and brain function in a fairly short period of time. It's not revolutionary, but this is a good study in the sense that it documents this in a different way."

Benjamin Bikman, Ph.D., an associate professor of cell biology and physiology at Brigham Young University, added that research around Alzheimer's disease is changing, even examining if Alzheimer's disease is a metabolic disorder affected by insulin.

"The brain is an energy hog, with among the highest metabolic demands of any tissue in the body," Bikman explained. "In order for the brain to get all the energy it needs, the hormone insulin must be able to do its job. Insulin, among many roles, opens glucose doors into parts of the brain involved in memory and learning, helping those brain cells get all the glucose they need to function." "Exercise has many beneficial effects, but among the most relevant with Alzheimer's disease is that it drastically improves insulin sensitivity, allowing insulin to work better in the body and allow more glucose to feed the hungry brain," Bikman explained. "While we should certainly [do] mental exercises to keep our brain sharp, such as studying a new language and learning a new instrument, this shouldn't replace whole-body exercise, which helps the myriad metabolic functions in the body, including the brain, run optimally."

Kesari said the potential implications of this study and others like it are massive. "Simply exercising could improve your brain function in the long run, and it's good for you at the end of the day. The health economic implications are huge. It could reduce severe dementia in the long run and reduce healthcare costs.

A slightly fading memory is not unusual as you grow older, but dementia is so much more than that. It's not a normal part of aging. There are some things you can do to lower your risk of developing dementia or at least slow it down. But because some causes are outside your control, you can't totally prevent it.

A 2019 study showed that aerobic exercise may slow atrophy in the hippocampus, the part of the brain that controls memory. Another 2019 study revealed that active older adults tend to hold on to cognitive abilities better than those who are less active. This was the case even for participants who had brain lesions or biomarkers linked to dementia.

Regular exercise is also good for weight control, circulation, heart health, and mood, all of which could affect your dementia risk. If you have a serious health condition, talk to your doctor before starting a new exercise regimen. And if you haven't exercised in a while, start small, maybe just 15 minutes a day. Choose easy exercises and build up from there. Work your way up to:

- 150 minutes a week of moderate aerobics, such as brisk walking or

- 75 minutes a week of more intense activity, such as jogging.

Twice a week, add some resistance activities to work your muscles, such as push-ups, sit-ups, or lifting weights. Some sports, like tennis, can provide resistance training and aerobics at the same time. Find something you enjoy and have fun with it. Try not to spend too much time sitting or lying down during the day. Make movement a priority every day.

Dementia is a group of symptoms affecting memory and other cognitive functions. The top cause of dementia is Alzheimer's disease, followed by vascular dementia. Some types of dementia are due to things you can't change. But lifestyle choices that include regular exercise, a balanced diet, and mental engagement can help lower your risk of developing dementia.

Regular exercise changes the structure of our bodies' tissues in obvious ways, such as reducing the size of fat stores and increasing muscle mass. Less visible, but perhaps even more important, is the profound influence exercise has on the structure of our brains – an influence that can protect and preserve brain health and function throughout life. In fact, some experts believe that the human brain may depend on regular physical activity to function optimally throughout our lifetime.

Here are just a few ways exercise changes the structure of our brain. Many studies suggest that exercise can help protect our memory as we age. This is because exercise has been shown to prevent the loss of total brain volume (which can lead to lower cognitive function), as well as preventing shrinkage in specific brain regions associated with memory. For example, one magnetic resonance imaging (MRI) scan study revealed that in older adults, six months of exercise training increases brain volume.

Another study showed that shrinkage of the hippocampus (a brain region essential for learning and memory) in older people can be reversed by regular walking. This change was accompanied by improved memory function and an increase of the protein brain-derived neurotrophic factor (BDNF) in the bloodstream. BDNF is essential for healthy cognitive function due to its roles in cell survival, plasticity (the brain's ability to change and adapt from experience), and function. Positive links between exercise, BDNF, and memory have been widely investigated and have been demonstrated in young adults and older people.

BDNF is also one of several proteins linked with adult neurogenesis, the brain's ability to modify its structure by developing new neurons throughout adulthood. Neurogenesis occurs only in very few brain regions – one of which is the hippocampus – and thus may be a central mechanism involved in learning and memory. Regular physical activity may protect memory in the long term by inducing neurogenesis via BDNF.

While this link between exercise, BDNF, neurogenesis, and memory is very well described in animal models, experimental and ethical constraints mean that its importance to human brain function is not quite so clear. Nevertheless, exercise-induced neurogenesis is being actively researched as a potential therapy for neurological and psychiatric disorders, such as Alzheimer's disease, Parkinson's disease, and depression.

The brain is highly dependent on blood flow, receiving approximately 15% of the body's entire supply – despite being only 2-3% of our body's total mass. This is because our nervous tissues need a constant supply of oxygen to function and survive. When neurons become more active, blood flow in the region where these neurons are located increases to meet demand. As such, maintaining a healthy brain depends on maintaining a healthy network of blood vessels.

Regular exercise increases the growth of new blood vessels in the brain regions where neurogenesis occurs, providing the increased blood supply that supports the development of these new neurons. Exercise also improves the health and function of existing blood vessels, ensuring that brain tissue consistently receives adequate blood supply to meet its needs and preserve its function.

A team led by researchers from Massachusetts General Hospital says it might have found evidence suggesting Irisin-based therapies could help combat Alzheimer's disease. Irisin is a muscle-derived hormone that increases in the body following exercise. It regulates glucose and lipid metabolism in fat tissue and increases energy expenditure by accelerating the browning of white fat tissue. Studies have shown Irisin is present in human and mouse brains, but its levels are reduced in people with Alzheimer's as well as in mouse models of Alzheimer's.

The team involved in the latest study, which was published today, September 8, 2023, in the journal Neuron, have previously developed the first 3D human cell culture models of Alzheimer's disease that display two major hallmarks of the condition: the generation of amyloid beta deposits (plaques) and neurofibrillary degeneration (tangles) of the protein tau found in brain cells (neurons).

In their new study, researchers said physical exercise has been shown to reduce amyloid beta deposits in various mouse models of Alzheimer's, but the mechanisms involved have remained a mystery. They used the same model to investigate whether exercise-induced increased levels of Irisin affect amyloid beta pathology.

To test whether Irisin plays a causal role in the link between exercise and reduced amyloid beta, Se Hoon Choi, Ph.D., and Eun Hee Kim, Ph.D., both researchers at the Genetics and Aging Research Unit at Massachusetts General Hospital, along with their colleagues, applied Irisin to their 3D cell culture model of Alzheimer's.

"First, we found that Irisin treatment led to a remarkable reduction of amyloid beta pathology," said Choi in a press release. "Second, we showed this effect of Irisin was attributable to increased Neprilysin activity, owing to increased levels of Neprilysin secreted from cells in the brain called astrocytes." Neprilysin is an amyloid beta–degrading enzyme that is elevated in the brains of mice with Alzheimer's that were exposed to exercise or other conditions leading to reduced amyloid beta.

The researchers uncovered more details about the mechanisms behind Irisin's link to reduced amyloid beta levels. For example, they identified a receptor that Irisin binds to, triggering the cells to increase neprilysin levels. They also discovered Irisin's binding to this receptor causes reduced signaling of pathways involving two key proteins: extracellular signal-regulated kinase (ERK) and signal activator of transcription 3 (STAT3).

Reducing the signaling of ERK and STAT3 is critical for Irisin to enhance Neprilysin, which fights the brain-damaging amyloid beta. Previous studies have shown Irisin injected into the bloodstream of mice can make its way into the brain, creating a new pathway for targeted therapies. "Our findings indicate that Irisin is a major mediator of exercise-induced increases in Neprilysin levels leading to reduced amyloid beta burden, suggesting a new target pathway for therapies aimed at the prevention and treatment of Alzheimer's disease," said Rudolph Tanzi, a senior author of the study and director of the Genetics and Aging Research Unit at Massachusetts General.

Ryan Glatt, a senior brain health coach and director of the FitBrain Program at Pacific Neuroscience Institute in California, told Medical News Today the research is still in the early stages, and there's much more work to be done. "Prior studies in adult humans have demonstrated increased levels of Irisin as the result of exercise, particularly resistance training, which may mediate some of the benefits of exercise on brain health," Glatt said. "The exact mechanisms require further elucidation, so studies like these can get us closer to that understanding. More human research is needed, and future studies could compare the mediating effects of Irisin in comparison to other growth factors, such as insulin-like growth factor-1 (IGF-1) and brain-derived neurotrophic factor (BDNF).

Glatt added that future research should also seek to clarify what modes of exercise (i.e., aerobic versus resistance training) as well as what intensities and what durations lead to in terms of the concentration of certain Myokines such as Irisin. "The responses from adults who are cognitively healthy in comparison to those with existing cognitive impairment needs further research, and the cognitive outcomes as the result of the expression of Myokines, such as Irisin, need to be better understood," Glatt said.

Nick Voci is a doctor of physical therapy at Manchester Physical Therapy in Vermont. Voci told Medical News Today that he works with many people who have Alzheimer's for various health issues, such as decreased activity tolerance, balance deficits, and/or decreased strength. "While this may be big news as to the 'why' exercise helps, in the physical therapy world, this just adds to the growing evidence of why we need to continue to promote physical therapy, as well as activity and exercise in general," Voci said. He added the study may lead doctors to try finding medications to mimic the effect of exercise without actually requiring physical activity.

"While this research shows promising results, a lot more research would be needed to show how much of an impact it would make on people with Alzheimer's and how much would be needed for a preventive effect," Voci said. "But I would argue that this gives more evidence to the broad spectrum of what exercise can treat. Exercise is medicine."

Finally, regular exercise can prevent, and even treat, hypertension (high blood pressure), which is a risk factor for the development of dementia. Exercise works in multiple ways to enhance the health and function of blood vessels in the brain.

With these studies and information at hand, I decided to couple our desire to run races with new and exciting experiences through travel and tours. That lent itself to many opportunities to socialize with like-minded individuals.

Since I'm not doing a clinical trial, I can't give a scientific answer as to whether running all over the world helps, but it certainly doesn't hurt. Our travels, coupled with our exercise routine, had given us the ability to run marathons in the past and now other various race distances. It will allow us to continue this lifestyle as long as feasible. It satisfies Catherine's desire to regularly exercise, compete in races, and see new sites.

It definitely wears her out so she can get plenty of sleep, which is highly recommended for people with Alzheimer's. More on sleep in a later chapter. The time horizon for the progression of the disease depends on so many factors, so I felt it was crucial for us to tackle this as a team effort.

CHAPTER 7

Spring is in the air

♦ ♦ ♦

"Spring is the best life coach: It gives you all the energy you want, all the positive thoughts you wish, and all the boldness you need!" ~Mehmet Murat Ildan

This means it is time for the spring racing season for Catherine and me. It was a tough winter, but we could run outside all but 2 weeks of it when we paused in the Louisville, Kentucky, area. Previously, we have been in the Caribbean, but you do what you must do when COVID is in the air.

The first stop is to a little town of Cookeville, Tennessee, about 80 miles east of Nashville. There, we got the state of Tennessee accomplished. This is state number 25 in our new quest to run a half marathon in all 50 states. I figure it will take us until the end of 2023. Catherine often says, "What else do we have to do."

Cummins Falls State Park Half Marathon, this race had it all. The first stop was the drive-thru packet pickup. A gentleman wished us luck, and I replied, "Luck has nothing to do with it; it takes pure skill and determination." His reply was classic for the time. "Lucky you weren't here last week; we had an ice storm and no power." With on-and-off rain in the forecast, I would have to agree.

For dinner the night before, we met up in the hotel breakfast area to meet up with some new and old friends. Lois Berkowitz, the president and newsletter editor of the 50 State Marathon club, drove over from Michigan for her 4th crack at the marathon. She already has some 400 marathons under her feet. Not bad for a 72-year-old. She is working on the spring newsletter, featuring Catherine's 50-state finish while fighting the good fight with Early Onset Alzheimer's.

In Lois's own words, 50 State Marathon Club Profiles, Cathy Popp & Tony Copeland-Parker. Catherine began marathoning at age 36 and has been marathoning for 23 years. She has completed 83 marathons plus one ultra. She completed her 50 states on 10/25/20 at Narragansett, RI. Her marathon personal record, PR, was at Louisville in 2002, a 3:49:15, and her personal worst, PW, was at Casper in 2019, a 6:12:22. Her ultra was the JFK 50 miler, completed in 11:41:55. Catherine started swimming at age 6 and was on her high school swim team. She used to ride a bike and has completed numerous triathlons.

Tony has completed 68 marathons. He has put the plan to finish on hold while running with Catherine. Tony has also completed one ultra, the JFK with Catherine. Tony ran track in high school before he gained his full height. He did not do sports regularly. Tony's daughter completed two marathons with him when she was 17. Tony says he started running marathons because he "did not want to be one of those dads yelling from the sidelines who couldn't run a mile themselves—so I trained anywhere my sons' soccer games were." He coached his daughter in soccer until she entered high school.

Numbers: Tony loves numbers; he did the JFK 50 Miler when he turned 50. When he turned 55, the two ran from their condo

27.5 miles out and then back the next day for a total of 55 miles. At age 60, Tony did his 60th marathon at the Medoc Marathon in France. He did 65 marathons prior to age 65 and now has a total of 68. He thinks about going back to make it 70 before he turns 70.

Tony and Cathy have run in 35 countries outside the U.S. Most of their international marathons were with Marathon Tours and Travel, but Tony selected many based on where they were in the world at the time (He traveled as a commercial pilot). Tony has been working on completing all 50 states but had a bad experience in Wyoming in 2018 with back problems, which took over 6 hours to finish, and various knee problems. He decided to focus on the states Catherine needed.

The additional 8 states he needed, the two completed as half marathons. He says, "I decided also to let that be one more thing she has over me—her fastest marathon time is 8 minutes faster than mine, and she qualified for Boston in 2012 at the inaugural Louisville Marathon, whereas I went the charity route, sort of. She has 15 more marathons than me, but we have crossed the finish of 55 marathons hand in hand." Tony added that all of their travels, races, and tours give Catherine plenty of opportunity to socialize, which helps retard the progress of Alzheimer's.

Running Stories: In 2010, they attended the 2500th running of the Athens Marathon. The race was a bit tough, with boring switchbacks. They finished in just under 5 hours. Everyone dressed up for the race, with the highlight being the finish at the coliseum. Around mile 20, Tony had noticed that they would finish just short of 5 hours. He grabbed her by the hand, and they sprinted.

The picture at the finish shows her completely airborne! "Catherine is a dog lover, and they were everywhere. Many suppliers brought their dogs and left them there. The government had them fixed, and the society took care of all the strays until their death. You would see people stopping and feeding them every-where."

Running Stories: One small problem they have when running together is that someone will pass them on the course; if it is a woman, Catherine will often try to chase after that woman and drop Tony. Tony had open heart surgery in 2014 to replace a faulty aortic valve and has been slowing down. Tony and Catherine's new shared goal is to do a half marathon in all 50 states, with 24 states already completed.

He is planning the rest now, and they hope to complete it in 2022. "Unlike many couples, we always train and race together, and no matter who is having a good day or a bad day, we stay together the entire time. We are side by side 24/7. I am the perfect person for Catherine during this ailment. I cared for my Mom in her last 9 years, and she taught me how to care for others."

As stated earlier, Tony is retired after 37 years as a manage-ment pilot for UPS and Catherine was a scheduling officer with the Transportation Security Administration, TSA, After their re-tirement, they sold their home, and since have been running all over the world.

Lisa, who was with us back in October for Catherine's 50th state in Rhode Island, had nothing else better to do, so why not add to her 260-plus marathon total? She was flanked by B-Rod, who is no slacker with over 300 marathons. One day, I will do one of my unscientific studies on why people like them do so many marathons.

The rain on race day was on and off for us, but they kept it interesting with HILLS, HILLS, and more HILLS. At the 4-mile marker, the half split off from the Marathon, and we went through a field for a half mile, then straight up for almost 2 miles on a muddy, leafy, rocky, and extremely steep hill. All that slowed us down a bit, but that was only the beginning. I must have sounded like a freight train, huffing and puffing for the next 4 miles as we climbed and climbed our way to what I thought was to heaven.

We did level off for a few miles, but then there was a part I could have done without. We turned onto a major road with cars going 50-plus miles per hour in both directions with no shoulders. If that was not enough, why not throw in one more steep hill for about 1/2 mile? No one was hurt in the making of this chapter, so all was good. To make it all worthwhile. It was a gorgeous course overall. We both ended up getting 2nd in our respective age groups. There were only 100 of us running the half marathon.

Instead of going straight to Atlanta, why not make an overnight stop in Nashville? As Catherine puts it, "We have to stay somewhere." We have an old friend, Jen, who was a travel coordinator with Marathon Tours. One of our best trips with her was to Prague.

She recently relocated back from Utila, Honduras to Nashville. We visited her in Utila back in 2018. It sounds like she got out just before COVID hit that small island. They did not let anyone on or off the island for almost a year when they went into lockdown. Catherine and I got stuck in St. Kitts for a month in March last year due to Covid.

After Atlanta, we are off to Guymon, Oklahoma, another city I have never heard of. I went to flight school in Tulsa in the late 70s, and we ran the marathon there in 2011. This time around, we will have to fly into Oklahoma City and drive 4 hours each way to get there. I don't like driving much, so knowing me, it will take us all day.

Mainly Marathons held the race at the only park in the city, Thompson Park, and we ran around the lake there, Sunset Lake. The course was set up so that you would run almost all the way around the lake and then reverse course back to the start. Since we were doing the half, that meant 7 times out and back.

The lake was the home of thousands of ducks and geese in all shapes, sizes, and colors. The continual honking, I thought, would have gotten on my nerves. In actuality, it was rather soothing. I gave up early on, trying to avoid their poop on the concrete path. The path was only about 6 feet wide so the 70 of us were back and forth and back and forth with people coming and going. It was not as hectic as the race we ran in Texas on the first of January, but it was pretty darn close.

The premise behind Mainly Marathons is to bring together like-minded serial racers to knock off 5 to 7 states in a row over the course of the week. This particular series was called the Dust Bowl series. We only needed Oklahoma for our quest to get a half marathon in all 50 states. We had also planned on New Mexico, which was canceled due to continual COVID concerns in that state.

One gentleman, Greg, whom we met last year back in Rhode Island when Catherine finished getting her 50th state as a full marathon, was there. He got a trophy for completing 100 marathons, just with Mainly Marathons. He has over 300 in total. Some were out and out racing either against others or against previous times. Most were out there to race against themselves into their own history books. One lady wore a T-shirt proudly stating she had done 500 half marathons.

I did not know it then, but one gentleman who mostly walked but would occasionally break into a slow jog was one short of 1,600 marathons. He did get the 1,600th one done in Ulysses, Kansas, the next day. Henry is in his early 70s, and we went by each other repeatedly. He always had a big grin surrounded by his long grey beard and mustache and would cheer us on.

I tried my best to wrap my head around the fact that at an average pace of 8 hours per race, he has spent much of his adult life on his feet, all while moving forward. Even if he started doing marathons 40 years ago, that would require 40 marathons a year. That can be easily done since Mainly Marathons puts on over 80 races a year.

In May, I am looking at us doing 3 half marathons in a week with us doing one every other day with Mainly Marathons so we can get the states of Nebraska, South Dakota, and Missouri done. I don't think we are ready to do a complete race circuit with them in a week, but you never know—baby steps for now.

There was literally nothing else to do in Guymon, so as many of the folks there do, we went to the local Walmart Super Center. I try to avoid Wally World, as I call them, in our travels and got to see up close and personal how they come into these little towns and become the only place to shop. They had it all and then some. We got everything we needed for our meals for the 3 days there.

I like to recycle while on the road, and the hotel did not have a bin for recyclables, so I looked around town and found none. I did notice that there were no trash cans but just these big tan containers for garbage scattered all over town. That made perfectly good since the wind was 30-35 miles per hour on race day. Garbage cans would not stand a chance in this town. That would also explain why there are no two-story homes.

On the 4-hour, mostly straight, drive back to Oklahoma City, I had to dodge the many tumbleweeds trying to cross the major road out of town. I had to come to a complete stop on this 75 miles and hour-two-lane road when two tumbleweeds joined up. When they got to the middle of the road, they kept going back and forth until the wind won out, and they went on their way across the road like all others.

Guymon was a place I will most definitely not return to, but at the same time, I'm glad we got to experience it. I had to wonder what people do for fun and entertainment there. We could tell that Wally World was probably their biggest employer. I was just glad this small town was willing to let 70 of us serial racers come to town and try to figure out why we do the things we do.

Our next stop is Lafayette, Louisiana, for our third half marathon in three weeks. Back in the spring of 2019, we did 8 races in 9 weeks, so I feel pretty good about getting these done. I look forward to getting back on the road at the pace of moving around every 3 to 4 days like we have been doing for the last 6 years.

The Zydeco Marathon and half marathon were next with a great Lafayette Louisiana race. This was our first race that was held on the streets in a major city since October 2020. It was nice to run on closed streets and not have to loop on paths or on the side of the road with cars racing by.

The flat course was laid out around town, through the University of Louisiana at Lafayette, and some nice neighborhoods. Some folks were sitting in the yards and cheering us on. They tried their best to do a Covid-compliant start to the race. They had spots painted on the street where we were supposed to line up six feet apart, but as soon as the race started, everyone bunched up like it was going to make a difference.

Catherine, Lisa, and I lined up in the back, and we were the last to cross the start line, about 10 minutes behind the 500 of us who laced up for this race. Lisa ran the marathon and was the only one in her age group, and there were only about 50 who ran that distance. I am still trying to figure out why she is on her fifth time around all 50 states.

Covid slowed us down a bit, but we got our second shot in the arm when we came through Atlanta before Tennessee. I don't plan on doing anything much differently regarding masks and eating out. Catherine and I have worn our masks from when we left the current place we are staying in until we return. We have also not eaten indoors at a restaurant over the last year.

We will still wipe down our airplane seats and hotel rooms, and it turns out we have been doing that for 5 years. After the first year of our travels, Catherine and I were getting sicker more often than usual. That all stopped when we started with our cleaning routine and held over when COVID-19 hit.

We both double mask on airplanes and wear eye protectors. Since I flew for over 37 years, I feel pretty comfortable still doing so. We have only been flying on Delta. They do a great job of keeping us all safe as they have updated the air filtration systems on their airplanes. It is a risk-reward situation for me. The minimal risk is well worth the overwhelming reward of getting out there and experiencing all the world has to offer.

Also, while in Atlanta, Catherine and I both participated in separate Alzheimer's studies. Mine involved two MRIs while looking at pictures. I was asked to take pictures of Catherine for ten days and asked to write down what she might be thinking at the time. They will use this information to help caregivers like myself be more empathetic toward their loved ones.

Catherine's study involved her giving blood and saliva so that they could use it from her and others with Alzheimer's to possibly identify something in their blood and saliva to predict Alzheimer's early on. We both got compensated for our time and effort. Catherine had been asking for years to participate in such a study. So she was very happy to help out.

After a few weeks of visiting family back in the Kentuckiana area, as they call it. The next stop will be Carmel, Indiana, for state number 28. Why stop there? So why not a combo trip to Virginia? My middle child, Shawn, took a new job in Harrisonburg. Luckily, there is a half marathon in nearby Charlottesville in the same time frame for our visit to see him and his growing family. He and his wife, Cassie, are due for baby number 2 within two years, at the end of July. Don't worry; I have it on the calendar this time around, especially since I was in Patagonia during the birth of their first child, Lily Ann.

I can't say I like the spring race season better than the fall, but suffice it to say, I am just ready to get out there and see what this old body can still do. Knock on wood, especially since all the parts are in good working order. I went almost two years with a right knee that gave me problems on and off, which started back in September 2017 in Detroit Lakes, Minnesota.

I just want to take a minute to thank everyone for all your support over the years. We have met some great people and refer to many as our new best friends. A few are mentioned by first name in our first book, and still, more will recognize themselves as we run all over the world.

Cookeville, Tennessee
February 27, 2021

CHAPTER 8
Why Do We Do the Things That We Do?

♦   ♦   ♦

"Because we can" ~Catherine Elizabeth Popp

That is always Catherine's answer when I start questioning myself about some of my hair brain schemes. I will put a plan together for a week or a month at a time. Review it with her and then ask myself out loud. "Why do we do the things we do"?

Speaking more broadly. Why does anyone do the things they do? In this respect, I am talking about what I commonly call serial racing. Some reading this know exactly what I am talking about. But for those few others, I will try my best to explain.

If this does not describe you, I am sure you may know someone who always seems to be going somewhere to do a race. Catherine and I had a funny discussion about "racing" the other day. She wanted to know why, when we "race," we are not out there trying to beat someone else, as the term implies. I explained to her that even though she was faster than me, we were a team. I help her stay on course, and she helps me by dragging me along the way. She has the heart, and I have the brains, as it were. We both got a good chuckle out of that.

I am very goal-oriented, and in turn, I set goals to keep her going. I know it must be extremely tough to keep going with the terrible hand she was dealt with, Early Onset Alzheimer's. With a race on the horizon, I hope it gives her something to grasp a hold of that is very good for her. The race increases endorphins, helps wash away the amyloid and tangles, and wears her out to aid in sleep.

I must admit that I tend to think outside the box. I prefer the term counterintuitive. I worked on many projects within Flight Operations at United Parcel Service, UPS, where I would develop policies that were applicable to left-brain, right-brain, and, as I would joke, no-brain thinkers. Right-brain thinkers are more creative, intuitive, artistic, non-verbal, emotional, musical, and imaginative. Left-brain thinkers are more logical, analytical, linear, verbal, factual, and sequential.

I try to be as unique as possible. I believe it might have to do with the fact that I am often pigeonholed into being a basketball player. Being a 6 foot 6 African American might have something to do with it, but the fact that I am athletically built has more to do with it. Because I have lived with that continual question, "Do or did you play basketball." Did, when I was younger and do nowadays.

In actuality, I was a Commercial Management Pilot for over 37 years, a Marathoner, a Blogger, a Podcast guest, an Author, a father, a Care-Partner, and a world-traveling nomad. With those varied experiences, I am always looking for ways to be even more unique to deflect the quick analysis by others that I must have simply played basketball. When asked that question, now my answer depends on the setting and circumstances at the time. Most times, "a long-distance runner." is my answer.

Being in Management as a pilot is also very unique. Most folks become pilots for the sheer love of flying, whereas I saw it as a means to an end. It was a great career, and at the same time, I could schedule my flights around my kid's schedules. I rarely missed any family events, which is highly unusual. Less than 4 percent of all commercial pilots are African American and coupled with being a Manager, the majority of my career was even rarer. During my 27 years at UPS, which is the 9th largest Airline, I had 16 different jobs. I called myself the Jack of all trades and masters of none. Come to find out, there is another line to this famous quote from William Shakespeare. It goes on to say that oftentimes, it is better than a master of one, which in turn is actually a compliment.

All of these experiences served a valuable purpose as I moved through life but must admit being a caregiver for Catherine as nomads was the most rewarding. It gave us experiences that will last a lifetime. As we move along the disease progression, I will continue to look for ways to weave these experiences into our daily lives. At the same time, we look for counterintuitive ways to make our lives as enriching as possible.

With my first book, I would always read portions and show pictures to Catherine to spark that smile I so much fell in love with. I made sure I had it turned into an Audio Book so a hired professional could instill that excitement we once shared as we toured the world, one footstep at a time.

The Guymon, Oklahoma race was a prime example of me asking myself, why do we do the things that we do? Catherine often jokes about a line in our song by the Dave Matthews Band called You and Me. The particular line talks about taking a boat to the end of the world. We both think we have done such when we reflect on destinations like Antarctica and Madagascar. In this case, we were in the middle of nowhere in Guymon, Oklahoma.

It's time for two weekends off to visit with family, and then we will be back at it with 3 races. That will be 3 weekends in a row, starting with Carmel, Indiana, Charlottesville, Virginia, and New-ton, Iowa. The plan is for us to meet up with some of our new best friends and family while there for the particular races. That will take us up to 30 states. I am now projecting us to have the 50 states plus DC all done by the end of spring 2022.

Maybe my next goal will be for me to go back and get my last 8 states done as marathons. That will take me to 76 marathons. I will be ahead of the game for 70 marathons by 70 in 4 years and have me all set for 75 marathons by 75. One of the many great things about Mainly Marathons is that they have a leave-no-run-ner-behind policy. So, as I continue to get older and slower, I won't have to worry about them pulling up the mats like they did in Istanbul, Turkey.

I will continue to ask and try to answer why we do the things we do. I probably will just have to go with what Catherine always says, "because we can."

CHAPTER 9
This Naked Mind

♦ ♦ ♦

"We need to stop asking ourselves if we have a problem with alcohol and start to get curious about how much better our lives could be." ~Annie Grace

To celebrate my 1 year of being Alcohol-Free, AF, as of April 6, 2021, I would like to share my thoughts on this book, This Naked Mind. I shared some in the last chapter of my first book on how we became AF, but I would like to elaborate more in this chapter.

With Catherine's early onset Alzheimer's, I have always thought it would be a good idea for her to stop drinking, but for many years, I could not find it to be a recommendation. Contrary to that, I would run across the benefits of red wine, putting that thought on the back burner. On top of that, when I suggested to her, she would remind me that I would have to join her. That made perfectly good sense to me. I could not ask her to do something I was unwilling to do myself.

So we continued our nomadic lifestyle with her Prosecco or two at dinner and my beer, Jack Daniels and Sprite, or Gin and Tonic right by her side. Some days, the drinks would start right after our late morning runs or walks, but at this point, who is keeping count? I first ran across this book, This Naked Mind, in mid-February 2020. Since I have a subscription with Audible, for a small fee, I get one book a month. I found it a great way to listen to a book while working out or on a plane, train, or automobile. This way, I can kill two birds with one stone.

I was not sold on the idea, so I returned to my one or two-drink habit since they are not easily broken. I noticed that almost everyone we ran across was a drinker, as I put it. Occasionally, you would run across the downright drunks and the few that could hold their liquor. I guess you could call them functional alcoholics.

The people that intrigued me were the folks who would abstain in a social setting. By now, we were back on a Windstar Cruise in the Caribbean, so there were plenty of opportunities to have a few drinks before, during, and after dinner.

Over the years, I remember striking up a conversation with those who abstained from alcohol. I do love to do my unscientific surveys. Some were recovering alcoholics with being AF as their badge of honor. A few just did not get into alcohol, as they would put it. For some strange reason, it did intrigue me. No one touted the benefits, so I just filed it away.

The book dissected the hypothetical pros and the real-life cons of Alcohol. There is a whole chapter where the author goes over the ill effects of Alcohol on every organ of the body, which I found to be fascinating. When I had my yearly cardiology appointment last July, I mentioned to my cardiologist the fact that my blood pressure was now normal and that I no longer needed to take one of the medications he prescribed. He said that made sense since I had stopped drinking. I have to ask myself why no one suggested that I stop drinking instead of just prescribing blood pressure medications.

There also was a chapter on how advertising has tricked us into believing having one or two drinks with dinner is beneficial. They did not need to provide proof to make that claim. No wonder alcohol-related deaths account for 5 percent of all deaths worldwide each year.

The bottom line is that I do remember that there were, in fact, times I could not remember exactly how I got back to wherever we were staying at the time. I am sure some of you know exactly what I am talking about. However, we can all somewhat recall how much fun we had that particular night, so all was good.

Recently, I ran across several articles related to alcohol and Alzheimer's that might be of interest.

Alcohol Consumption Linked to Acceleration of Alzheimer's Disease, Featured Neurology Neuroscience·February 17, 2023

Summary: Even modest consumption of alcohol can accelerate brain atrophy and increase amyloid plaque formation. The findings reveal alcohol consumption can accelerate Alzheimer's disease pathologies.

Source: Wake Forest University

Alzheimer's disease is the most common form of dementia, accounting for 60% to 80% of dementia cases, according to the Alzheimer's Association. While current research suggests alcohol use disorder is a risk factor in Alzheimer's disease, the impact alcohol use disorder has on Alzheimer's disease pathology is an area of continued research.

In a new preclinical study, scientists at Wake Forest University School of Medicine showed that even modest amounts of alcohol can accelerate brain atrophy, which is the loss of brain cells, and increase the number of amyloid plaques, which are the accumulation of toxic proteins in Alzheimer's disease.

The study appears in Neurobiology of Disease.

"These findings suggest alcohol might accelerate the pathological cascade of Alzheimer's disease in its early stages," said Shannon Macauley, Ph.D., associate professor of physiology and pharmacology at Wake Forest University School of Medicine. The study was a collaboration led by Macauley and Jeffrey Weiner, Ph.D., professor of physiology and pharmacology at Wake Forest University School of Medicine, through the medical school's Alzheimer's Disease Research Center and Translational Alcohol Research Center.

Using mouse models of Alzheimer's disease-related pathology, researchers used a 10-week chronic drinking approach where mice were given the choice to drink water or alcohol, mimicking human behavior regarding alcohol consumption. They then explored how voluntary, moderate consumption of alcohol altered healthy brain function and behavior and whether it altered the pathology associated with the early stages of Alzheimer's disease.

The researchers found that alcohol increased brain atrophy and caused an increased number of amyloid plaques, including a greater number of smaller plaques, potentially setting the stage for increased plaque proliferation in later life. Even modest amounts of alcohol can accelerate brain atrophy, which is the loss of brain cells, and increase the number of amyloid plaques, which are the accumulation of toxic proteins in Alzheimer's disease. Interestingly, researchers also noted that acute withdrawal of alcohol increased the levels of amyloid-beta, which is a key component of amyloid plaques that accumulate in Alzheimer's disease.

Further analysis showed that chronic alcohol exposure poorly regulated brain and peripheral metabolism—another way to accelerate Alzheimer's disease pathology. Macauley previously showed that elevated blood sugar increases amyloid-beta and amyloid plaques. In the current study, researchers found that even moderate drinking caused elevations in blood sugar and markers of insulin resistance, which increases the risk not only for Alzheimer's disease but also for other diseases such as type 2 diabetes and cardiovascular disease.

The study also found that moderate alcohol use altered anxiety and dementia-related behaviors. "These preclinical findings suggest that even moderate consumption of alcohol can result in brain injury," Macauley said. "Alcohol consumption may be a modifiable risk factor for Alzheimer's disease and dementia."

About this alcohol consumption and Alzheimer's disease research news. Author: Press Office. Source: Wake Forest University

Ethanol exposure alters Alzheimer 's-related pathology, behavior, and metabolism in mice. Epidemiological studies identified alcohol use disorder (AUD) as a risk factor for Alzheimer's disease (AD), yet there is conflicting evidence on how alcohol use promotes AD pathology. In this study, a 10-week moderate two-bottle choice drinking paradigm was used to identify how chronic ethanol exposure alters amyloid-β (Aβ)-related pathology, metabolism, and behavior.

Ethanol-exposed mice showed increased brain atrophy and an increased number of amyloid plaques. Further analysis revealed that ethanol exposure led to a shift in the distribution of plaque size in the cortex and hippocampus.

Ethanol-exposed mice developed a greater number of smaller plaques, potentially setting the stage for increased plaque proliferation in later life. Ethanol-drinking mice also exhibited deficits in nest building, a metric of self-care, as well as increased locomotor activity and central zone exploration in an open field test. Ethanol exposure also led to a diurnal shift in feeding behavior, which was associated with changes in glucose homeostasis and glucose intolerance.

Complementary in vivo micro-dialysis experiments were used to measure how acute ethanol directly modulates Aβ in the hippocampal interstitial fluid (ISF). Acute ethanol transiently increased hippocampal ISF glucose levels, suggesting that ethanol directly affects cerebral metabolism. Acute ethanol also selectively increased ISF Aβ40, but not ISF Aβ42, levels during withdrawal.

Lastly, chronic ethanol drinking increased N-methyl-d-aspartate receptor (NMDAR) and decreased γ-aminobutyric acid type-A receptor (GABA$_A$R) mRNA levels, indicating a potential hyperexcitable shift in the brain's excitatory/inhibitory (E/I) balance. Collectively, these experiments suggest that ethanol may increase Aβ deposition by disrupting metabolism and the brain's E/I balance.

Furthermore, this study provides evidence that a moderate drinking paradigm culminates in an interaction between alcohol use and AD-related phenotypes with a potentiation of AD-related pathology, behavioral dysfunction, and metabolic impairment.

FAQ: Do symptoms of Alzheimer's get worse when you drink alcohol?

Alcohol and Alzheimer's

Alzheimer's disease is a progressive neurodegenerative disorder that affects memory, thinking, and behavior. While there is no cure for Alzheimer's, individuals with the condition can take steps to manage symptoms and improve quality of life. One factor that can have a significant impact on symptoms is alcohol consumption.

Does drinking alcohol increase your risk of developing Alzheimer's?

When it comes to drinking and Alzheimer's risk, the jury is still out. Alcohol use comes with plenty of other lifestyle factors that can be variables in risk of negative effects on the brain, including the long-term risk of neurodegeneration, and studying the long-term effects of alcohol use in a controlled environment is virtually impossible. So, while study after study shows that chronic drinking is linked to higher dementia risk, other studies have found some alcohol consumption—if not just neutral. Long story short, more research is needed to determine the link between alcohol and brain health definitively.

For people living with Alzheimer's, does alcohol make symptoms worse?

In the meantime, for people already living with Alzheimer's, scientists do have more solid data to go on. While Alzheimer's disease typically progresses through seven stages, every individual with Alzheimer's experiences a different journey, and care plans for people living with Alzheimer's and other forms of dementia should be individualized. That said, research shows that excessive alcohol consumption can worsen symptoms of Alzheimer's disease. Alcohol is toxic to the brain and can lead to brain damage, which can result in a decline in cognitive function, memory, and motor skills.

Further, alcohol can interfere with medications used to treat Alzheimer's, making it harder to manage symptoms. Alcohol consumption can also lead to dehydration, which can exacerbate symptoms of Alzheimer's. Dehydration can cause confusion, fatigue, and difficulty with coordination, which can be especially challenging for individuals with Alzheimer's.

Given the potential negative effects, experts recommend that people living with Alzheimer's avoid alcohol consumption. This can help with the management of Alzheimer's symptoms—and it can improve one's quality of life.

With this information now in hand, I am glad we stopped drinking when we did. At the same time, I wish, for Catherine's sake, I had taken her up on the offer to stop drinking much sooner.

I am not saying this lifestyle, just like putting everything in storage and running all over the world, is for everyone, but if you read or listen to this book, it just might be for you. As I often say, to each their own. In closing, one thing to consider is that just because you decide to be AF does not mean you have or have had a problem. Maybe you will realize like I did, that Alcohol no longer does anything "FOR" you. Also, if you are caring for someone with Alzheimer's, sooner is probably for the better.

CHAPTER 10
Running With Cat

◆ ◆ ◆

"Running Buddies There are friendships that have been forged by dedication and by, pain by defeat and by accomplishment, by mud, and by sweat, by laughter and by tears. Friends who have seen each other when we look our worst, when we look our best when we feel like we could collapse, and when we've won our biggest victory. Friends who encourage us when we want to stop but stick with us when we're about to fall and run beside us not just in races but every day. These are the types of friendships that don't fade with time and don't dwindle with distance. These are Running Buddies." ~Ellen Gass

This will be the third time I have changed the name of my blog. The first one was at blogspot.com, and then, for many years, I have used PlayHard-HaveFun.com. The story behind that name came from the fact I used to tell my kids to simply play hard and have fun at the beginning of their various games. I always wanted them to win, but at the same time, I wanted to keep things in perspective by telling them to play hard and simultaneously have fun, and everything else will take care of itself.

I decided that I needed a more functional website, and since I hired someone to develop it, this would be a good time to change the name. I also did not want to have to explain in great detail for someone to remember. It turns out that PlayHardHaveFun was already bought by someone who was not actually using it but was offering it for sale. So that is why I had to use the hyphen or dash between hard and have. For the life of me, I cannot remember where I heard that phrase before, but I can assure you that I did not think of it all by myself.

I have mentioned several times that, unlike some couples, Catherine and I always run together in training and races and always finish hand in hand. It was not always like that since she is faster than me, but we have found it more enjoyable to share those moments together over the years. Now, it has become more of a necessity due to her Early Onset Alzheimer's, but it is still a very enjoyable experience.

The first thought was to call the website runningwithcatherine.com; however, the name Catherine is more often spelled Katherine, so once again, I would have to explain the name, thus the chance of someone forgetting. Catherine's family calls her Cathy; however, I have always called her Cat, my pet name for her. Some might think I am talking about running with Cats, the animal, but those folks probably would not be interested in what I have to say. So RunningwithCat.com is the new website.

The Carmel Half Marathon signified the official beginning of the spring race season since there were over 3000 participants in the 11th annual race in Carmel, Indiana. The start was a bit chilly and windy for my taste, but we had on the proper layers of clothes, so all was well. The feel-like temperature was in the mid-twenties at the start, and we started and finished with a 15-18 MPH headwind.

We were able to drive up the day before the race to Lafayette, Indiana, and have a home-cooked meal at Mike and Kay's house. It was nice to catch up with them; they are members of "The Band," as we called ourselves. We met on a running cruise ten years prior in the Caribbean. There are two other members, Kim, who lives in Loretto, Mexico, and Debra, who is from Chicago. It turns out we are doing another half in Schaumburg, so hopefully, we will meet Debra, Mike, and Kay there.

The Carmel Half Marathon race itself was not much to write home about, but we got it done. It was not very memorable. We did get to spend some time with Jim and Janet also from several runningcruise.com trips, and the last time we saw them was back in 2018 on a Hawaii cruise.

Charlottesville, Virginia, was the next stop after a touch-and-go in Atlanta for three days. This will be state number 29. The first sentence of the course description for this race is that it is very hilly. No flat and fast here. To keep it interesting, they say half the race is on gravel. I bought some shoe gaiters to keep the rocks out, so I will get to try them out during this race.

We kept with the theme of seeing old friends, acquaintances, and family as we bounced around from race to race. This time, we will see my son Shawn and his family in nearby Harrisonburg, Virginia, the day after the race. The race started and finished at the local favorite winery called Knights's Gambit Vineyards. Since I am now over a year AF Alcohol-Free, I am sure there will not be a temptation to partake. They had free beer at the finish of the last race, and the thought of having some did not even enter my mind.

This was a fantastic race, and I really enjoyed the overcast, slightly foggy weather. In other words, the temperatures were perfect. The rolling hills kept it interesting, and the off-road portion made me very happy to have our shoe gaiters on. It was not as rocky as I had expected, but I am sure without them, I would have had to stop to pull rocks out of my shoes. I only saw one other runner as smart as us with them on.

Since the entire race was foggy, we did not get any spectacular views of the nearby mountains, but we will get plenty on our hour-long drive through the Shenandoah Natural Park to and from Harrisonburg. They had a barbecue truck at the finish. Cat and I scarfed down the perfectly prepared pulled chicken sandwiches, and Cat had her happy face on with the sweet potato fries. The only downside was that we had to park 1/2 mile from the start, but that was no big deal since we were very happy with our finishing time and full bellies for the walk back to the car.

Some people have asked what we do with ourselves for the other 2 or three days when we drop in these towns dotted across the US. First, we go to the nearby grocery store to get the essentials since most hotels nowadays have limited offerings for breakfast and dinner. Depending on when we arrive, we either do the shoe leather express tour of the city or simply unpack and head for bed.

The next day is either packet pickup, finding the start line, or visiting someone we know in the area. We are not big into museums or monuments, but we can't pass up a botanical garden, arboretum, or nearby park. They say the connection with nature is very therapeutic for folks with Alzheimer's. Then there is race day with laundry to follow with nothing else besides dinner from somewhere that caught our eye during our walks or even the race itself. We rarely leave the day after the race, so that gives us a much needed down day, or once again if someone we know lives within an hour, we try our best to make that connection.

Well, here we are in Newton, Iowa, to get state number 30 under our feet. This time, it was a charity run called Run for Her Life put on by the Phoenix Phase Initiative, which is an Iowa-based non-profit dedicated to helping women who have been sexually trafficked around the world. These women are rarely given a chance to escape, and when they do get the chance, they RUN for it! The Phoenix Phase Initiative is there so they have a place to run to where they can be accepted, receive counseling, and learn job skills to break the cycle and create new lives for themselves.

About 50 of us, the total for the 5k and a half marathon, lined up for the 9 am race start around Newton. What a contrast from the last two weeks. Here, we had one cop car block one street, and most times during the half marathon, you had to wonder if you were headed in the right direction. We got to see the entire town up close and even made our way back out to Agnes Patterson Memorial Park, where we went for a walk out there the day before.

Before the park, we did two loops around the high school's very spongy track, and while at the park, we were able to visit the beautiful botanical gardens and past a soccer field where the "we ones" were chasing after the ball. That brought back memories of me getting my miles in while my kids warmed up for their many games or between games.

Cat and I only had five people finish behind us. I know this for a fact since we were dead last at the start, and we only passed 5 people the entire race. That said, I know that we were first in our age groups simply because no one else was as old as we were.

It was suggested that we visit Pella, Iowa, after the race, so off we went to this very quaint Dutch town about 30 miles away after doing the usual laundry. Who knew? There, we found tulips in various stages of bloom everywhere. Simply stated, they were magnificent. The central park area, adorned with its tulips, was adjacent to the tallest working grain windmill in the United States, The Vermeer Windmill.

This town is also home to its annual Tulip Time festival that occurs each May, featuring parades where the community dresses up in authentic Dutch costumes. This also includes where Pella Windows is based. This town is a must-see and experience if you are ever in the area. I have often talked about the benefits for folks with Alzheimer's, and even though we had just run a half marathon, Cat was all smiles the entire time we were there.

Once again, we reunited with some new best friends, Sue and David, from our last Windstar Cruise just before the Pandemic hit in February 2020. They live outside Iowa City, which is only an hour from our hotel. Getting an up-close tour of their 8000-acre farm of corn and grain was a lot of fun. One of their newly purchased huge John Dear, 8 tire, tractor was even very intimidating to me, a former airline pilot. It was great to catch up, but the climate was far different from when we first met in the Caribbean. There were snow flurries and 30-degree weather for our drive back to the airport the next day.

We were back in Atlanta from Iowa for a few days, then to Bloomington and Louisville for the 147th Running of the Kentucky Derby. This was planned some 11 years ago when we figured out that this year's Derby would be on Cat's 60th birthday. She says she was also there when she turned 21, but back then, she did not see a single race. I wonder why.

This is not our first experience with the Derby. When we lived in the area, we would go and experience the follies of the fillies from the infamous infield, but for her birthday, I spared no expense, and we viewed the extravaganza from our seats near the Derby Museum.

CHAPTER 11

Three Half Marathons in Five Days

♦ ♦ ♦

"Have we lost our minds?" ~Tony Copeland-Parker

Cat chuckled while she answered, "Yes." That is how we roll. On the edge of sanity and sometimes, but not very often, over the edge. Not to worry, I have everything under control. Oops, I forgot to book a rental car in Atlanta, and because the travel boom is beginning to heat up, Hertz and others are a bit behind in getting their hundreds of thousands of vehicles back out of storage. No big deal. Mass transportation will be our mode of travel this time around, and I will have to plan better moving forward.

For those of you with Mainly Marathons, this is nothing for you folks. We are doing three races with them every other day with the Prairie Series. Most of them are doing all eight states as Marathons. They have a race for those that want to do a 50K, Marathon, Half Marathon, 10K, and 5K or a combination over the 8 days.

2021 Prairie Series
Series Dates
Sunday, May 9 – Sunday, May 16, 2021
Race Locations

- Days 1 & 2 (Sunday, May 9/Monday, May 10): Brecken-ridge, Minnesota/Wahpeton, North Dakota
- Day 3 (Tuesday, May 11): Baltic, South Dakota
- Day 4 (Wednesday, May 12): Sioux City, Iowa
- Day 5 (Thursday, May 13): South Sioux City, Nebraska
- Day 6 (Friday, May 14): Hiawatha, Kansas
- Day 7 (Saturday, May 15): St. Joseph, Missouri
- Day 8 (Sunday, May 16): Miami, Oklahoma

Once again, the rental car shortage hit me, with Hertz wanting a total of $5,000 for the week, thus discouraging someone from picking up a car in South Dakota and dropping it off in Missouri. So we flew in and out of Kansas City and then drove to South Dakota and then did the races back south to Missouri. Being the driving wimp that I am, I stopped overnight in Omaha on our way north.

Day 1
The first race, for us, was in Baltic South Dakota at River Park; the course description was a gravel path with scenic views of a water-fall. We had to do 11 out and backs, and our Gaiters once again came in handy to keep the gravel out of our shoes.

I was very satisfied with our performance on the first race, but I have to wonder how our bodies will fare moving forward. It was a good idea to take a day off between races, but who knows, maybe one day we will try to do multiple races back to back. I am now starting to see the allure of this type of racing.

Day 3
The second race, once again, for us, was in South Sioux City, Ne-braska, at Crystal Cove Park, and the course description was a wide

concrete path around a lake with moderate shade. We had to do 6 back and forth and around the lake, and it was perfect weather. Lisa and Rick met us there along with two other folks, Marie and Rosa, from our Marathon Tours days. They were doing multiple days back to back as half marathons.

I was shocked at how well our bodies responded to doing another half marathon with only one day off. We cut our time by 8 minutes, which was unexpected. Each mile faster than the one prior. That helps when you start really slow. I also wondered why, when doing a race around a lake, why they don't just go all away around. Now I understand. It is because this allows everyone to interact with others with many taking walking breaks to socialize with their friends or just walk the entire race with them or others as they go by.

We had 222 miles to cover the next day back to St. Joseph, Missouri, for our last race with Mainly Marathons this time around. We will meet up with them again in June on their Independence series in Maryland and New Jersey.

Day 5

The course description was a smooth concrete path along the river with moderate shade at Heritage Baseball Park. Turns out there was about a half-mile section that was packed dirt and gravel with some water and mud hazards from the rain the night before. No big deal; at least it didn't rain during the race. This time, it was 7 laps for us. Little known fact, at least by me. St. Joseph is famous for the Pony Express, and this is where Jesse James lived and died.

We have decided that we like the every other day idea. Especially since we pretty much bring everything we own with us in two 55-pound bags. That makes packing and unpacking every day a bit much. It turns out that in this series, there were two opportunities to stay in one hotel and do two states, but we already had those states.

We might try it when we go and do the Independence series. They do New Jersey, which we are planning on doing, and then New York the next day, so I might have to look at the hotels and see if we can stay in the same hotel and do both states.

This race was once again a negative split, thanks to Denise Sauriol. She suggests that in her book Me, You and 26.2, which I highly recommend. We started, once again, really slow on this race and got faster by the mile, which felt great. Turns out we were only 1 minute slower than the first race. She also suggests that runners not clinch their hands, which I did not realize I have been doing all these years. I think the track work Denise suggests in her book helped us for these races.

We are headed back to Atlanta on Monday, then off to Chicago for the Chicagoland Spring Half Marathon next Saturday, and spend some time with our dear friend, Deborah. They had a lottery for this race in Schaumburg, Illinois, and then you had to verify that you were going to actually run the race. That will be state 34 for us and our 11th half marathon this year.

St. Joseph, Missouri
May 15, 2021

CHAPTER 12

Hot, Hot, Hot!!!

♦ ♦ ♦

"What doesn't kill you, makes you stronger."
~Friedrich Nietzsche

Well, sometimes you get what you ask for. For some time now, I have been complaining about how the temperatures have been bouncing around this spring, with it being 30 one day in one place, then 80 the next day somewhere else. We have run races recently with many layers at the start, with long tights and pants being the standard.

Well, it finally caught up with us with our race in Schaumburg, Illinois. The temperature at the start is predicted to be 84 and 88 by the time we get finished. This race took socially distancing to the extreme, with being assigned start times depending on your predicted pace. So, for us, that was 11:31 am. I guess I should have fudged my pace. Oh well, I am sure we will get it done.

We are not only here to get the state of Illinois done. This will be number 34 with our 12th race this year, but we also want to visit our dear friend, Deborah. We first met her nearly 11 years ago on a running cruise with Marathon Expeditions in Alaska.

It has been 18 months Since we last saw her in Loretto, Mexico, with our fellow "Band" members, Kim, Mike, and Kay. She currently lives in the Oak Park area of Chicago, and she was able to give us a great tour of the Frank Loyd Wright, 1889-1909 homes, and the Unity Temple he built, including his home and now a museum.

Wright's bold design, with its cubist features and use of poured reinforced concrete, broke all the rules of American religious architecture. The all-concrete building was entirely cast here at this site, including the distinctive columns near the top, which support the overhanging roof. The design creates an imposing facade and the concrete muffles street noise.

Unity Temple has been in continuous use since 1908 by the congregation that commissioned it, now a Unitarian Universalist Congregation. It fits right in with the area's all-concrete post office right across the street. In July 2019, Unity Temple, along with seven other Wright buildings, was inscribed as part of the "The 20th Century of Frank Lloyd Wright" UNESCO World Heritage designation, among only 24 sites in the U.S. representing significant cultural and natural value.

Deborah correctly decided not to run with Cat and me, so that meant we were able to be dropped off and picked up right at the start/finish line. We arrived at 11 and were then told that we could start right away. I now wished that I had arrived an hour earlier. As fortune would have it, the temperature at the start was only 77 degrees and 82 at the finish, but still, it was, Hot Hot Hot.

During the Chicagoland Spring Marathon and Half Marathon, in an effort to get this race over with, I pushed us a bit at the start of the race so there was no negative split for us. The first 3 miles were on a mostly concrete, two-lane, closed road that was slightly downhill. So no way I was going to be able to do any faster coming back up it in the heat of the day. We did come in right at our usual race time of 2:44, which is not bad for a soon-to-be 66-year-old.

After that portion, we did go off onto their bike and running trail system for 3.5 miles, which was asphalt and very scenic. I now see why they spaced starts so much since the trail was not very wide. It was an out-and-back, and other runners, walkers, and bikers were using the path.

I must say, when it was all said and done, I did not much like this race. It was much harder than the third half-marathon we did in 5 days last week. I am sure as time goes on; I will feel better about it. That is how it always happens, or who would do these races more than once? I used to say the same about marathons and that it must be like childbirth. I have often been corrected.

The next day we did do some more sightseeing, this time by boat, on the Architectural tour by Wendella Sightseeing Company. Here, we got an up-close perspective of Chicago's internationally known architecture as seen from the Chicago River. We ventured through the Chicago Lock to gain a new perspective of Chicago's architecture from Lake Michigan.

We finished off the day with a walk around Millennium Park and had to take some pictures of us in front of the sculpture called, cloud gate. Cloud Gate is a public sculpture by Indian-born British artist Sir Anish Kapoor that is the centerpiece of AT&T Plaza at Millennium Park in the Loop community area of Chicago, Illinois. Constructed between 2004 and 2006, the sculpture is nicknamed The Bean because of its shape, a name Kapoor initially disliked but later grew fond of. Made up of 168 stainless steel plates welded together, its highly polished exterior has no visible seams. It measures 33 by 66 by 42 feet and weighs 110 short tons.

Tomorrow, we are off to Atlanta to meet up with my younger-looking older Sister, Gwen, and then drive down to see my daughter, Mariah, in Athens, Georgia. After 3 days there, we are on our way to Bloomington for Memorial Day to get together with Cat's daughter and family.

Cat will have her first speech therapy appointment with Fox Rehabilitation, which has an office in Bloomington. They also have one in Atlanta, but right now, they do not have any therapist available. They also have telehealth, so while we are on the road, the therapist and Cat can connect.

From there, a few days stop in the Jeffersonville area, then off to Maryland, New Jersey, and Massachusetts for three more half marathons, this time in 7 days with Mainly Marathons. We hope to see some friendly faces out there and maybe a new best friend or two.

Schaumburg, Illinois
May 23, 2021

CHAPTER 13
The Only Thing You Can Control
Is Your Attitude

♦ ♦ ♦

"You cannot control what happens to you, but you can control
your attitude toward what happens to you, and in that, you will
be mastering change rather than allowing it to master you."
~Brian Tracy

I try to keep that thought close to my heart and mind as Cat
and I face the day-to-day challenges of Early-onset Alzheimer's. The announcement of the new drug, Aduhelm, by
Biogen is very concerning to me, but it took me a few days to figure out exactly why.

Here is an article on Aduhelm for your reading pleasure.

Today, June 7, 2021, the U.S. Food and Drug Administration
approved, Aduhelm (aducanumab) for the treatment of Alzheimer's, a debilitating disease affecting 6.2 million Americans.
Aduhelm was approved using the accelerated approval pathway,
which can be used for a drug for a serious or life-threatening illness
that provides a meaningful therapeutic advantage over existing
treatments. Accelerated approval can be based on the drug's effect
on a surrogate endpoint that is reasonably likely to predict a clinical

benefit to patients, with a required post-approval trial to verify that the drug provides the expected clinical benefit.

"Alzheimer's disease is a devastating illness that can have a profound impact on the lives of people diagnosed with the disease as well as their loved ones," said Patrizia Cavazzoni, M.D., director of the FDA's Center for Drug Evaluation and Research. "Currently available therapies only treat symptoms of the disease; this treatment option is the first therapy to target and affect the underlying disease process of Alzheimer's. As we have learned from the fight against cancer, the accelerated approval pathway can bring therapies to patients faster while spurring more research and innovation."

Alzheimer's is an irreversible, progressive brain disorder that slowly destroys memory and thinking skills, and eventually, the ability to carry out simple tasks. While the specific causes of Alzheimer's disease are not fully known, it is characterized by changes in the brain—including amyloid plaques and neurofibrillary, or tau, tangles—that result in the loss of neurons and their connections. These changes affect a person's ability to remember and think.

Aduhelm represents a first-of-its-kind treatment approved for Alzheimer's disease. It is the first new treatment approved for Alzheimer's since 2003 and is the first therapy that targets the fundamental pathophysiology of the disease.

Researchers evaluated Aduhelm's efficacy in three separate studies representing a total of 3,482 patients. The studies consisted of double-blind, randomized, placebo-controlled dose-ranging studies in patients with Alzheimer's disease. Patients receiving the treatment had significant dose-and time-dependent reduction of amyloid beta plaque, while patients in the control arm of the studies had no reduction of amyloid beta plaque.

These results support the accelerated approval of Aduhelm, which is based on the surrogate endpoint of reduction of amyloid beta plaque in the brain—a hallmark of Alzheimer's disease. Amyloid beta plaque was quantified using positron emission tomography (PET) imaging to estimate the brain levels of amyloid beta plaque in a composite of brain regions expected to be widely affected by Alzheimer's disease pathology compared to a brain region expected to be spared of such pathology.

The prescribing information for Aduhelm includes a warning for amyloid-related imaging abnormalities (ARIA), which most commonly presents as temporary swelling in areas of the brain that usually resolves over time and does not cause symptoms, though some people may have symptoms such as headache, confusion, dizziness, vision changes, or nausea. Another warning for Aduhelm is for a risk of hypersensitivity reactions, including angioedema and urticaria. The most common side effects of Aduhelm were ARIA, headache, fall, diarrhea, and confusion/delirium/altered mental status/disorientation.

Under the accelerated approval provisions, which provide patients suffering from the disease earlier access to the treatment, the FDA is requiring the company, Biogen, to conduct a new randomized, controlled clinical trial to verify the drug's clinical benefit. If the trial fails to verify clinical benefit, the FDA may initiate proceedings to withdraw approval of the drug.

Aduhelm was granted Fast Track designation, which seeks to expedite the development and review of drugs that are intended to treat serious conditions where initial evidence showed the potential to address an unmet medical need.

Some experts are questioning whether a newly approved Alzheimer's drug is less effective for women. The results from Leqembi's clinical trial were published in the New England Journal of Medicine last year and concluded that the drug slowed clinical decline by 27%. Another way to look at it is that it only slowed down progression by 5 months.

However, in a supplementary appendix also published in the NEJM, analyses of subgroups found that the rate the disease was slowed was lower for women than for men in the study.

The drug slowed cognitive decline in women by 12% compared to 43% in men. "To me, males are likely benefitting more from this drug than females are," said Madhav Thambisetty, senior investigator and chief at the clinical and translational neuroscience section at the National Institute on Aging.

"I think these are important subgroup analyses in a clinical trial that was very adequately powered, and I think we can make interpretations from these," he added. Yes, but: The gender disparities were not found to be statistically significant, which essentially means the observed difference happened by chance, Eisai said, adding that the study was not designed specifically to measure efficacy by sex.

For both males and females "treatment is effective in the positive direction," said Shobha Dhadda, senior vice president of biostatistics and clinical development at Eisai. What they're saying: "You would get data that looks like this if you were flipping a coin," said Christopher van Dyck, the lead researcher on Leqembi's clinical trial and the founder and director of the Alzheimer's disease research unit at Yale University School of Medicine.

But at the same time, based on this data, if you had to make a bet on a male versus a female subject, how well they would do or likely to benefit you'd bet on the male. The big picture: Some clinicians said those results will influence the conversations they have with female patients weighing whether to take the drug.

"I don't think that it's enough to say no woman should be treated with this. I think that would be the wrong take-home message. But the risk benefit ratio, which is always complicated because of lots of things, will need to weigh gender as part of the equation," said Alvaro Pascual-Leone, a neurology professor at Harvard Medical School.

Other researchers pointed to their already-existing concerns about the drug's safety. "I would be hesitant even more so with [women] to prescribe it because I just don't see that the benefits outweigh the risks because there's just not a benefit that is being shown here," said Reshma Ramachandran, an assistant professor at Yale School of Medicine.

"I think it is a point of caution. It's one of those things where you shouldn't view this as a definitive answer, but it does temper their results, where you're looking at this and saying, it doesn't look like the women benefitted nearly as much as the men did," said Matthew Schrag, an assistant professor of neurology at Vanderbilt University Medical Center.

But Schrag said the benefit is small for all subgroups, especially in the context of the drugs' risks. "I don't think that there's any group of patients that I would recommend this drug to." Since patient gender were not a primary consideration and it's possible that the patients were not comparable enough, "you really can't draw conclusions from that difference," said Constantine Lyketsos, an Alzheimer's researcher at Johns Hopkins School of Medicine.

"Keep in mind that what you don't know is whether men and women at baseline differed on severity of illness or a variety of other variables that would have predicted the outcome, so this might have nothing to do with gender," he added. Although the results suggest male patients benefited more, limitations in the analyses mean they are "not adequately powered to allow for firm conclusions on treatment effects for inclusion in labeling," an FDA spokesperson told Axios. The spokesperson added that "female patients benefit from treatment with Leqembi."

Eli Lilly this month is due to release full clinical results for its experimental Alzheimer's treatment Donanemab, which works similarly to Leqembi. It'll be worth noting whether there are any gender discrepancies there. "If it seems to be a pattern across studies with different drugs, there may be an issue," Lyketsos said. "But you still have to resolve the question as to whether men and women coming into the study are comparable in their risk.

Groundbreaking treatments for Alzheimer's disease that work by removing a toxic protein called beta amyloid from the brain may benefit whites more than Black Americans, whose disease may be driven by other factors, leading Alzheimer's experts told Reuters. Two other drugs – Leqembi, from partner biotech firms and Biogen, and an experimental treatment developed by Eli Lilly, Donanemab, are the first to offer real hope of slowing the fatal disease for the 6.5 million Americans living with Alzheimer's.

Although older Black Americans have twice the rate of dementia as whites, they were screened out of clinical trials of these drugs at a higher rate, according to interviews with 10 researchers as well as 4 Eisai and Lilly executives. Prospective Black volunteers with early disease symptoms did not have enough amyloid in their brain to qualify for the trials, the 10 researchers explained.

Hispanics, who experience dementia at one and a half times the rate of whites, were also excluded at a somewhat higher rate due to low amyloid, though the issue was not as pronounced as for Black people, five of the researchers said. The growing evidence of a disparity around amyloid, a defining characteristic of Alzheimer's, is raising questions among some scientists about who will benefit from the two new treatments – the first ever proven to slow the rate of cognitive decline, the researchers said.

Referring to Leqembi, Dr. Crystal Glover, a social psychologist and expert in equity in aging research who leads clinical trial recruitment of the Rush Alzheimer's Disease Research Center in

Chicago, asked: "Is this even applicable to the groups that are most at risk?

About 20% of older Black people are estimated to have Alzheimer's or another dementia, twice the rate of white people and above the 14% of Hispanics.

Some researchers are asking whether Black patients are experiencing dementia due to causes other than Alzheimer's or whether the disease manifests differently in diverse populations who have higher rates of chronic conditions. The disparity in beta-amyloid is adding to evidence that some health metrics may not work the same in diverse populations as they do in white people.

A US Food and Drug Administration spokesperson said the agency was aware of the potential exclusion of some African Americans from the new treatments due to insufficient amyloid levels. The spokesperson said the FDA encourages companies to increase enrollment of diverse populations in their ongoing trials. In April of 2022, the FDA recommended companies submit a diversity plan for enrollment.

Eisai said it is working to understand why so many Black people seeking to enroll in its clinical trial for Leqembi were screened out due to a lack of amyloid. The company told Reuters that 49% of Black volunteers did not meet the trial's amyloid threshold requirements compared to 22% for whites and 55% for Hispanics. That left just 43 Black participants out of 947 people enrolled in the US portion of the trial, or 4.5% of the total—a stark underrepresentation since the disease is most prevalent for Black Americans and they make up 13.7% of the U.S. population. Despite the amyloid screening failures, Hispanics made up 22.5% of the U.S. arm of Eisai's trial, an overrepresentation compared to the US population.

"Is it because MCI (mild cognitive impairment) or early dementia type-symptoms in Blacks are caused by other reasons more so than Alzheimer's?" Eisai's U.S. head Ivan Cheung told Reuters in an interview. "We're looking into it." Only people who are amyloid positive should get Leqembi "irrespective of race and ethnicity," Cheung said: "The drug was not designed to help specific ethnic groups or races." Eisai, which is based in Tokyo, is working with the National Institutes of Health (NIH), a US government health research agency, to test Leqembi's effectiveness in preventing Alzheimer's dementia among people with elevated amyloid but normal cognition. The company is targeting Black enrollment of at least 8% in the 1,400 person trial, Shobha Dhadda, Eisai's global head of biostatistics, told Reuters. So far, 95% to 98% of Black candidates are failing to meet the amyloid threshold required for inclusion, she said.

Eisai's partner Biogen did not participate in Leqembi's development but has the rights to sell the drug. Black people and Hispanics were also screened out at somewhat higher rates in the trial for Lilly's experimental drug Donanemab, said Dr Mark Mintun, Lilly's group vice president for neuroscience research and development. The drug is currently being reviewed by the FDA. In the US, 4% of the participants were Black and 6% were Hispanic, Lilly said. The company said it recognized those numbers were low despite its efforts to increase recruitment and that it aims to have enrollment in its US trials overall reflect the make-up of the population. Lilly said the research into why Black and Hispanic people were screened out of trials at higher rates is ongoing and that there were many hypotheses, including that their dementia is not caused by Alzheimer's, or that they are in an earlier phase of Alzheimer's but that their disease is complicated by other factors such as small strokes.

Clinical trials typically have low enrollment of diverse populations: Among US trials that reported race and ethnicity, about 80% of participants were white, 10% were Black, 6% were Hispanic, and 1 percent were Asian, a 2022 study found. In 96 dementia trials from 2000-2017, diverse populations only made up around 11% of enrollment, according to a 2018 study.

Alzheimer's researchers have moved away from using outward signs, such as memory loss, for identifying patients with the disease towards detecting Alzheimer's-associated proteins in the body, including amyloid, that can occur long before dementia sets in. Yet some tests that are used to identify these proteins may perform differently among Black and white patients.

Differences in the drivers of Alzheimer's were noted in a small 2015 study comparing brains of Black and white individuals who died of the disease. The study, led by Dr Lisa Barnes, who is also at the Rush Center, found that white people were more likely to carry Alzheimer's associated proteins as the primary driver of their dementia. Among Black people who died of Alzheimer's, their dementia was more likely to result from multiple causes, such as vascular disease. Subsequent studies involving brain scans, spinal fluid, and blood tests—many citing Barnes' work—have also found differences.

In a 2021 paper published in Nature Reviews Neurology, Barnes argued that scientists need a better understanding of Alzheimer's in Black people or else effective treatments would not be available to this at-risk, but under-represented population. "We're seeing that come to light with this recent drug," Barnes said in an email to Reuters, referring to Leqembi.

"We need to know what the other pathologies are beyond amyloid that leads to dementia in Black people, and how risk factors, especially socially constructed risk factors, relate to those pathologies," Barnes said.

Dr. Joshua Grill, a University of California, Irvine, Alzheimer's researcher, who collaborated with Eisai and other researchers to analyze two trials for Leqembi and two for an earlier anti-amyloid drug, also found that Black, Hispanic, and Asian people were more likely to be screened out of clinical trials because the amount of amyloid in their brain was below the trial's threshold. The researchers intend to submit the findings for publication.

"Is it that it's not Alzheimer's disease? Is something else causing their cognitive problems across all these studies? Is it that the biomarkers don't quite work the same in those communities, or is it something else that we're not able to measure?" Grill said.

Two researchers told Reuters one possible explanation for the differences in amyloid is APOE4, a variant of a gene that regulates amyloid deposits in the brain and that is associated with a greater risk of late-onset Alzheimer's. The risk of developing the disease among people with the variant is higher in those of Asian or European ancestry and lower in people of African and Hispanic ancestry, according to the National Institutes of Health (NIH).

Differences in APOE4 could help explain why more Black people are failing to meet the amyloid thresholds required for recent drug trials, said Dr. Reisa Sperling of Brigham and Women's Hospital, who is leading the trial of Leqembi to prevent Alzheimer's dementia. Other factors could be at play, experts said.

In the United States, more than 75% of Black Americans are overweight or obese, increasing their risk of hypertension, high cholesterol, type 2 diabetes, and sleep apnea—factors that raise the risk of vascular dementia, according to US government data. Socioeconomic factors play a role in obesity and may also play a role in dementia.

A number of recent studies are finding that racism, and resulting inequities in income, access to high-quality medical care and healthy food, exposure to pollution, and chronic stress affect the health and possibly the underlying biology of different populations.

My thoughts on this drug are that the internet has blown up over this decision by the FDA, and the drug company stock went up 30% on the news. I see several stumbling blocks concerning this drug, but that does not explain why it bothers me as much as it does. Cat and I were involved in a Clinical Trial back in 2015 and 16, and we did see some improvements for her, but the drug never went to market since the drug company was not satisfied with its results.

Everyone is touting the benefits of this drug; however, the panel that reviewed the clinical trial data did not recommend its approval, and two doctors resigned from the panel. Part of my fear is that with this tentative approval, other drug companies will give up on their research. I am not sure how they will get folks to sign up for another clinical trial since those folks might get the placebo when they can go get the actual drug with the doctor's approval.

I have always felt Cat would be cured, but I feared that the first drug would only help a subset of sufferers, and this is the case here. This drug is only approved for folks with mild symptoms, and unfortunately, she is more in the moderate range. Also, she has both APOE4 genes from both of her parents which would exclude her from this treatment. There was a drug that helped her, but it did not go to market when she was still in the mild range, and now this one will not help her. I believe that is my major rub with this announcement.

They say that it probably will be prescribed to only 2% of sufferers after a $6K PET (positron emission tomography) scan to help confirm the disease and then $56K a year for the monthly infusions. Also, you will need continual PET scans to make sure you do not have any brain swelling and bleeding, which can be life-threatening.

Fast forward to January 2024, Aducanumab, a pricey drug approved for the treatment of early-stage Alzheimer's disease, was withdrawn from the market. Aducanumab received accelerated approval in 2021 from the Food and Drug Administration after a pair of late-stage trials showed skimpy enough results that neither Medicare nor private insurance companies would cover the drug at a price tag of $56,000 a year.

While its withdrawal comes as a disappointment for patients and advocacy groups, it probably made good financial sense to its owner, Biogen. Aducanumab has netted a mere $3 million in sales to date, implying that fewer than 100 people have reached into their pockets to pay the full price since its approval.

A similarly acting drug, Lecanemab, (Leqembi), marketed by Biogen in partnership with Eisai, was approved in 2023. Only about 2,000 individuals are receiving Leqembi, which costs $26,000 a year. Lecamemab is covered by Medicare and some private insurers. Medicare projects the cost to the traditional Medicare program to be around $500 million in 2024, and the entire Medicare program 3.5 billion in 2025.

In March 2024, Eli Lilly announced Friday that the U.S. Food and Drug Administration (FDA) had established a committee to evaluate Donanemab, the Alzheimer's drug that had its approval blocked last year. Donanemab is one of three monoclonal antibody treatments for Alzheimer's including aducanumab (Aduhelm) and Lecanemab (Leqembi). All three drugs work by clearing the amyloid plaques that are characteristic of Alzheimer's, but there was scarce evidence in early trials that clearing the plaques slowed cognitive decline.

The three drugs attack plaque at somewhat different stages of its formation but are all meant to remove these deposits from the brain. And this they undoubtedly do.

"All are quite adept at pulling amyloid plaques out of the brain," Mike Greicius, who is also a steering committee member of the Knight Initiative for Brain Resilience at Stanford's Wu Tsai

Neurosciences Institute. "Just because A-beta plays some kind of role early on—and it clearly does—doesn't mean removing plaque is going to be helpful". "But none of these drugs makes much of a difference to the patient's wellbeing. The effect is tiny," said Greicius.

First, amyloid plaque may be a lousy tracker of Alzheimer's progression. Lots of people get lots of plaque but show no sign of anything more than normal age-related cognitive losses. The plaque deposits aggregate not within, but between, nerve cells. And the places where these deposits show up aren't necessarily the brain structures whose deterioration is most directly relevant to cognitive and memory loss, Greicius said.

Much more closely tied to nerve-cell breakdown and associated cognitive loss are another kind of deposit known as neurofibrillary tangles: stringy aggregates composed largely of a protein called tau. Neurofibrillary tangles are situated within, rather than between, nerve cells, and their presence strongly correlates with nerve cell and nerve-circuit damage to brain structures implicated in memory and the ability to think. So, then, why didn't drug developers initially focus their efforts on neurofibrillary tangles instead of amyloid plaque?

While most Alzheimer's cases occur late in life, a small fraction of cases begin much earlier and are clearly heritable. Examination of these familial early-onset cases has pinpointed mutations in the protein whose A-beta snippets aggregate to form amyloid plaque. That drug developers might contemplate a method of removing amyloid plaque from the brain was reasonable. There was no similar early genetic tie-in with tau-rich neurofibrillary tangles, which manifest later in the course of Alzheimer's pathology than amyloid deposits do. But there's little to no evidence that removing amyloid plaque from the brain actually improves cognitive function. The plaque-attack drugs' clinical trials did achieve what researchers call "statistical significance," meaning the observed effects were unlikely to have been illusory. But the size of the effect matters, too.

"Even assuming the plaque-attack drugs' observed effects on cognition were real, it was so small a clinician wouldn't notice it," Greicius said. This holds true even for Donanemab, as evidenced by a late-stage trial that recorded the largest cognitive improvements.

This takes me back to the title of this chapter. The Only Thing You Can Control Is Your Attitude. With these promising drugs and their setbacks, for us, that means that we will continue to concentrate on enjoying life as much as we can for as long as we can and not get wrapped around the axle when it comes to finding a cure. That is something we can not control, but we still hold out hopes that it will one day happen.

We can control our effort and with that, we will continue to use that effort towards achieving our goals. Presently, that is to do a half marathon in all 50 states. Right now we are in Simsbury, Connecticut, for a 10K and on to Holyoke, Massachusetts, for our 37th half marathon state on Sunday. The 10K will be applied towards our next goal of a 10K in all 50 states, with one in Connecticut being the 6th State.

My middle child, Shawn, and his wife, Cassie, are having their second child in July, with my youngest, Mariah, having her first child a month later. We are planning a trip to Juneau, Alaska in August for a 10K and half marathon while there in August of 2021.

In September, Cat and I are hopefully off to Germany and Scotland with Marathon Tours and Travel. With that said, I am sure we will be mastering change rather than allowing it to master us. I will continue with my research for a cure rather than just another treatment that merely slows the progression. I am pretty sure our lifestyle does that all by itself.

CHAPTER 14

The Brain and the Heart: Understanding How to Prevent and Treat Alzheimer's Disease

♦ ♦ ♦

"What's good for the heart is good for the brain, and this might be even more true for women."
~Dr. Michelle Mielke

D
r. Michelle Mielke has devoted her career to answering Questions like: Can we predict who will develop Alzheimer's disease (AD) and other dementias? Can we identify biomarkers to predict disease development early? What are the most promising treatment targets? And importantly, how do sex and gender affect risk factors, symptom onset, and disease progression?

In the United States, two-thirds of adults with AD are women, and experts still ponder how much of this gender difference can be attributed to the average longer lifespan of women compared with men and how much stems from biological or environmental factors.

AD is particularly cruel to women, and Cat, was in the prime of her life, so this Chapter will be devoted to the difference between the sexes.

"As we have learned with many diseases and conditions, women and men can have different risk factors, different mechanisms underlying disease, and different responses to treatments," said Mielke, chair of the Department of Epidemiology and Prevention and a professor of epidemiology, gerontology and geriatric medicine, and neurology at Wake Forest University in North Carolina.

"We need to continue studying sex-and-gender differences in Alzheimer's disease to uncover what's best for women and men."

Dr. Mielke found a link between cardiovascular conditions, risk factors for cardiovascular disease, and cognitive decline in mid-life that is stronger for women than men.

Women's Health Research at Yale Director Carolyn M. Mazure, Ph.D., invited Dr. Mielke to discuss her research on this topic at a virtual Grand Rounds presentation in April sponsored by the Women's Behavioral Health Division of Yale School of Medicine's Department of Psychiatry. Before leaving her faculty position at the Mayo Clinic in March, Dr. Mielke was the senior author of a study published in the journal Neurology, finding that the link between cardiovascular conditions, risk factors for cardiovascular disease (CVD), and cognitive decline in mid-life was stronger for women than for men. This was true even though men generally have more heart conditions and cardiovascular risk factors in mid-life, such as high blood pressure, diabetes, and obesity.

"There is still a lot of work to be done about the mechanistic, biological underpinnings of Alzheimer's disease," Mielke said. "But what our study and prior research are telling us is that what's good for the heart is good for the brain. And this might be even more true for women."

Reasons for this difference could include the influence of sex hormones on heart health and cognition as well as social differences that often vary between women and men, such as exercise and education. Women are also more likely than men to have types of CVD that decrease small vessel blood flow to the heart without a co-occurring cholesterol blockage in the larger arteries. Such sex differences in the biology underlying CVD might affect cognition differently for women and men.

Dr. Mielke said the data increasingly point toward a need to treat cardiovascular-related conditions early and to more closely follow women with these conditions over time to optimize both heart and brain health. For example, women with preeclampsia, a condition of high blood pressure in pregnancy that can damage organs and threaten the pregnancy and the life of the mother, often have worse cognition in their 60s and 70s.

"If we know that these associations exist between heart health and cognition, even if we do not yet know the precise biological connection, we can follow women with these conditions more closely," she said. "And see if by treating their cardiovascular disease, maybe the cognitive issues can be prevented."

Similarly, Dr. Mielke's team has demonstrated how the surgical removal of a woman's ovaries—and thus the hormones they produce—before natural menopause is associated with poorer cognition and dementia. She cautioned against the unnecessary removal of ovaries for women without ovarian cancer or who are not at high risk of developing the disease. She also pointed to a larger lesson about how to perceive hormonal fluctuations across the lifespan.

"Some have said that menopause is a risk factor for dementia, but I don't believe that is correct," she said. "All cisgender women, a person whose gender identity corresponds with the sex registered for them at birth, go through menopause. To blame menopause would be like saying puberty is a risk factor for heart disease."

Instead, Mielke likens menopause to a "stress test" in which evidence is starting to show that women with more severe menopause symptoms, such as intense hot flashes, are more susceptible to developing cardiovascular disease and potentially at a higher risk for AD or vascular dementia. I am unable to speak to the intensity of Cat's hot flashes, but I will point out that she was at the beginning stages of menopause when she was diagnosed with Early-onset Alzheimer's.

Mielke's work also focuses on identifying blood-based biomarkers for AD that can aid diagnosis through primary care as opposed to the more expensive, harder-to-access visits to specialists with more expensive tests, such as neuro-imaging or a lumbar puncture. At the same time, Mielke wants medical providers to understand how such a test could be effectively utilized in the general population, particularly as other diseases and conditions might affect the levels of certain biomarkers and how to interpret the results.

For example, experts have long focused on proteins called beta-amyloids that can collect between brain cells and form plaques that disrupt brain function. Another target protein called tau can form tangles inside neurons that prevent proper communication between the cells. Although previously not feasible, with new technology, beta-amyloids, and tau can now be measured in the blood. However, recent evidence suggests that people with chronic kidney disease have higher levels of beta-amyloid and tau than people without kidney disease, even though they do not appear to have a greater risk for AD. Similarly, other groups of people develop high levels of these blood markers but no symptoms of cognitive dysfunction.

In addition, if an accurate predictor of AD were to be established, Mielke stressed the importance of understanding how to present the results of such a test given the implications of a positive biomarker. For example, how might this new knowledge affect an individual's mental health or their ability to obtain life insurance?

"It would be phenomenal if we could eventually develop an effective method for screening potential susceptibility to Alzheimer's disease, as this could lead to possible preventive strategies," she said. "But, in any event, we would definitely need to educate health care providers about the meaning of a positive biomarker, so they understand how to discuss with patients what this means."

Research has identified differences in the way Alzheimer's disease affects the brains of women and men. For example, women who develop AD experience higher neuro-degeneration, a condition in which brain cells become damaged or die at accelerating rates. Dr. Mielke also stresses the importance of discussing how environment and experience filtered through gender contribute to disease.

A 2019 study from UCLA found that mothers between the ages of 60 and 70 who never participated in the wage-base labor force showed far more rapid declines in memory than women who worked. This was true for married women and single women who experienced a prolonged period without paid employment.

The authors suggested that mental stimulation and financial and social benefits could have contributed to the observed difference. With such factors in mind, Dr. Mielke has helped form a group on sex and gender at the Alzheimer's Association to take a global perspective on whether and how sociocultural factors contribute to the disease. "We have had so many changes in society over the last 50 years," Mielke said. "It's important to understand what effect these social transitions might have, so we can better protect people from this disease."

CHAPTER 15
Hope For the Best

♦ ♦ ♦

"To be hopeful that a positive occurrence will happen. This can be an expression of hope or insight after something has gone awry or when circumstances seem bleak." ~The free dictionary

That is all I could ask for. This is the furthest we have gone from our home base in nearly two years. We are still nomads and travel a lot by anyone's standards, but usually, it is only a couple of hours by plane or car. I had a lot of apprehension about still doing trips this far from our home base of Atlanta, Georgia.

This 5-night trip took us to Juneau, Alaska, to add one more state to our quest to run a half marathon in all 50 states. While there, we also did a 10k. This is state number 38 for us and our 19th race this year. When we were doing marathons, we did Anchorage for the state of Alaska many moons ago.

So far, so good, another idiom: everything is satisfactory or developing as planned up to the current point or moment in time.

Idiom: A group of words established by usage as having a meaning not deducible from those of the individual.

The race series was once again put on by our new running family at Mainly Marathons. The 10K was done at Savikko Park (Treadwell Trail), across the bridge in Douglas, Alaska. It was a beautiful, wooded, somewhat muddy, and occasionally rocky course. I am glad we opted for the half marathon the next day on the paved asphalt course at Twin Lakes Park back in Juneau.

While there, I did ask Greg and Kevin, a long time Mainly Loonies, why they do it. To be a Loonie, you must complete 100 races with Mainly and each of the races they put on. You know me and my unscientific surveys. The bottom line is, "It's the people stupid." Whatever works for them. We have our eye on getting two more states with them next month.

Maybe next time, we will do all four days since running still has a very positive effect on Cat, which did help compensate for the long flight days and 4-hour time change.

As many know, there is so much to see and do while in Juneau, but we picked the following five.

Gold Creek Salmon Bake

Cat is a salmon connoisseur, whereas I can take it or leave it. Sometimes, it is good, and other times, not so much. So, I never order it off the menu. I figured since this place had salmon as part of its name, why not give it a try?

We got there right when it opened at 5 pm and were able to beat the busloads of people off the cruise ships that were finishing up their tours for the day. Outstanding was one word I would use. The outdoor, buffet-style dinner hit the spot. It was so good I even had seconds of the freshly grilled salmon over an open fire pit. The specially prepared glaze topping tantalized my tastebuds. The blueberry cake to finish off the fabulous meal was the cherry on top. We took a stroll of the surrounding property, and it was cool to see the spawning salmon in the nearby creek and waterfall area.

Mount Robert's Tramway

They say you have to experience Mount Robert's Tramway, so we did. We have taken tours on many a tramway to the top of some mountain in the area around the world, so no real surprises here. They had a trail system up and down the mountain and probably would have gone either up or down that way if the on and off again rain had not persisted.

Shrine of St. Therese

Cat and I are not very religious. We think of ourselves as more spiritual, but it was nice to go inside the National Shrine of St. Therese to once again pray for Cat as we usually do from time to time all over the world. The magnificent adjacent gardens were an unexpected treat. The huge bulldozer making small work of the nearby cabins was a stark contrast.

Jensen-Olson Arboretum

Right down the road was the Jensen-Olson Arboretum, and we never missed an opportunity to walk amongst the local vegetation. They say walks or hikes like these are very beneficial for folks with ALZ. It takes the sufferer to fond memories in their minds and crowds out the daily frustrations they commonly experience.

Mendenhall Glacier

You can't come to Alaska and not experience a glacier up close and personal. Unfortunately, with climate change, the Mendenhall Glacier, like many others, is receding, so instead of being right out the visitor center observation deck's window, it is now about a half mile away, but still worth the visit.

The trip back to the lower 48 started with a 5 am departure from Juneau with a 90-minute connection once again in Seattle. The day ended with a very respectful arrival time of 6 pm back in ATL. Needless to say, we were both worn out. Cat did well, and this was a good training run for our trip back over the pond next month to Berlin and Scotland. I learned a few things to be aware of for that trip to help Cat as much as possible.

It does make it all worthwhile as we thought about all we witnessed in Juneau. In two chapters in our first book, I talk about possible places to live, and Juneau made it to another list of places we could not live. The reasons why are too numerous to mention here. It also made it to a short list of places we will never return to. Been there, done that, and we even got a tee shirt for running two races while there.

Juneau, Alaska
August 5, 2021

CHAPTER 16

Why We Travel

♦ ♦ ♦

"If your dreams don't scare you, they're not big enough."
~Unknown

Travel has been in my blood my entire adult life, but it goes deeper than that. I have come to the realization, that certain things about travel intrigued me. I'm a planner and manager by heart. I have spent most of my adult life managing assets, money, and people. I find that to be a better fit for me than actually flying airplanes from point A to B safely. I enjoy the planning part of travel and then putting those plans into action. The points of interest are nice to look at, but figuring out how to get around on my own is where the real thrill exists.

During our travels, I have been asking random people why they travel, and here are some answers that I have been given:

- It's something I have always done
- For the excitement
- To meet new and different people
- To see it for yourself
- Because my father didn't

- Because my parents did
- Because we can
- For the adventure
- It makes for a good story to tell others
- You only live once
- To get a better perspective of the world

Another reason to travel is to learn. As we age, our brains don't do as well as when we were younger. Seeing new and exciting things keeps those synapses fired up, especially for folks like Cat with younger-onset Alzheimer's. I have noticed the difference for myself, too. These memories will stay with me for a lifetime, as opposed to who said what to whom on the latest TV show.

Something occurred to me the other day. As a caregiver for someone with Early Onset Alzheimer's, EOA, it can be frustrating sometimes. For me, I use travel as a way to escape or, in other words, keep myself occupied with the planning, the actual new views, and perspective while caring for Cat.

I have talked previously about how it benefits Cat. It is hard for either of us to obsess about our current situation while walking through a botanical garden in some far-flung country. Cat and I are looking forward to our trip to Berlin and Scotland later this month with Marathon Tours and Travel.

Berlin is particularly special for me since it was the first marathon I ran after open heart surgery seven years ago. That was only 3 months after my surgery. It is also bittersweet since it was around the same time we realized that our lives would forever be changed by the diagnosis of EOA for Cat. We are not running the marathon this time around, but we will be doing the breakfast run. In Scotland, we will be doing the Lockness 10K.

COVID has put a bit of a hitch in our Giddy-up. The lack of socialization has negatively affected both of us. We did some travel to Mexico and Aruba this time last year, but besides that, we have been mostly stateside. We have nothing against the good old "US of A," but there is something special about the sights and sounds of a foreign land. We miss the socialization you get when touring a new place along with making new best friends along the way. I realize the travel across the pond will be tough on both of us, but I hope it will be well worth it.

In the meantime, we are off to the states of Washington and Idaho with Mainly Marathons to get them both checked off our Half marathon and 10K's lists. That will be state numbers 39 and 40 in our new quest to run a half marathon in all 50 states. I still have 8 states to go, but still undecided if I am going to go down that road.

Here is a great article to drive home all the various reasons why even folks with Alzheimer's should consider traveling as long as possible, even after the dreadful diagnosis.

"'Travel therapy' may offer treatment for dementia and benefit mental health. There are two types of people in this world: those who would take an Alzheimer's patient on a joy ride and those who would say it was a waste of gas. Which one are you?" ~2016 National Society of Newspaper Columnists' contest finalist

- Dementia impacts many people's abilities to think, remember, and function.
- Since dementia has no cure, care is often supportive to help people with dementia have a higher quality of life for as long as possible.
- New research shows that tourism, or "travel therapy," may be beneficial for mental well-being and may have several components that can positively impact brain health.

Many people like to travel for rest, relaxation, and inspiration—but there may be significant cognitive benefits as well. A study published in the October 2022 edition of Tourism Management presents the thoughts of a cross-disciplinary team of experts in both dementia and tourism.

The research has not yet been peer-reviewed, but experts have proposed there may be significant benefits of travel for people with dementia, particularly in the areas of mental health and well-being. Researchers are still working out how to best help those with dementia, but many elements of promoting overall well-being may be helpful. One area of interest is how traveling may benefit people with dementia.

The study authors proposed the potential benefits of tourism, sometimes called "travel therapy," in treating people with dementia.

One definition of tourism the researchers used was "visiting places outside one's everyday environment for no longer than a full year." They note that the experience of tourism has four main components to it:

- How it impacts feelings, emotions, and mood (affective experience)
- How it affects thoughts and memories (cognitive experience)
- How it impacts behavior (cognitive experience)
- How it impacts the senses (sensorial experience)

The study authors concluded that tourism may have a potentially positive impact on well-being and quality of life through a variety of components. Still, literature supporting this in the treatment of dementia is limited.

Based on their literature review and expert opinion, the researchers proposed how tourism may address components of nonpharmacological interventions in people with dementia. Tourism could impact the following areas and many other elements of treatment:

- Cognitive and sensory stimulation: Travel stimulates thoughts and knowledge, which may benefit people with dementia. It could also involve experiencing sensations that improve behavior and well-being.

- Environment: Travel puts people in a new environment and can increase social interaction, which can stimulate brain function for people with dementia.

- Exercise: By its nature, travel involves movement and exercise. Maintenance and improving physical function can help people with dementia.

- The use of musical therapy: While travel doesn't always involve music, music can help to improve brain function and boost mood in people with dementia. Travel that has more of a musical focus could, therefore, be beneficial.

- Reminiscence: Talking about and remembering past experiences can be helpful for people with dementia. Tourism may help stimulate memories in people with dementia.

The study authors added that focusing on components of positive psychology, such as what people can do, positive experiences, and well-being, may also benefit people with dementia. They proposed a few ways to implement components of tourism to help people with dementia, such as group travel that promotes social interactions or traveling to locations that stimulate the senses.

Study author Dr. Jun Wen, a lecturer in tourism and hospitality management at the School of Business and Law at Edith Cowan University, noted the following to Medical News Today:

"All tourism experiences offer elements of anticipation and planning, both of which stimulate brain function.

Exercise is often an important component of tourism experiences, and it is frequently included in dementia intervention plans. Tourism experiences such as a beach visit offer dementia patient's sensory stimulation, boosting one's mood, exercise, music therapy, and instilling a sense of freedom as non-medicine dementia interventions. Group travel may simulate psychological interventions, and music at a destination is in line with music therapy programs for those with dementia." ~Dr. Jun Wen

While there is limited data, the idea of the benefits of travel is not new.

For example, Andrea Robinson, PhD, wrote in a 2017 Psychopharmacology and Substance Abuse newsletter about the benefits of travel to mental health:

"Vacations can also improve our mental health by reducing depression and anxiety. Vacations can improve mood and reduce stress by removing people from the activities and environments that they associate with stress and anxiety. A Canadian study of over 800 lawyers found vacations reduced depression and buffered against job stress. Even a short vacation can reduce stress. A small Japanese study found a short, three-day leisure trip reduced perceived levels of stress and reduced levels of the 'stress hormone' cortisol." –Andrea Robinson, PhD

Dr. Wen's paper discusses many ideas that could lead to further research and the development of more diverse treatment options for people with dementia. And it proposes that researchers can more thoroughly explore tourism's medical benefits.

Further research can focus on the benefits of travel therapy in people with dementia. The authors note that there is limited research on how travel benefits tourists with vulnerabilities like dementia. The other component is how to best implement these practices. Dr. Wen explained that not every person with dementia would be able to travel.

"A team approach to dementia treatment helps to ensure the best possible care, and decisions about tourism as an intervention should be made with the input of the full team, including medical staff, caregivers, and family members," he said. "From a tourism destination perspective, many opportunities exist for marketing a destination as 'dementia friendly.'"

Dr. Wen added that hospitality staff could strive to accommodate guests with psychological conditions in a positive atmosphere. "Certain destinations may be able to incorporate some additional sensory exhibits that would provide a richer experience for visitors with dementia," he said.

When Cat was diagnosed with Early Onset Alzheimer's in 2014. We elected to retire, sell our home, and became nomads running marathons and half marathons all over the world. We have used two different tour companies during our travels. One is Marathon Tours and Travel, where we have done, soon to be, 27 trips with them, and Marathon Expeditions, where we have made 12 trips with them.

We have also gone on over 20 weeks of cruises from everything from River Cruises with AMA Waterways, The Caribbean, and Europe on small ships with Windstar Cruise Line to a few of the bigger ships. The most memorable would be crossing the Drake passage to and from Antarctica on a Russian Research Vessel.

I am not suggesting everyone take as drastic a step as us, but I do suggest that you give travel a try. I am sure there are places you have always wanted to go and visit, and there is no better time than the present. The travel industry is very accommodating, and they are trained to handle any conditions, including dementia.

A word of caution. If you buy insurance for you and your loved one, it will not cover any Alzheimer's/Dementia, mental illness-type claims. Recently, I bought insurance for the first time, and when I submitted my claim, it was at first denied. They were quick to point out the relevant exclusion. They ended up paying the claim after I reiterated the fact that it was the seizures, which is a medical condition, that was the reason for the cancellation. As a bonus, Delta also gave me eCredit for our canceled flights. I have since checked with several other insurance companies, and they all have that exclusion.

The time horizon for this disease varies from person to person, so I would suggest starting as early as possible. They say those with ALZ need a lifestyle that encompasses routine. Since travel has been in both of our blood. Travel is both our routine and medicine. It does get more challenging as the disease progresses, but for me, I love a good challenge.

Lewiston, Idaho
September 7, 2021

CHAPTER 17

Marathon Woman
Catherine Elizabeth Popp

◆ ◆ ◆

"The marathon is a long-distance foot race with a distance of 42.195 km (26 mi 385 yd), usually run as a road race, but the distance can be covered on trail routes. The marathon can be completed by running or with a run/walk strategy. There are also wheelchair divisions. More than 800 marathons are held throughout the world each year, with the vast majority of competitors being recreational athletes, as larger marathons can have tens of thousands of participants." ~Wikipedia

Less than one percent of the world's population has ever experienced running a marathon, and even fewer have run more than one. Only 5,000 people have run a marathon in all 50 states with only 1/3 of them being female. Little known fact. Less than 4,000 females have done all 6 major marathons, those being New York, Chicago, Boston, London, Tokyo, and Berlin. Needless to say, Catherine has all of that and more.

This is a chapter I wrote for the book Before the Diagnosis: More Stories of Life and Love Before Dementia. Creator and Editor Ginny Heins.

Catherine was diagnosed with early-onset Alzheimer's in 2014 at the age of 53. She is now in the moderate range in terms of the progression of the disease; however, she is still enjoying life to the fullest. Marathons don't define her but do describe her. The same determination and grit that is required to complete 26.2 miles on foot, nonstop, in a race have been her guiding light through the trials and tribulations of her current condition. April 2014, she was handed the detailed 29-page report from her neurologist that described her condition as early-onset Alzheimer's or like condition. They say you don't know for sure until the autopsy, so the three letters, EOA, will work for us for now. We could have done some more expensive testing to rule out other word-salad ailments, but how we tackle the daily challenges would still be the same.

Catherine Elizabeth Popp grew up amongst her four highly competitive siblings when even having a meal was a competitive sport. At the dinner table, you got what you could, and sharing was a personal foul. That attitude made its way to the football field for the three boys, with swimming and track for all five of them. Catherine's deceased dad, Tom, who succumbed to vascular dementia in his 70's, threw her in the pool at six and simply said, "Swim or drown." She has been doing all the strokes possible ever since then in this race we call life, her favorite being the butterfly because of its level of difficulty.

As a child, Catherine swam like a fish, earning a multitude of ribbons and trophies that had to share space with her sister's awards in the bedroom they shared. As an adult, one sport was not enough for her, so biking and running were added for one simple reason: because she could. For Catherine, winning was not as important as doing. The feeling of pushing herself was what made her feel the most comfortable.

Catherine is determined to live a full life even though there are many parts of it she may not clearly remember without a reminder. She definitely does not need to be reminded of the motorcycle ride she made to and from the West Coast from her hometown in Indiana. She soundly repeats that story every time she sees or even hears a motorcycle go by, her smile as wide as ever, which includes her beautiful, sparkling blue eyes. Catherine made the trip with a friend, each of them riding their own bike. It was an experience Catherine will never forget.

A college degree was something Catherine always wanted to earn and for her, no time was like the present. At the age of 32, she put the plan together to get it done in five years. That meant working at night, tossing packages, some the size of her, at UPS, and going to school during the day. Many thought that was a daunting task, but for her, it was just a way of life. That's the way Catherine approached everything, with enthusiasm and a detailed plan.

Catherine's daughter was in high school at this time, so she took care of her daughter, made meal preparations, and slept, along with working full-time and going to college. My head swims with thoughts of how she was able to do this all by herself! It does explain how she can handle the daily changes to her mind and how it currently processes information. This gives a picture of how determined Catherine has always been, even now. Just like the attitude she takes towards running a marathon, she just puts her head down, puts one foot in front of the other, and never gives up.

Catherine and her daughter are only 18 years apart in age, and she did the majority of the parenting all by herself. I still remember, to this day, when we first met, Catherine told me that she did not need a man, and she went through most of her life proving it in her own way. She lost her husband when she was in her 30s after only being married for a year. That is when marathoning came into her life like a guiding light. Her oldest brother took her under his wing to save her from the spiral of despair, and they began the journey of running a marathon in all 50 states. They began with 5K, 10K, and 13.1-mile half marathon races as they worked up to the 26.2-mile marathon distance at the Chicago Marathon in 1997.

I met Catherine by chance, as I overheard her talking to others about running marathons. I joined in on the conversation, and I knew in an instant that she was the one. Her stories took me back to my years growing up in New York, watching the New York City Marathon on TV. I dreamed of one day running in that race, not as one of the elite runners, the multitude of cameras following their every step, but as one of the masses of humanity that followed way behind. When Catherine talked about running a marathon, determination oozed from her pores, and I knew then that no matter what, she would always land on her feet.

I convinced Catherine to train me to run the New York City Marathon in 2000, and as they say, the rest is history. My thoughts were like most that complete a marathon, one and done, but she had other plans. Not sure if they included me but I was willing to tag along, as long as I could. Race after race became more daunting to me but seemed effortless to her.

In 2001, after 9/11, the Transportation Security Administration was spooled up in response, and Catherine, with an extensive scheduling background, joined forces as a Scheduling Operations Supervisor. She was responsible for the scheduling of all the agents in three airports in Kentucky. She was in her element, with everyone loving her even if they did not get exactly what they had hoped for on their daily schedule. She had a way to make everyone feel like they were her best friend and that she sincerely had all their best interests at heart.

Dogs, anything furry, and babies are her true weakness. Catherine took care of our two 90-pound dogs with ease, often having to referee between the two. Her days often started at 5:00 AM with these two highly rambunctious dogs. They frequently trained with her, with the Doberman completing a marathon with Catherine. My dog, which was a Weimaraner, had little interest in running that distance. He was more of a sprinter from one fire hydrant to the next.

I did take Catherine off course when it came to completing her goal of getting a marathon done in each state plus DC when we went to Athens, Greece, to run our first international marathon as my 50th birthday present to her. We went in 2010, which was a big deal for the Athens Marathon. It was merely 2500 years prior, in 490 BC, when Pheidippides ran from Marathon to Athens and later died. We were no longer getting faster, so when the thought of finishing the race in over 5 hours became apparent, we grabbed each other's hand and sprinted across the finish line. Being over a foot taller than Catherine, the finisher photo had her completely airborne, as if I was pulling a rag doll. The timing clock overhead read 4 hours and 59 minutes.

During conversations with others about our running prowess, Catherine was always quick to point out three things that separated the two of us.

One—that her fastest marathon time is eight minutes faster than mine. Catherine's is 3 hours and 49 minutes.

Two—that she actually qualified for the Boston Marathon. A runner has to accomplish a previous marathon within a specified time limit for their age and gender. I, however, donated to charity to get the opportunity to run the coveted marathon.

Three—she has run 15 more marathons than me. These three points will forever be.

One of Catherine's greatest accomplishments is her only daughter. She has grown into a successful lawyer who runs a law firm with her husband. Together, they have raised three fantastically ambitious children who all love to run, which gives Catherine much joy. Before her diagnosis, they lived close by, and she would visit them often to participate in many of their daily activities.

We enjoyed the adventures of travel to foreign lands as we would go on race-cations to places we could only imagine years prior. These international races slowed down the pace of Catherine's goal of finishing a marathon in all 50 states, but it was something she kept a keen eye on. Goal setting is an integral part of who she is.

I started to notice that she was not on her usual A-game, and she would begin asking me to repeat plans jointly made. Catherine got a new boss, and he was a "shake things up" type of guy. The routine was now her cornerstone, so he made life at work more difficult, which, in turn, made it easier to help Catherine realize that something was just not right. To help protect her government job, I made sure she saw and documented visits to the neurologist so that a simple firing by her new boss would not sweep the now obvious problem under the rug.

She was able to get a nice severance package, including a timely pension with health care. Social Security followed suit with a disability determination. The diagnosis, as it often does, changed our lives, as it does all, but our reaction to the news was counterintuitive.

We both retired, sold our home, and became nomads running all over the world. Catherine's resilience or reserve, as it were, is anything athletic, so we combined that with our love of travel. Together, we have visited 82 different countries and run at least a half marathon in 35 of them, with these events covering all seven continents. Catherine has completed 83 marathons, one Iron Man Competition, a 50-mile Ultra Marathon, and many races and triathlons of various distances. Before her diagnosis, she completed four of the six major marathons in New York, Chicago, Boston, and London. Since her diagnosis, she was able to achieve the other two in Tokyo and Berlin.

In October 2020, I had the pleasure to once again cross the finish line hand-in-hand with Catherine, but this time, it was when she completed her 50th state, in Narragansett, Rhode Island. She now has a fourth accomplishment to hold over my head and to brag to others about, but now, I doubt she will ever do so.

We celebrated Catherine's 60th birthday, along with her 86-year-old, highly energetic mother, at the Kentucky Derby, which falls on Catherine's birthday every five to six years. She was quick to remind us that she was also there when she turned 21 but did not actually see a single race. I wonder why.

Catherine's new goal is to finish a half marathon in all 50 states, and as of September 2021, she has 40 of them under her feet, with five more, for a total of 45, planned by the end of the year. Catherine expects to reach her goal in spring, 2022. You can follow her continued adventures at RunningwithCat.com and read all about our life as nomads in my book, Running All Over The World, Our Race Against Early Onset Alzheimer's.

Smyrna, Georgia
November 14, 2020

CHAPTER 18
This is it!
♦ ♦ ♦

"Nothing happens next. This is it." ~Zen saying.

I have a chapter in my previous book called This Is It or Is It. I am not going to give away the storyline in that chapter, but obviously, it wasn't. Since that chapter was written, we are still nomads moving about every 4 or so days. This chapter, however, is going to give you some insight into where Cat and I are going from here.

Once again, we are getting on a shiny Delta jet headed across the pond to Berlin with a 2-plus hour layover, first in Paris. My sister, Gwen, is meeting us there, so that will be a big help. I was able to use our global upgrades to get First Class, i.e., Delta One, but not quite sure how this is exactly going to work out.

In a previous chapter, The Road to Recovery, I talked about the importance of deep, restorative sleep for people with ALZ, and Cat has been getting 8-9 and sometimes as many as 10 hours of restorative sleep a night. She is hard to get going with less than 6 hours, so I probably will just let her nap for a few hours and then wake her with breakfast on the descent.

I did discuss this trip with her Nurse Practitioner at the Integrated Memory Center, and her response was simply, "Of course you are." She did give me some great tips for the flight over and back and also, in general, moving forward. She also gave us some cards to give to the flight attendants of the long-haul flights, simply saying that my companion has Alzheimer's. It brought Cat and I much joy to give her an autographed copy of our book, and we all shed a tear or two.

As you can already see, I am planning this whole trip out just like I was flying the plane overseas myself. Back when I did that, we always had contingency plans laid out throughout the flight with the goal of getting to the destination safely and on time. In this case, this 14-day trip to both Berlin and Scotland is chalked full of tours with the Lock Ness 10k in Scotland.

With no race in Berlin, some might be already wondering why we are even going in the first place. There are several very good reasons. 7 years ago, this past June, I had open heart surgery to replace my leaky aortic valve. Three months later, I ran the Berlin Marathon, so this race and place hold so many special memories.

We don't do marathons much anymore, so I figured it would be great to just sit back and cheer others on. We were to do a breakfast run, but due to Covid, it was canceled. Speaking of Covid for a minute. Germany and Scotland are not playing around when it comes to allowing foreigners in their country. I don't plan on giving many details, but no telling as this plan unfolds.

Another reason is that this trip was about 5 months after Cat was diagnosed with Early-onset Alzheimer's and just 1 month before her retirement. I followed suit 3 months later, and as they say, the rest is history. Cat has been looking forward to seeing all her buddies who work for Marathon Tours and Travel, along with the dozen or so new best friends we have met touring and running with them over the last 10 years.

Lastly, I was asked to speak during one of their dinners. Actually, three times since the group of 500 can only seat 150 or so at a time. More importantly, I do love talking about our experiences and hope maybe I can inspire others to look at life just a bit differently. Especially if they are ever faced with a life-altering ailment like ALZ. Unfortunately, unless a miracle happens, this will be our last trip to Europe.

Over the last month, I have done about a dozen podcast interviews. Most, not specifically, about ALZ but more about our attitude toward life in general and our counterintuitive approach towards the disease. Several suggested that I start my own podcast, but that sounds too much like work.

I try my best not to go into many details when it comes to Cat's health. It has always been a sine wave in decline, with some days being better than others but still in a slow decline. On a positive note, she is usually very cooperative, loves to go for a run, race, or long walk, and asks me several times a day, "Did I tell you today that I love you?" So, all is good from my perspective.

While we were in Atlanta before this trip, we did go up to Roswell, Georgia, to run the Team Maggie's Dream 10k. and had a fabulous time running along the Chattahoochee River. They have running, walking, and biking paths all along it. As always, we crossed the finish hand in hand, and I even came in second in my age group. Granted, there were only two of us, but thousands my age did not even bother to try, so all is good in my book.

The flight over went better than I could have hoped, but the transition to the six-hour time change was an entirely different story. It took three days for Cat's circadian rhythm to switch over, and since we were doing a lot of tours during that time, we were not able to get our usual dose of endorphins from our exercise routine.

The speeches were well received, and I only choked up three times during the first one and only once during the last one. I did have a line about how Cat and I always finish hand in hand, but every time I tried to go there, I could feel myself getting ready to cry outright. I am sure most got the sentiment of my speech anyhow.

After Berlin, we flew over to Edinburg, Scotland, for more tours for two days and then on to Inverness by bus for the Lock Ness 10K on Sunday, with more tours prior. To be able to stay in Scotland, you have to test within two days of arrival, and the form they had you fill out was one that you really have to be motivated to be there, to complete entirely.

Cat and I had been to Edinburg before, and it is my first book, so I won't go into details here. It is a bit chillier than I expected, so it is once again a layer-up type of trip. Right before we left, our previous book was recommended by ALZAuthors.com. That is a big deal for me since it is the only site that vets books about Alzheimer's.

We took a leisurely bus ride from Edinburg to Inverness, stopping multiple times along the way, which included a very nice stop for lunch in Pitlochry. The little town was very quaint. The walk along the river that they had damned but provided a Salmon Walk so the Salmon could make their way around the damn to their spawning area was pretty cool.

Once in Inverness, we had two full days of tours, which included multiple tours of Castles. We even took an hour-long tour of Lake Lock Ness. Unfortunately, no Nessie sightings. I gave another speech to the 40 of us in this tour extension, and several came up to tell us their own stories.

One gentleman had just had brain surgery to remove a tumor. His chances of living through the operation were less than 50/50, and they doubted his chances of talking and walking and had zero chance of completing a marathon, which he did. He starts Chemo next week.

Another world traveler, Cyrus, with whom we had been to Madagascar together, completed his 50th marathon in a different country for a total of over 200. His wife, Ardie, joined him on this trip, and I followed her successful battle with cancer through Cyrus's Facebook posts. As I mentioned during my speech, everyone has a story, and you cannot tell what they might be by simply looking at them.

The 10k race was mostly slightly downhill, and the Sun Gods were out the entire time for us. I understand the Marathoners were not so lucky. Our time was 20 seconds faster than the last 10K in Georgia, but we were not there for the time. It was the scenery and the people that brought us to this neck of the woods. I just wish it had been a tad warmer and sunnier, but when you travel the world, you have no control over the weather.

We are now starting our trek back to the States. Our route has us overnight in Amsterdam, so not only did we have to provide a negative COVID test 72 hours before departure to get back in the States, but we also had to use the same test to overnight in the Netherlands, 48 hours before departure.

Overall, it was well worth all the paperwork, multiple testing, and vaccination requirements because, at heart, Cat and I were born to roam. But I do have to admit having to wear our masks for 17-plus hours there and back was a bit nerve-racking. However, Cat handled it like the true trooper she was.

It is interesting that when I started writing about this trip, I was certain this would be our last trip overseas, but now, as I reflect on the last two weeks, I am more prone to take a never-say-never-type attitude. It would definitely be with a group, including tours and most likely to someplace new.

We have a trip planned to Costa Rica for a week in the middle of January with Marathon Expeditions, so for now, it is a go as we take it one day at a time. There will be plenty of running on that trip. In retrospect, I probably should have planned better so we could get more exercise in, but deep down, I did not want to miss anything on the many tours. I will make sure to make up for it when we get back to Atlanta.

We usually have an easier time transitioning when we get back to the States, but this will be a very long day with the stop in JFK. I had to go this route to ensure we both got the upgrades, so it is well worth the extra few hours of travel time. It only took Cat one day to transition her body clock, but on night two, I still have a ways to go. We did get in a good, hard 4-mile run yesterday, and we are off to our all-time favorite place to run, The Silver Comet Trail.

Since we don't drink Alcohol anymore, we traded that vice for a Mocha Green Tea for Cat and a Pumpkin Spice Latte for me. I know the perfect place near the Silver Comet to enjoy on the way back to the hotel after another not-so-hard 5-mile run/walk. The other indulgence is dessert, but I figure with us running or walking just about every day, we deserve it. Calories in equal calories out.

I have our schedule planned out through Thanksgiving with trips to Connecticut, Kentucky, Indiana, Oregon, California, Washington, and another Half Marathon in New Mexico. I pretty much decided to take December and parts of January to get our Motor Home, "The Crib", back up and running. It has been sitting up now for several years in Fort Myers, Florida, so no telling what I am in store for.

As they say in the movie Nomadland, see you down the road.

Inverness, Scotland
October 1, 2021

CHAPTER 19

How Do You Overcome Doubt When Chasing a Dream?

♦ ♦ ♦

"Doubt kills more dreams than failure ever will."
~Suzy Kassem

I would like to share with you an article I ran across on LinkedIn by Richard Branson. He is one of my idols. We have a shared philosophy. We both believe that we don't have to know everything; we just need to know where to find that information and surround ourselves with very smart people. Einstein once said, when asked a question, "I don't know. I don't burden my memory with such facts that I can easily find in any textbook."

When I used to teach pilots at UPS, I had a huge book that I would bring to each class, and it contained all the reference materials for what I would be teaching that day. Also, as a manager at UPS, I would make sure to surround myself with the smartest people for whatever project I was working on.

I learned from the first version of my first book that It is not always possible in the real world. I hired people to help me with that project, but unfortunately, you don't always get what you pay for. No big deal: I have learned a lot in the process. I did not let that stop me. Since I was not perfectly satisfied, I found a different publisher for the abridged version. Practice makes perfect.

So many times, with the book project, I wanted to throw up my hands and walk away, but as you will read in this article, there are very good reasons why you should not do so. At the same time, there are reasons you should reevaluate your decision to continue down that path.

~Richard Branson

What I've learned throughout my life is that every success is built upon a thousand failures (or 'opportunities to learn', as I like to think of them). Whenever doubt creeps in, I remind myself that dreams aren't linear. I also think of all the brilliant innovations and discoveries that would have come to nothing if their inventors had given in to their doubts. I'm sure everyone from Thomas Edison to Gertrude Stein doubted their dreams from time to time, but the difference is they didn't let it knock them off course.

It's always a good idea to discuss any doubts you have with colleagues and friends and to really listen to their feedback. If you feel more confident after these conversations, take a 'screw it, let's do it' attitude and push your doubts to the side.

It's also healthy and perfectly human to have a little bit of doubt. It's how we make progress and stay in touch with reality. Your doubts may signal a niggling problem that needs to be addressed. If you demand proof from your doubt, you'll be able to either squash it or solve the problem. Either way, your dreams and ideas will be better for it.

The day after we launched Virgin Atlantic, the bank manager came to my house and threatened to shut us down. I managed to get him out of the door and brought my team together to find a solution. It was a very sweaty moment, but I didn't let doubt creep in, and we quickly fixed the issue.

If things really start to get you down, my advice would be to step outside, get some fresh air, and have a cup of tea. Whenever doubt starts to get the better of me, I find exercise really helps. I'll get on my bike, play some tennis, or have some downtime with my family. This is often when my best ideas come to me as well!

For me, some of my best ideas come to me while I am running. The bottom line, I did not give up, and overall, I am very happy with the outcome. Many ask why I wrote a book in the first place. I have several answers depending on who is asking.

I love listening to books as opposed to sitting down and reading one. I listen to many while traveling, running, or right before bed. I thought it would be great for Cat and me to listen to our travels, so I reverse-engineered the project. For that to be possible, first, I had to write the book. I did a lot of writing articles at my old job, and that continued through my open-heart surgery. I wrote to a journal and shared with other open heart surgery patients at Heart-Valve-Surgery.com.

It was very therapeutic, and reading other journals gave me a great insight into what to expect. As you will read in a later chapter, journaling plays a very important role in the mental health of full-time care partners, such as myself. That morphed into a blog I wrote to while traveling. When I decided to write a book, I simply took that material, edited it myself while stuck in St. Kitts due to COVID-19, and then hired a professional editor. I then selected a publisher and planned on doing the same with this book without the stuck-in St. Kitts part.

I must admit the most rewarding part was working with the narrator, Lucas, who did a great job. He had it done on time and under budget, which was very refreshing since some other experiences with the book did not go as well. The other day, we were driving to Richmond, Virginia, and it was with great joy to hear

Cat's laughter and see her smiles as we listened to our book on Audible on the car radio. It made all the fits and starts worth it.

Lastly, I plan on donating a portion of the proceeds on the sale of both books, in all formats, to organizations that provide support to Alzheimer's patients and their caregivers.

CHAPTER 20
Are you taking care of yourself?

♦ ♦ ♦

"It is a common misconception that thinking taking care of your-self means having a "me first" attitude, it isn't, it means having a "me too" attitude." ~eventgreetings.com

Everyone keeps asking me that question. Are you taking care of yourself? I am sure they all mean well, but for the life of me, I can not figure out exactly what they mean by that. I ran across an article entitled, A Helicopter Style of Alzheimer's Caring, which I will include here for context. The premise is that we, as caregivers, should not hover over our Loved One's like parents do with their kids.

A Helicopter Style of Alzheimer's Caring
By Nikki Nurse

Welcome to Caregiver – You are Doing Too Much 101. In today's lesson, we are going to discuss the helicopter style of caring and the importance of taking breaks for self-care as you care for your LOWD (loved one with dementia). Alright class let's sharpen those pencils and get to work!

A helicopter style of caring comes from the term helicopter parenting, which often refers to a style of parents who, like helicopters, hover and oversee every aspect of their child's life. Yup, overhead, oversee, and overdo. I was an overly focused caregiver to my mom with Alzheimer's, and I was doing too much! In my own defense, I used this style of caring to prevent my mom from experiencing getting hurt, being misunderstood, and protecting her independence but all that attention was just a recipe for my own burnout.

Are you helicopter-caring?

Yes, attention. That is the keyword especially when we are speaking about a helicopter style of caring, am I right? Well, it is also the key question that I would like to propose to you. How much attention do you give to yourself? How much attention do you give to your loved one?

If you are like me then, you are giving them A LOT – so much that it takes away from the attention you should give to yourself. This was the case for me. I made it incredibly difficult to prioritize any type of wellness in my life specific to my mental and physical health. My reasoning for justifying this? I was preserving as much normalcy for my mom as possible.

Why does helicopter caring happen?

As mom's caregiver, I felt the enormous weight of keeping her busy, entertained, and mentally stimulated. Admittedly, I gave my mom all my attention to the point that I became a helicopter caregiver. I did not realize then that monitoring my mom's everyday engagement and interaction, in a sense, was preventing me from being present to my own needs. But I love my mom, and I wanted to give her purpose and hope after being diagnosed.

At the age of 58, my mom was living with early-onset Alzheimer's, and life became very different from the one she was accustomed to living. Never one to catch sitting down relaxing, my mom was on the go from before the sun came up to after the moon was shining bright in the sky. At the time, I admired this about her, her energy, her grind, but I realized later on when I became her full-time caregiver that it may not have been the healthiest form of living.

How do we prevent overbearing care?

To be honest, the first step for me was to extend grace to myself for neglecting my needs. My second step, giving myself permission to prioritize my focus on my immediate needs, both mental and physical. Creating a wellness routine that I could easily practice daily; whether that was staying active every day or sitting with a book to read at night. It made a difference in the style of care for my mom.

Who knew that by making an effort to prioritize your own health, you create the space to rock out caring for others? OK class, did you get all that? I'm curious to learn what your style of caring is! How do you prioritize self-care practices for your life?

My thoughts on taking care of yourself.

I am a firm believer in, "Do on to others as you would want them to do on to you." As Cat's care partner, I would hope she would do the same for me. When we embarked on this adventure that is coming up on 7 years, I had a choice to make. Should I continue to work and have her fend for herself during the day or, as I did, retire and be by her side 24/7? As I say to her all the time, where I go, she goes, and where she goes, I go.

This has helped me to be more responsive to her ever-changing needs. The little nuances that I would have missed while away at work 8-10 hours a day. At the same time, what would she be doing during that time besides walking around the house trying to find one item after another that she misplaced? Only for me to come home and put the house back together as she tore it up trying to find those items.

Since exercise is our passion and we both love to travel, I have combined the two so that we can enjoy these activities as long as we can. From time to time, it is frustrating trying to figure out how to navigate the maze of Alzheimer's. Since I am truly a manager by heart, it always intrigues me to try to figure out what is best for her and, by extension, me.

I take care of myself by solving the puzzle of travel minute by minute. What are the best flights to catch, hotels to stay at, restaurants to eat at, and, of course, what races to run? We both enjoy a good walk in a beautiful park and on top of that, they say, that is also good for her brain.

I did a podcast the other day, and the gentleman pointed out that I use travel as a form of medicine. I have often heard that movement is medicine, so I will have to add travel to our medicine cabinet. I probably have learned as much from each of these podcast interviews as from their host and guests. I have done over a dozen so far and have another half dozen on the schedule. Cat enjoys listening to me doing them. So much so that you can hear her giggling in the background on one.

I also know that by taking care of myself, I can be there for Cat. It turns out that over half the caregivers die before their loved ones. I don't want to contribute to that statistic. I don't think much about that possibility since the more you think about something, the more the likelihood it will happen.

I am going to take a moment to talk about how Cat is doing. I don't do this very often, but I hope this snapshot is useful to others traveling down this road with us. I have often talked about the importance of sleep for folks with ALZ, and back then, she was starting to have problems getting her normal 8-9 hours of sleep, so she started to have delusions from time to time.

All was well on the sleep front because of the supplement Mind Restore by Alchemy, and the delusions, in turn, went away and have not returned. I sometimes refer to our health issues as whack a mole. As soon as I figure out a solution to one, another one raises its ugly head. That is for both of us. We are presently headed to the West Coast for two half marathons; more about that later. Also to have my gut checked after an operation that was done several years ago to repair an aneurysm on my right iliac artery.

Well, for Cat, she started to fidget quite a bit and twisting her fingers. Unfortunately, this is pretty common for folks with ALZ progress. Working with the Integrated Memory Center folks in Atlanta, we tried some different prescribed medications. Over the years, I have tried my best to keep her off actual medications and try to find a supplement for the solution. It turns out that some of the hard-core medications can accelerate the downward spiral. It had gotten so bad that it was once again preventing her from sleeping, which in turn would not allow the "wash cycle", as I call it, to take place in her brain.

During sleep, if you can get into deep sleep, the brain releases a fluid that helps remove accumulated toxins. In her case, Amyloid Plaques. With her continuing to wake up several times a night, that "wash cycle" can not take place. Back to taking care of myself, it also prevented me from getting a good night's sleep.

As always, I researched for a solution, especially since she had a very bad reaction to one of the medications. They say that the fidgets and twisting of the fingers are a reaction to stress and anxiety, so I looked for an over-the-counter solution. For the sleep solution, I was able to find and add Sleep 3+ by Nature's Bounty. It is listed for stress support. It has three benefits in one. Benefit 1: GABA helps support occasional stress. Benefit 2: Quick-release melatonin helps you fall asleep fast. Benefit 3: Time-release melatonin works with your body's natural sleep cycle to help you stay asleep.

We are now back to 8-9 hours of sleep for her and my usual 6-7 hours of sleep for me. I don't take it, but I do take 1, Mind Restore, and a gummy 10mg of melatonin 30 minutes before bedtime. Since she is now getting to experience the "Wash cycle" of sleep, her days are much better, and we are back to where we were 6-8 months ago. She is still very cooperative, and with the cooler weather, we have been out running or some other form of exercise just about every day.

With that said, occasionally, the fidgets and twisting of the fingers do come back during the day, and for that, I give her Olly, Goodbye Stress Gummies. It also has GABBA, L-Theanine, and Lemon Balm. They say it is to keep you calm and stay alert. I give her one of the two recommended and the second one later in the day if they come back.

Right now, we are headed to Portland for what I am calling the West Coast Swing. We are to do the Columbia Gorge Half Marathon for the third time in 5 years. That is highly unusual for us, but you can't beat the views along the course, and the fall colors should be in full bloom. They encourage dogs on the course, and the first year, we started behind the dog wave, and Cat was in heaven running ahead, petting them while waiting for me.

We also have some friends who have been on several Marathon Tours trips with us in the past who all live in Portland, so it will be great to catch up with them. The first part of the race went well as we climbed 500 feet along the mountain on one side and the Columbia River on the other side. The views and fall colors were spectacular, but the rain Gods had their way with us on the way back down.

As the intensity of the rain increased, the temperature continued to drop, and we were now soaked with about 2 miles to go. Cat was starting to experience mild hypothermia. We ended up walking the last mile, and that did not help matters. We did manage to finish once again hand in hand, and she snapped back pretty quickly after a few cups of well-needed hot Apple Cider.

From there on to Los Angeles to catch up with our friend, Wendy. We will also have lunch with Susie and Dan with the Podcast Love Conquers ALZ, which I was a guest on several months ago. I will also be doing a podcast interview from our hotel. One of the things that is great about Podcasts is that I can be anywhere in the world, or they can be. I did one where the gentleman was in London and another one where the lady was in Paris.

On one of their Love Conquers ALZ podcasts, they interviewed Elizabeth Miller, Certified Caregiver, and Consultant, on the topic of taking care of yourself as a caregiver. She talks about how her writing is part of her self-care. I also find writing and talking about my book helps me a lot. I can express how I feel from time to time as opposed to keeping all those feelings bottled up.

After a scenic drive from Los Angeles to San Diego, we met up with my eldest son, Aaron, and daughter-in-law, Kelsey. We were also able to get in a good slow 6-mile run at Mission Beach and a 3-mile walk at Mission Regional Park. Two of my favorite places to run and walk while in San Diego. Unfortunately, my right calf is giving me fits, so I will have to take a few days off for it to heal before a half marathon in New Mexico in a week.

The next stop is Seattle for the gut check. I brought along my doctor's own personal autographed copy of our book, especially since she is mentioned by name in the book for the outstanding repair job she and her staff did. However, I think I am going to find someone in Atlanta for the routine yearly checks from now on.

Back to Los Angeles for two days, then on to New Mexico to once again meet up with my sister, Gwen, and my sister-in-law, Joan, to do another half marathon, this time in Farmington, New Mexico, with, once again, Mainly Marathons. This will be state number 41 for us in our goal to get a half marathon in all 50 states. They are both going to do the 10K while there. I think I might have them both hooked.

The Farmington half marathon went well as we ran along the Animas River on the Berg Park trail. Little did I know that there was a War Memorial right across the river, and we had to go back the next day to visit the site. I must say they did a great job of memorializing the sacrifices that were made over the years for our freedom. On our way back to Albuquerque, we had to stop at the Bisti/De-Na-Zin Wilderness Area to get a gander at a big hole in the earth. It was about an hour out of the way but well worth it.

Back in Atlanta, that will be stop number 650, still averaging 4 days per stop in almost 7 years. Time flies when you are having fun, and it goes by even faster when you are retired. Speaking of which, my previous employer set aside just enough money to pay out for 5 years, so now I am on the plus side of the actuary game.

During this 19-day trip, we were able to meet up with 13 different people we knew from previous trips. That is another way I take care of myself. That and the fact that during this trip, I did make a stop to get my gut aneurism repair checked out.

Back to the title of this chapter. I think I might have figured out what people mean when they ask if I am taking care of myself. They are not offering to help out, especially since we can't seem to stay put for more than a few days, but more of a reminder for me to also do what is good for myself. I look at this disease as a team effort to hold it off for as long as possible. I would love for Cat to be in a position to be one day cured, and she will have to be in relatively good mental shape to participate in that cure.

In the meantime, we will continue to do what we are doing as long as we can and enjoy ourselves as best we can along the way. Back in 2015, after the failure of the Mindset Clinical Trial, I entertained participating in a protocol established by Dale E.

Bredesen, MD. We did some of what was suggested, but recently, I ran across his second book called, The First Survivors of Alzheimer's, How Patients Recovered Life and Hope in Their Own Words.

I could kick myself for not going all in with his protocol, but I always try to learn from my mistakes and now plan on following it to a T. First, we had to have some extensive blood tests done where they took 15 tubes of blood. I asked the folks at Quest Diagnostics what is the most they have taken and she said 75. They had to do so over about an hour to keep the lady from fainting. 15 tubes was the most I had witnessed, and I have given a bunch of blood with my two operations. After the analysis of the blood is done, they will recommend a strict supplement regime. We also might have to modify her diet somewhat, but we shall see.

He recommends 6 days of exercise, and in the book, he debunks all the excuses one might give for not doing so. Now that we have sleep back under control, they will also look at optimum thyroid levels and screen for possible toxins, pathogens, etc. Once again, going back to my love to manage and solve problems, this will be right down my alley and, at the same time, a way to take care of myself since if Cat is happy, I, too, am happy.

During some of the podcasts that I have done, the question of not following a routine lifestyle keeps coming up. I admit that what we are doing is counterintuitive, but it seems to work for us. What is routine, anyhow? Since I left home to go to college, I have been on the road ever since. Some places a few years longer than others, but as a pilot for 37 years, most of it was spent living out of a suitcase.

I believe some people use routine as an excuse since it does take more effort to live life the way we do, but by contrast, they say you must exercise your brain daily. They suggest brain games like crossword puzzles, etc. As Cat and I navigate the maze of travel from hotel check-out to hotel check-in, I can easily say I exercised her brain over the day. Following the commands from me and others is not easy for her, and sometimes it is frustrating, but at the same time, she knows when it is all over, she will be breathing the air in a new city with all its different sights and sounds. Also, there is probably one of our "new best friends" waiting for us when we arrive.

She will always have me by her side, and I cannot imagine it being any other way. Maybe one day it will be too hard for me to handle it by myself, and if that day comes, we will have settled down, and if someone comes up to me and asks if I am taking care of myself, I can then say, No, can you please help me? No one knows when or if that day will come, so until then, I will continue taking care of myself the best way I can, one day or footstep at a time.

CHAPTER 21

Beauty and The Beast

♦ ♦ ♦

"Do not take life too seriously. You will never get out of it alive."
~Elbert Hubbard

I often tell folks that for me, I have to come up with a title for a chapter before I can start writing it. Then, I find a quote like the one above, and that is how the story develops. Most titles have double meanings, and I hope you enjoy this one about our 12-day adventure to Costa Rica with our running buddies, Marathon Expeditions.

They say it is very beneficial for folks with Alzheimer's and ALZ to see and experience all the beauties of nature. Everywhere you turn here in Costa Rica, you are sure to experience the beautiful sights and sounds. This will be the 13th trip we have done with this running group over the last 11-plus years.

The original plan was for Cat and I to only do the 7-day trip, but the night after our arrival, I started to wonder why we were going to leave just because everyone else was. People often ask me if I miss flying planes myself, and the answer is always a very simple "Nope." After 37 years of going where and when my employer wanted me to go, I enjoy just sitting back and relaxing and letting someone else make those thousands of decisions to get the plane safely from point A to point B.

I must admit on the flight from Atlanta, ATL, to San Jose, SJO, I did go into pilot mode. A snowstorm had been predicted for the day of departure, and a few days prior, I went into contingency mode. I tried to figure out if there was a better way for us to get to SJO. When I originally booked our flights many months ago, I bought main cabin seats. We got upgraded to comfort plus seats. However, the two seats together were exit row seats. As time has moved on, I did not feel it was a good idea for Cat to be sitting there since she is no longer able to do all that is required to occupy those seats.

By now, there were no seats together, and First class was listed as full. I say listed since I was no longer able to pay for an upgrade, even though there were a few seats they were holding to the side for day-of-flight upgrades. So now the thought was to leave a day early and pay the extra price for First Class on that flight. The only problem with that idea was that I would have to pay twice the amount more than my original ticket. I was unable to swallow that pill, so I looked at flying to one of Delta's other hubs like New York's, JFK, Minneapolis, MSP, or Detroit, DTW a day early and then flying from there to SJO. Another problem with that idea was that they all came to ATL before going on to SJO. Lucky for me, by the time I was ready to bite the bullet and pay the extra fare for the flight the day prior, everyone else had already done so. No First Class, comfort, or main cabin seats together.

All I could do now was hope that the snow and ice storm did not start until after departure time and the few first-class seats would still be available for upgrade just before departure. The next morning, I woke up an hour before my alarm went off, and when I checked the Delta app, there were now 9 First Class seats. I can only speculate as to why. Since Cat and I are both Diamond Medallion and Million Milers, I felt pretty confident we would get two of those seats. It showed that we were, in fact, one and two for the upgrade.

The only thing left was for the weather to cooperate. At the ticket counter, 2 hours prior, six of those coveted first-class seats were now gone. Cat and I were still one and two for the remaining 3 seats, none of them together, but I was still in pilot mode, and I had a plan. At the gate, I asked if we could get the window and aisle behind each other, and I would simply ask either person to switch since they would still get their requested window or aisle, just in a different row.

No problem there; however, when we were all settled in about 15 minutes prior, and the snow and ice were now only about 30 minutes away, there were way too many empty seats for us to push on time. So yes, we did wait about 15 minutes for connecting passengers and came to find out those 6 first-class seats that vanished earlier were taken by folks who had gotten stuck in Buffalo and missed their flight the day prior.

I knew then we were not going to beat the weather and to make it more definitive, we had to wait an additional 15 minutes for a pushback tug. Just as predicted, after pushback, we went to the deice pad and ended up being 2 hours late. The beast of the weather just slowed us down. However, the beauty of San Jose, Costa Rica, was still there, waiting with all its glory.

As Cat and I have run all over the world for the last seven years, we have stayed at some very nice hotels and resorts. Many of them being 5 stars but the Springs Resort in La Fortuna at the base of the Arenal Volcano was 10 stars, if there is such a thing.

It is suggested, and we do this a lot during our travels, to visit botanical gardens, but until this trip, I cannot say I stayed at a hotel/resort that was in one.

Cat often says to me, "Build it, and they will come". Dubai was a prime example of that, with all the one-of-a-kind, biggest, and tallest of everything. That is not the case here. The resort was built next to an active volcano, but there has not been an eruption since 2010, and it feeds a multitude of hot springs. Of course, because of them, you have any outdoor adventure activities known to man. Too many to mention here.

Since grand adventures are no longer our forte, we chose an hour's hike across two of the four swinging bridges. Our guide kept trying to find snakes, which is not high on my list of things to see, but the Howler monkeys swinging and just relaxing in the trees was more my speed. The rest of the group went zip lining, and stories told of top speeds on the two miles of zip lines sounded exhilarating.

We also came here to run, so while at the first resort for 4 nights, we did a 5K followed by a fantastic and very informative coffee and chocolate tour. My new favorite is honey coffee. The winners of that race were the fastest male and female runners and walkers. For the next race, you could do either a 5 or 10k around Lake Arenal. We finished up at the Howlers Monkey Bar and Grill for librations.

We went for the 5k and caught the first bus back to the resort for some well-needed hot springtime. The winner of that race was whoever got Aces that were randomly handed out from several decks of cards at the finish.

Right now, we are at the back of the tour bus with me in the middle seat, obviously for the legroom. Today, we are going cross country to our beach resort for 3 nights.

We made it to the Si Como No Resort and Wildlife Refuge in Manuel Antonio unscathed. It was a 7-hour bus ride door to door with an hour stop for a nice lunch. It was a slight step down from the resort we just left but by far better than 90% of the hotels we have stayed at over the years. They have stairs everywhere, which is good for Cat's coordination.

Something else that comes to mind when thinking about the title is the beauty of Cat. Her beautiful blue eyes captivated me when we first met, and how they sparkled right along with her engaging smile. I point her toward the camera and say smile, and they both come alive.

She also has a beautiful soul. One that is always willing to help a stranger, someone she knows, or even whoever she talks to in the mirror. In reality, no one is a stranger to her, and she treats everyone like they are her best friends.

Then you have me as the beast. The one that has to ask and sometimes gently tell her what to do constantly. It is my fault since we are on the go all the time, and with exercise, showers, and all, I am there at every turn trying to get her to do such and such. We would not have it any other way. The constant changes to her environment, in my mind, keep her engaged and, with that, keep her brain cells wired as best as possible.

I take my role as the beast seriously. There is so much to see and do in this vast world, and since she might not live as long as most, however, she will still see and experience more than most, and that is okay with us.

We enjoyed a great run on the beach the following day with some pool time back at the hotel. The group did a relay race format for 4 or 6 miles a half mile at a time. It was a predicted race, with the winners coming in only a few seconds off their time. Since we now, always run together, we walked out 1/4 mile and then ran back for a total of 2 miles.

Many of us were out in the sun a bit too long, but I still find it funny that we are all getting tans in January. We ended up calling ourselves "the renegades" since, with COVID-19 doing its thing, the 50 of us banded together to make this adventure a reality.

John and Jenny filmed us all running/walking towards the water, and he commented on something I once said about them. "They could get this group of lemmings to jump off a Clift if they wanted". They would not even need a club.

The last day of this 7 mountains to Pacific coast trip included a tour of the largest National Park in Costa Rica called the Manuel Antonio National Park. We had Sloths, Bats, and Monkeys sightings. On the way back to the entrance to the park, we were also able to witness the most beautiful beaches in all of Costa Rica. They call them Beach 1,2 and 3.

The day ended with the awards ceremony, where Cat and I got the Courage to Love award and were given the coveted yellow hat. It took me a while to fully grasp the meaning of Courage to Love since, for me, the Love that Cat and I have for each other takes no courage at all. I, in turn, was able to give them their very own autographed copy of our book.

I was reminded, however, that some take the easy way out when going down this path. They throw up their hands and simply find someone else to do the daily tasks. You could also say, on Cat's part, it takes courage to love someone as much as she loves me, to trust me to the point she does, most times, while not knowing exactly where she is and what we are about to do. The same trust a blind person has for their cane or dog. The other way to look at it is that it takes a great deal of courage to throw caution to the wind and follow your love/passion for running and combine that with your love/passion for travel.

I get great joy when Cat musters up the words to express her thanks for all that I do for her or apologizes when the beast of ALZ raises its ugly head. I would not trade the journey with the love of my life for all the tea in China. It has taught me so much about myself and my real and perceived abilities.

I do a lot of my writing while in transit by planes, trains, and buses. Now, back to how this 7-night planned trip turned into 12 nights. As I sometimes do, I look at our schedule and see what we have planned and noticed I did have a Zoom meeting with a New Jersey running group. I had planned to do it back in ATL but had the same exit row seats with little chance of upgrades for the trip back. Now, with no real reason to have to leave, since all I need is the internet to do Zoom. I started looking at flights on other days and ran across plenty of first-class seats on Friday, 5 days later, for only 300 bucks more.

At my last job at UPS, I was responsible for the flight crews flying out of Miami for all parts of Central and South America, and I have very fond memories of layovers at the Costa Rica Marriott Hotel Hacienda Belen outside of San Jose, which was probably one of the best properties in our system. We ended up staying there near the beginning of our trek of running all over the world. We stayed there for a week before a Windstar Cruise through the Panama Canal. 100k points later, we were all set, and it turns out that by staying here an additional 5 days, it will turn out to be about 500 bucks overall cheaper, win-win.

Tomorrow, most head back to their homes and I am so happy I decided to stay 5 extra days and not have to set an alarm and just sit back and enjoy the pure beauty of Costa Rica. I am sure Cat will ask, when it is just the two of us, "Where is everybody else?" as she often does when these tours come to an end. My reply, as always, will be. "What am I, chop liver."

I am going to close this chapter out here since we will probably just be running and swimming for the next 5 days. Not much to write about there. I might get a haircut, shave, and her hair done. Maybe find a gentle horse for Cat to ride. They say that is very good therapy, and over the years, we have been on many horseback rides. I am always trying to find something to help her enjoy life as best she can for as long as she can. I don't dwell on tomorrow much since one thing I know for sure is that no one is getting out of this thing called life alive.

So, basically, for the next 5 days, we will continue to enjoy the beauty of Costa Rica and Cat's infectious smile and try to tame the beast of ALZ, one footstep at a time.

San Ramon, Costa Rica
January 19, 2022

Espadilla Beach, Costa
Rica
January 21, 2022

Aguirre, Costa Rica
January 23, 2022

CHAPTER 22

The Caregiver's Companion, Caring for
Your Mind, Body, and Spirit

♦ ♦ ♦

"You are the caregiver, not the cure-giver." ~Siegel & Yosaif

This is by far the most comprehensive guidebook that I have found during my journey with Cat. I refer to it often and only wish that I had found it right after she was first diagnosed. Back then, I did not realize how important it would be to take care of myself since I was "all in" when it came to the care of Cat.

I must admit I do not follow it step by step, but every time I review the material, I find another informative gem that I include in my tool belt. I hope each of you finds the information contained in this chapter as useful as it has been for me. You are no good to the person you are caring for if something were to happen to you during the process of taking care of them.

As a caregiver, you have a job that changes constantly depending on your loved one's health and needs. You deal with expectations and feel many emotions. Being a caregiver can be a long journey with many challenges. Taking good care of yourself, also called self-care, is essential to your health and sense of being well. It also helps the loved one you are taking care of.

Your emotions may include feeling overlooked by the healthcare professionals caring for your loved one. You might feel alone and unable to talk to your loved one about how the situation makes you feel. Perhaps you feel misunderstood by friends, family, and coworkers.

This guidebook is here to support you, whatever your relationship is with the person you care for. You are husbands and wives, parents and children, friends, relatives, and acquaintances. And you are not alone on this journey.

So often, you hear that it's important to take care of yourself. But for caregivers like you, who spend so much time and effort caring for someone else, how is that possible, and what does it mean? Another important group of individuals reading this guide are those coping with the loss of their loved ones.

This guide is based on scientific research and other caregivers' personal experiences. It walks you through the four areas of your life that are key to being at your best. These are your sense of self—who you are—your choices, your circle of support, and your relationship with the outside world. You can read the guide whenever you have a few minutes to yourself or need help and advice.

As you work with this guide, you may find healing. But you may not find a cure. "Cure" means the signs and symptoms of disease, injury, or loss are completely gone, and this is not always possible. For example, if your loved one was in combat, they may have permanent hearing loss or other changes. If you lose a child, you will always be conscious of the loss. However, healing is a process of recovery, repair, and renewal. It is personal, and it can continue throughout your life. Healing can help you and your loved ones live the best life possible.

In addition to the resources in this guidebook, you can find free videos, fact sheets, and journal exercises online. Visit drwaynejonas.com/caregiver for more information and to download the journal companion.

Although this guide helps you work through some of the challenges of being a caregiver, it is not meant to solve problems of abuse, neglect, someone using you, or you hurting yourself. If you or your children are in danger, get help immediately. Don't wait until your situation becomes a crisis. Talk to a friend or family member and make a plan to be safe when the problem happens again. Talk to a medical provider, crisis center, or spiritual leader. If they do not help, talk to someone else until you do find help.

Physical and emotional abuse almost always gets worse and worse unless you get professional help. Even with professional help, it might not change, and you might need to simply get away to a safe place. You and the person you care for are worth the effort.

When you think of self-care, you might think of exercise and eating well. But how well you feel in general comes from how you feel about yourself, your life, and your relationships.

Who you are includes the thoughts, feelings, and wishes that come from the mind. It also includes your spiritual life and having a sense of meaning or purpose. You can lose this sense of self when you are caring for a loved one. Even as you love and want to help them, you might feel their illness or injury has taken over your life.

Acknowledging that who you were before and who you are now may not be the same can be a painful process. The goal is to work toward accepting your new self as a complete person who has grown from your experiences.

Each day comes with new challenges that test and build your ability to bounce back, but this does not mean bouncing back to become the same person you were before. Instead, you become someone better, stronger, and more aware than you ever were before.

Caring for someone else teaches you compassion, love, and empathy as no other experience can. You also learn practical skills such as managing time, speaking up for the patient and yourself, listening, and communicating.

Give yourself credit for bouncing back from challenges and becoming stronger. This can create new meaning in your life and work—and finding meaning is important for your mind, body, and spirit. Writing in a journal is one way to take care of yourself. It can help you heal, grow, and thrive. Here are some reasons why it helps:

I started my journal writing before my open heart surgery, and it morphed into my blog and continued in this and my first book. I found it very therapeutic.

- Journal writing helps bring order to your deepest thoughts and fears. Writing things down creates order out of chaos.
- A journal is free therapy. It helps you have a conversation with the person who knows you best—you!
- You can keep track of your progress. Read what you wrote earlier to learn how much progress you have made on your journey.
- Sharing your journal with others might bring you joy. But whether or not you share your work is up to you.
- A gratitude journal is a journal with lists of things you are thankful for. This kind of journal relieves stress. Writing about what you are happy for is a powerful reminder of the good in your life.

For many, spirituality, faith, and religion are central parts of who they are. They can influence how you cope with trauma and loss. They help you find happiness and meaning within rather than from external influences such as money, belongings, work, fame, or food, which may leave you feeling empty, lost, and alone.

The same mind and body practices that help you develop a sense of spirituality can help stop stress and its harmful effects. A mind and body practice can help you relax through mental focus, controlled breathing, and body movements. The most important thing to know is that the same practice does not work for everyone. However, all of them can break the train of everyday thoughts.

Consider these factors when picking a mind and body practice:

- Physical energy—Do you enjoy being physically active?
- If yes, consider a moving meditation like tai chi, qi gong, yoga, walking, and running, or an active meditation like art therapy or writing in a journal.
- If no, consider breathing techniques, meditation, mindfulness-based stress reduction, loving-kindness meditation, guided imagery, or progressive muscle relaxation. These can all be done when your body is quiet and still.
- Self-based or Provider-based—Practices such as acupuncture or massage require making time to see a provider. For some caregivers, that time-out can be relaxing. Other caregivers may find it stressful to go to one more appointment. Some practices, such as breathing techniques or repeating a meditation mantra, require nothing more than your attention and a few seconds. Other practices can be done alone after you learn them. These include acupressure, reiki, yoga, or tai chi.

- Time—Consider what fits into your schedule. Do you have 30 seconds? Five minutes? An hour? There is a mind and body practice for every moment.
- Belief and conviction—Choose a practice that fits into your belief system. Whether you call it making time for prayer, meditation, or quiet reflection, what's important is that you are practicing self-care. It is not important to be convinced that the practice will work for you. However, it is important to set your doubts aside and look at it as an experiment. Often, taking that first step is the hardest, though the most important.

Make a list of 3 qualities you have that you consider weaknesses. Then, write a sentence or 2 about how you can also consider them strengths. For instance, if you think a weakness is having to manage every detail of everything, you could also consider that you have the strength of being organized and responsible. Once you determine the strength for each "weakness," write about a time when you used that strength in a positive way. If you can't think of a recent example, write down how you might use this strength positively in the future. Try to schedule this time regularly. Knowing that you have time set aside just for yourself can be helpful.

Not all stress is bad. Small amounts of stress can increase your focus and help you perform better. However, too much stress has the opposite effect on the body. You are less efficient when you work or concentrate, and you become more anxious. A regular mind and body practice helps your body use its natural ability to overcome the harmful effects of long-term stress.

"Over time, continued strain on your body from routine stress may lead to serious health problems such as heart disease, high blood pressure, diabetes, depression, anxiety disorder, and other illnesses." ~National Institute of Mental Health, 2016

The saying "No pain, no gain" does not apply to stress. Pushing yourself through it may lead to physical and mental burnout. Your stress response can get stuck in the "on" position, so you are always in a stressed and anxious state. It is important to learn ways to reset it. Stress management skills can help you to recover faster from stress. They can also increase your ability to handle challenging experiences.

Take Action: Commit to developing a mind and body practice. Healing Intent

Healing intent is a conscious choice to improve your health or another person's. It includes the belief that you can feel better and reach the goal you want. Belief and hope help you prepare to heal.

Developing healing intent includes awareness, intent (also called intention), and reflection.

You may frequently hear from friends or family, "How's your [ill or injured] spouse or loved one?" But you may rarely hear, "How are you?" You may be very aware of how the person you take care of is feeling but less aware of how you are feeling.

Awareness addresses the question, "How do I feel?" It helps you learn what your body is telling you and to connect what you think about to who you are.

You can become aware of your body's subtle signals, such as changes in energy level or mood. Bring these thoughts and feelings to your conscious mind. This allows you to change behaviors that don't make you healthier. You can also learn new skills to change your automatic responses. Physical symptoms are messages from your body telling you how it is doing and what it needs.

Some caregivers turn to active practices like jogging, yoga, or even repeating a single word that makes them feel "centered."

Others use religious prayer, practices, and services. You can also just take a few moments to be quiet or to meditate.

Once you know how you feel, it's essential to know what you want. If being a caregiver has changed your life from what you planned, this can be challenging. However, it is important to create new goals and plans. These may be different, but they can also be meaningful and fulfilling.

On a spiritual level, once you connect with your inner self, you can direct your intention to bring this sense of peace and healing to yourself or others in your life.

In your journal

Write about a moment when you felt a particular emotion and how you felt it physically. Were your palms sweating? Was your heart racing or head throbbing? How did you sense your environment through sight, touch, hearing, or smell? Was it dark, sunny, stuffy, or breezy around you?

What did you hear and smell? By expressing your emotional state through your physical experience, you can fully understand it. You can also write about your current state. What emotions are you feeling right now, and how is your body responding?

In your journal

List 5 qualities of your personality or outlook on life that you think define you. Write just one word, a phrase, or a sentence for each—not a summary of your whole life. Don't think too much! What seems most important now? You can do this exercise every now and then to see how the list changes. Then, write about each of those qualities.

The story you tell yourself about your life is powerful. It can help you understand the central themes of your life and find meaning in them. When your sense of meaning in life changes, it can lead to feelings of distress. Getting that sense of purpose back is important for feeling healthy in your body and mind.

Meaning and purpose help you deal with emotions such as loss and grief, hope and despair, and joy and sadness. They allow you and your loved one to accept the new normal, find a sense of feeling as well as possible within it, and control your outlook on life.

Writing in your journal, writing stories or poetry, doing art, working with someone who has been a caregiver, or talking to a hospital chaplain might help you consider questions of who you are as a person and a caregiver.

A hospital chaplain, or a military chaplain if your loved one is a veteran, can help you find meaning and purpose in yourself, your situation, other people, and a higher power or God. Some chaplains are also specially trained to support families in healthcare settings. They can counsel your loved one and help you speak up for them. They provide a safe place to grieve and can help you find ways to cope.

"It's not that mindfulness is the 'answer' to all of life's problems. Rather, it is that life's problems can be seen more clearly through the lens of a clear mind." ~Jon Kabat-Zinn, founder of the Mindfulness-Based Stress Reduction (MBSR) Program, in "Full Catastrophe Living"

You might think of "mindfulness" as being in a calm, Zen state. And it can be. To be realistic, you can also think of it as being aware of what your mind is doing in each moment but not letting those thoughts control you. It can even help to remind yourself: "My thoughts do not control me." Research shows that being mindful helps with depression, post-traumatic stress, and chronic pain. Mindfulness can improve the quality of your life.

Some specific skills to cope with stress and anxiety are positive thinking, a learning mindset, and living in the moment. Positive thinking helps you see opportunities where you felt anxious before. It can help build up your sense of self-esteem and value. This can keep you from doubting your decisions and being down on yourself during the ups and downs of caregiving. Tips for positive thinking:

- Start each day with the goal of learning something new.
- Give yourself permission to be wrong.
- Start a gratitude practice. Just get a journal and write down three things that you are grateful for each day.

"It is not happiness that makes us grateful. It is gratefulness that makes us happy." ~Brother David Steindl-Rast, monk and scholar

Gratitude turns what we have into enough. Even the smallest things, such as taking a bite of a beautiful strawberry or being welcomed home by a family pet, can make you smile. With practice, gratitude will come easier than grumbling. Some people take a moment each day to write down 3 things they are grateful for. Others like to think about what they are grateful for throughout the day. Do what feels right for you.

I listen to a gratitude meditation that can be done anywhere, even while running or walking. It is part of a 21-day meditation series by Aaptiv, narrated by Jess Ray, and can be found on Audible.

As you start being aware of your thoughts and feelings, notice how much of your day is spent thinking about the past or the future. Thoughts of the past can keep you from being present and making the most of your day.

You might feel extreme worry and fear when looking too far ahead. Knowing that you are not alone in these feelings can help. Other caregivers also have this experience. When it happens, spend a few moments in a mindfulness practice of your choice, such as meditating or taking a walk. Or connect with other caregivers in an online support group.

How often do you ignore what your gut is telling you? You may think, "I should call a friend for support," but decide not to because it's late. Or think, "I wish I could reschedule those plans," but do them anyway and regret it later.

Over time, as you become mindful of your thoughts and feelings, you will begin to trust your inner guidance. You may notice that when you follow your instinct, you feel better. On the other hand, when you fall back into old patterns of holding back and doing what you think you should, you feel worse.

Silently repeating a specific word that helps you feel "centered" or calm, or repeating a prayer word, is like pressing a pause button for your mind. It is a way to calm down, focus your attention, and think more clearly during times of stress or fear. Some people call this practice mantra repetition. It's as simple as pushing negative or "noisy" thoughts out of your mind by using a word or phrase you connect with. You don't need to sit quietly or close your eyes. You can do it anywhere and anytime. Use a phrase or word that feels right for your religious or spiritual beliefs.

The one I use is, "I am doing the best that I can," It helps me to center myself on the fact that I am not always going to do everything correctly, but what I am doing is all I can ask for.

In your journal

Think of a real or imaginary place where you feel safe and at peace. Create that place in your mind and write a detailed description of it using all your senses—what you see in this place but also what you hear, smell, taste, and touch. Then close your eyes and imagine you are in this place. See, hear, smell, taste, and touch everything you wrote about.

Being mindful of your emotions is an important part of self-care. What you feel affects your ability to make healthy choices. What is one realistic goal that you can set today to improve your relationship with yourself?

"Self-care is survival. It's not thinking about yourself more. It's thinking more of yourself." ~Gail Sheehy, Caregiver and author

As a caregiver, you spend most of your time thinking of and acting for others. This makes it hard to shift the focus back onto yourself. It can even feel selfish. Yet self-care is critical to surviving—making it from day to day. It is even more important to thrive—do well in life. Each time you fly on an airplane, you are told to put on your own oxygen mask before you help others with theirs. When you are your best self, you can share your best with your family.

But always remember you still have to put on the oxygen mask for your loved one.

"Seven of 10 deaths are from preventable chronic diseases." ~Health Affairs, Nolte and Mckee, 2008

Living a healthy life is one of the main things you can do to feel and be as well as possible. How you eat, move, relax, and connect to others are all important to caring for your body, mind, and spirit. If making healthy choices was tough for you before your loved one's illness or injury, it may seem nearly impossible now when you have so much more to do. But it is possible.

You probably know what you "should" do. But the problem is actually doing it, whether you want to stop smoking, lose weight, or take time for yourself. Finding a way to enjoy a new healthy habit can help. Try giving yourself a reward for drinking water instead of a sugary soda or finding a buddy to walk with once or twice a week.

"Just for today, do the next right thing and good things happen.

Your body is made up of 60-70 percent water, so you are what you drink. Even if you don't sweat, your body still loses water every day that must be replaced. Getting enough water is important for keeping a healthy weight, keeping your muscles working and your skin and kidneys working correctly, and keeping your digestive system regular. Carrying a bottle of water with you everywhere you go may help you remember to drink more often. Also, try to drink a glass of water with every snack and meal instead of another type of beverage. Flavored sweet drinks rarely contribute to better health. I talk about proper hydration in a later chapter.

The physical burden of caregiving can take a toll on your body. Eating good whole foods can help you stay at your best. A healthful anti-inflammatory diet like the Mediterranean diet, with a focus on vegetables and fruits with few whole grains and an occasional small portion of animal protein, will keep your body powered up. ~Dr. George Ceremuga

It can help to focus on adding good whole foods rather than depriving yourself of things that don't contribute to better health. An added bonus: Since vegetables and fruits contain mostly water, they will increase your hydration levels.

Consider the following when focusing on food:

- Instead of thinking about what you shouldn't eat, start with what you can add to your diet. A low-fat diet with moderate protein, high fiber, whole grains, and at least five servings of vegetables and fruits a day is best for your health.

- Try keeping a food journal on your phone or on paper to track what you eat throughout the day. We are often not aware of what and how much we eat. Some mobile apps help with this. They can help motivate you to choose a healthier diet.

- Foods with sugar, corn syrup, artificial sweeteners, and unhealthy fats have been linked to heart disease, cancer, and diabetes. Ask your doctor how much of these foods you should eat, and read labels to choose healthier foods. Eating a lot of foods with fiber, such as vegetables and whole-grain bread or cereal, can help lower some of the harmful effects of other foods.

- Eating too much and not exercising are the usual causes of obesity, but not the only ones. You might not be eating enough healthy food or not eating during the day. This can starve the body and affect the body's metabolism—your body's ability to burn calories.

Your healthcare provider or a dietitian may be able to help you design a healthy eating plan and set realistic weight goals to keep you healthy.

As important as knowing what to eat is knowing why you eat. For some, food can be loaded with meaning and emotion. Food is family, tradition, comfort, and sometimes even used to self-medicate. When you use food or alcohol for emotional reasons, you might overeat or make unhealthy choices. It can be easy to overeat or drink too much alcohol out of stress, anger, depression, anxiety, frustration, or loneliness.

What role does food play in your life? Are you filling an empty space with food or drink or using it as a friend?

Being healthy is not just about making good food choices. It's about having a positive relationship with food. As with other relationships in your life, it's important for your relationship with food to be a healthy one.

Having a positive relationship with food involves changing some thoughts and behaviors. Here are some ways to do that:

- Become aware of why you are eating.

- Ask yourself: Am I physically hungry, or am I eating to comfort, de-stress, please myself or others, or keep from feeling bored or lonely?

- If you aren't hungry, try to recognize the triggers and temptations that prompt you to eat.

- Be hopeful and trust that you can overcome any challenges that you are facing. You may be going against years of unhealthy behaviors, so be patient with yourself. If you make an unhealthy choice, treat yourself with love and kindness.

- Accept that the food rules of your past may no longer be needed or helpful for you anymore. For example, we are often told as children to finish everything on our plates. Give yourself the OK to no longer be a member of the "clean plate club."

- Understand that you are a unique person with your own needs and challenges. Learn to trust your hunger and listen to your sense of fullness. (See Hungry? Scan for Signs.)

- Comparing your habits and your body to others around you or in the media may be harmful.

- What you see in magazines and on TV is not always true. For example, you might see extremely thin or fit celebrities, but those pictures are often changed by computers to look "better" than reality. If you struggle with having a healthy body image, it may help to limit what you see in magazines, online, and on TV.

- Set positive health goals. Big weight loss goals can seem too far away to reach, so you stop trying. Try setting small goals, like a pound each week.
- Be positive, even in how you talk about food. Thinking of your food as a diet or bad adds judgment. Changing your language can help. Instead of seeing sweets as bad, see them as a treat. Allowing yourself a treat from time to time may prevent you from feeling starved and ready to quit.

Before you eat, stop and do a hunger scan.

1. Scan your body: Does your body need nutrition? When you need food, your stomach grumbles and feels empty. You may feel dizzy or unable to focus. Are you actually hungry, or are you thirsty and need to drink water?
2. Scan your mind: Did you just see or hear an advertisement that made you crave a certain food?
3. Scan your feelings: Is your hunger coming from emotion? Emotional cravings like loneliness, pain, and pleasure-seeking can never be satisfied with food. Understanding if and why you are hungry helps you to react less to the urge to eat.

Too often, because of the stress of daily life, food is eaten without even a thought. It's easy to eat what's in front of you without paying attention to whether you are hungry or when you become full. This is especially true when you are a busy caregiver. Keep these tips in mind:

- Eat slowly. Most meals are eaten in an average of 7 to 11 minutes. Fast eating can lead to overeating. The body doesn't have time to tell your brain that you are full. Putting in your journal,

- describe a recent food craving. Were you really hungry? Scan your body for its food needs. What does it feel like right now to be hungry, full, or in between?
- Putting your fork down between bites will help. If you tend to eat too fast, focus more on enjoying the meal rather than just slowing down.
- Eating includes all the senses—taste, touch, smell, sound and sight. Paying attention to the experience of eating is called eating mindfully. Mindful eating can help with a healthy lifestyle.
- Tune in when you are full. This is another part of mindful eating. Your body's signals might be small. If something is so delicious that you want to keep eating, try saying, "I can have more later. I don't have to eat it all now."

Planning what you will eat and when can be good for your budget, your stress level, and your waistline. Knowing what you're going to eat or having snacks on hand can also make preparing food less overwhelming. When you come home from work with a meal already planned, cooking won't feel like one more thing at the end of an already long day.

Be flexible. Have some ingredients in your pantry or freezer so you can make meals if you don't have time to stop at the store. Know where you can stop for a healthier take-out option if an appointment or workday is long.

Are you so hungry that you grab a snack on your way home before mealtime? Try having a piece of fruit, a bag of healthy popcorn, or a handful of nuts on the way home so you aren't starving when you walk in the door. Are you too tired to make the healthy meal you planned, so you find yourself ordering pizza several times a week? Maybe having easier meals like sandwiches or soup on the schedule would help.

It's important to have realistic expectations for yourself in meal planning.

- Try to shop only once a week. The time you take in planning your meals before you head to the grocery store may result in fewer trips to the grocery store and drive-through. Running into the store to pick up an item can lead to overbuying and more stress.

- Do the kind of cooking you like best. Do you like using the Crock-pot in the morning? Cooking a week's worth of meals on Sunday? Using the freezer? Cooking from what you have in the pantry? Don't fight your cooking style. Cook the way that works for you.

- Keep healthy food on hand. Having your pantry, fridge, freezer, and cabinets stocked with healthy foods makes it easier to cook and eat healthy.

- Involve your children so they will be more likely to eat and help with meal prep. If they can see the meal plan, it will cut down on the questions of "What's for dinner?" or "What can I eat?"

- Don't start the plan from scratch. Begin with a two-week or one-month rotation of your favorite recipes and add a new recipe occasionally.

- Make sure your plan is realistic. Plan for occasional take-out.

- Look for meals that include similar ingredients to avoid waste and cut down on prep time.

- Consider starting a small, manageable garden. Use pots on the balcony for easy-to-grow herbs or vegetables. This provides a chance for children to learn and get involved.

Your healthy changes can help your family as well. Children see their parents as their biggest role models. Be what your children should be.

Meals planned, prepared, and shared together at home tend to be healthier and more balanced than meals eaten at restaurants or on the go. Meals eaten out are often fried or highly salted. Plus, soda and other sweetened beverages are usually consumed more often when eating out. But there are more benefits to eating together than just health.

What are some positive family traditions that you would like to go back to or start for your family? Are there any unhealthy traditions that you can change or let go of altogether?

Meals Bring Family Together

In a busy family, it isn't always possible to eat together every day. But when you can, making time for family dinner is good for the mind, body, and spirit. Eating meals as a family several times a week can help children get better grades. Also, children who eat regular family meals tend to use less alcohol or illegal drugs.

Family meals help increase feelings of belonging, security, and love. This is especially important during times of change, like when you are someone's caregiver. Eating together builds a sense of tradition that can last a lifetime. Family traditions can affect your ability to make healthy choices. Becoming a caregiver might mean you need to change or develop some healthy new traditions like taking a walk after a shared meal.

Being a caregiver can be very hard on your body. Caregiving can be physical, especially if you have to do a lot of cleaning or laundry, take over new chores, or even lift the person you are taking care of. Stress and lack of sleep also affect your body. Exercise is a great way to refresh your body and help your mind work more smoothly.

At least 30 minutes a day of exercise is important. Ask your doctor for advice on the best type of exercise and how much is right for you. It is important to ask, especially if you are trying to lose weight or have certain physical conditions, such as a knee problem or diabetes. Try fitting physical activity into your day, even when you can't go to the gym or an exercise class.

Your doctor or a physical therapist may be able to give you a list of exercises and stretches to do when you have a few minutes to spare. Can you do leg lifts or ankle circles while waiting in a doctor's office? Can you park farther from the store to get a few more steps in? Use the stairs instead of the elevator? These activities add up.

Just going on walks can be good for your health. Walking gives you many of the same health benefits as running. If you can do it with your loved one, family members, or friends, then it can be a fun activity to share. Having a regular walking partner or group also helps get you out on your walks and gives you a way to have fun and be social.

You might know that 7 to 9 hours of sleep is the recommended amount for adults. But if you are someone's caregiver, it can be hard to get this much sleep. Or you might get up several times each night to help your loved one. Your sleep affects many areas of life, including your health, pain level, memory, weight, and mood.

Sleep can be especially challenging if you sleep with a partner who has sleep problems. These can include not sleeping much at night (insomnia or being unable to sleep), restless leg syndrome, teeth grinding or clenching, sleep apnea, and sleepwalking. Sleep disturbances are common in people who had a traumatic brain injury, or TBI.

Consider these tips for sleeping:

- Have a bedtime routine. In the hour before you go to bed, do quiet activities such as taking a bath or shower, reading a book, or listening to music. Avoid exercising, playing video games, working, or using your phone.
- Go to bed and wake up at the same time each day—even on weekends.
- Sleep in a dark room without a computer or other electronics, if possible.
- Avoid smoking, chewing tobacco, or having foods and drinks with caffeine or a lot of sugar for several hours before you go to sleep.
- Exercise in the morning or early afternoon.

Ask your doctor for help if these tips are not enough. You could have a health condition that is causing your sleep problems. Many things can cause sleep problems, including physical changes, breathing problems, medication, pain, and depression. Other causes include using too much alcohol, caffeine, or nicotine, being stressed, and not getting enough physical activity. You might also have sleep problems if you are a caregiver and worry or think a lot about your loved one. So, talking to your doctor or other health care provider is important. Let them know if you have any sleep problems. They might be able to help you make the most of the sleep you get, even if it is not as much as before.

Feeling grateful can help you deal with the challenges of being a caregiver, even in difficult times. It can keep you from feeling helpless and hopeless. Also, forgiving yourself, your family, or even God and the person you are taking care of can help you cope with feelings of blame or regret.

Instead of worrying about what you can't control, spend it finding moments of joy. Here are some ways to do this:

- Dream new dreams. You may have had to put past dreams aside, but that doesn't mean you can't come up with new ones. Focus on new goals and dreams that you can work toward.

- Find a creative way to let your emotions out. Doing a puzzle, finding a coloring book and some colored pencils, or playing music are great ways to take care of yourself. Other ways to find joy and release emotions are crafting, sewing, drawing, writing in a journal, gardening, and photography.

- Look forward to the future. Hope is important, even if the person you are taking care of feels hopeless. Have something to look forward to, such as meeting a friend for coffee, taking a vacation, or taking a full day away from caregiving.

- Keep inspiration on hand. Call a friend, visit a place of worship, or carry inspiring quotes or pictures with you. All these can help during rough times.

- Do things that make you happy. Join a walking club. Say yes to an invitation to do something with a friend. Spend time with people who give you energy and help you feel rested or hopeful. Go back to a hobby you used to enjoy, like reading, knitting, or doing woodworking.

- Laugh and play. Try a game night at home, play fetch with your pet, do a crossword puzzle, or listen to a comedian on TV. Laughter and play can lower your stress level, give you more energy, and help you connect with other people.

- Don't compare your life to others. Allow your life to be unique.

In the first phases of caregiving, you may always feel rushed. Family caregivers of severely wounded loved ones may even feel guilty about leaving the room or taking 30 minutes to run to the grocery store.

If your loved one has an emergency, keep taking care of yourself. Let yourself leave the hospital or rehabilitation center for 15 minutes to get some fresh air. You can go home, take a shower, and get something to eat without rushing back to the hospital. Taking care of yourself, even when things are very stressful, helps you stay healthy so you can keep taking care of your loved one.

List 5 things that you're grateful for—people, positive experiences now or in the past, places, and things. Then, write a few sentences about each one. Describe what you are grateful for in detail, perhaps at a particular moment in time.

List 3 activities that bring you joy. Write a few sentences about each one. When did you do it recently? Did you get totally involved in it?

If you have difficulty doing these activities as often as you want now, write down 1 or 2 ways you could do each of them more often.

You need balance in your life to keep from getting depressed. Balance can be more important after you have been a caregiver for a while. Balance is also important to get out of "crisis mode." This means dealing with one crisis or emergency after another and just waiting for the next one.

Adding personal time to your schedule of work and responsibilities is important for balance. Activities you enjoy can help create the balance you need. Find activities that are fun and rewarding so that you want to do them regularly. This can be anything from walking with friends and playing with your kids to taking your dog for a walk, playing a team sport, or going on picnics. Try joining a club or faith-based organization, volunteering in your community, or learning a new skill or craft. Living a balanced life can keep you from feeling "burned out."

Focus on love and forgiveness—and start with yourself. If you do not love and forgive yourself, you probably cannot inspire, motivate, and encourage anyone else.

A technique called loving-kindness meditation can help you cope with anger and emotional pain. If you struggle with shame, guilt, fear, chronic pain, problems with other people, or feeling like you have no support, try a loving-kindness meditation.

Loving-kindness meditation involves silently repeating phrases that help you heal. Close your eyes and repeat the following words to yourself:

May I be safe.

May I be happy.

May I be healthy.

May my life unfold with ease.

Then, think about helping the people around you heal by saying:

May you be safe.

May you be happy.

May you be healthy.

May your life unfold with ease.

How can you finish your to-do list? The first piece of advice might surprise you. Take a nap, meditate, go for a walk. Taking 20 minutes to practice self-care makes you more productive and able to do everything else. When you feel good in mind, body, and spirit, you are a better caregiver.

With this in mind, make your own physical and mental care a top priority. Get help with some of the other things on your list, or just decide not to do them—even if just for now.

List 2 things you often say "yes" to or said "yes" to recently. Then, list 2 things you often say "no" to or said "no" to recently. By each "yes," write whether you were taking good care of yourself when. you said yes, or not. Do the same thing with each "no" answer. Think about whether you say "yes" when you don't want to or say "no" to things you would really enjoy. Write 2 ways you might change your answers next time to take good care of yourself or write 2 reasons you made a choice that helped you.

- Do what is most important, and let the rest go. Don't feel like you have to do everything at once. Divide large jobs into smaller parts you can do one at a time. For example, you might not have time to clean the whole kitchen. But having the counter cleaned off makes you feel better. So, clean off the counter and leave sweeping the floor and other jobs for later.

- Think of a comforting saying, such as "Perfect isn't real" or "Good enough is great." This can put your mind at ease.

- Make things simple. Do errands and go to appointments all at once, if you can. Learn if you can get your loved one's regular appointments, such as blood draws, done close to home. Get prescriptions filled when they are ready so you do not need to rush and make extra trips at the last minute.

- Take a deep breath when your day is not going the way you planned. Getting upset won't help you or the person you take care of.

Caregivers live high-stress lives. You can feel anxiety and fear with even everyday activities. For example, you might feel panic when you hear a ringing phone, or checking on the person you care for can make you start thinking, "What if?"

Breathing techniques can help you calm down. This is because your breathing causes changes in your nervous system, and these changes help you manage stress better. Research shows that deep breathing techniques can help service members with post-traumatic stress and help emergency workers do their jobs better.

Try this deep-breathing technique. Put one hand on your chest and another on your stomach. As you breathe in and out, your stomach should rise and fall. If not, you might not be breathing deeply enough to be calm.

You might find yourself doing things that the person you take care of does. For example, if you have always been outgoing and social, but you take care of a veteran or law enforcement officer, you might start being extra alert, such as by checking the exits when you go somewhere. You might do this even when they are not with you.

Senator Elizabeth Dole wrote, "Those caring for individuals suffering from [post-traumatic stress] and TBI become hyper-alert for potential triggers. They must be sensitive to what may cause mood swings, anxiety attacks, or angry outbursts. In many cases, the caregivers become more sensitive than the veterans themselves. Veterans may only occasionally react to triggers, while caregivers put up their guard with every potential risk factor. This is a real and debilitating phenomenon facing our caregivers—many for the rest of their lives." The TBI that Senator Dole refers to is a traumatic brain injury.

If her description sounds like you, remember that you aren't alone in this—reach out for help. It's also OK to feel joy during the difficult times. You may think, "How can I feel happy when my loved one is in pain?" It's important to let this guilt go and focus on how you feel. Taking on someone else's suffering doesn't help you or them.

Let's face it: we all do things we know are not healthy. What is important is avoiding letting them become habits. Once they do, they are very hard to break, and sometimes we need professional help. Groups can help. You might find a group, though the important thing is to be aware of your behaviors and seek help. If you are a very private person who hesitates to share personal issues, taking that first step to look for help is the most difficult. Getting someone to go with you can make it easier.

In your journal
List 3 strengths that you value in yourself. Then list 3 strengths that you would like to have. Write 2 or 3 sentences about each strength. For the ones you already have, when did you use them recently? For the ones you would like to have, how can you develop them?

Use people you have good relationships with to fix behaviors before they become habits. Break bad habits so they do not become addictions. Find healthy habits to fill the space the bad habit used to take up. For example, if you quit smoking, you might chew sunflower seeds when you crave a cigarette. You might take up walking to relieve stress instead of smoking.

Healthy behaviors can help you feel better overall. They can also help you avoid getting sick or get better when you have a health condition. Making good food choices, exercising, coping with stress, and avoiding unhealthy behaviors are important for your lifelong good health. What is one healthy behavior you would like to add to your life?

Sometimes, our light goes out but is blown again into instant flame by an encounter with another human being. ~Albert Schweitzer, Nobel Peace Prize-winning Philosopher and Physician (1875-1965)

You are a social being. Your relationships with others and your role within your community provide a sense of belonging, care, and support. Positive relationships can also be good for your health and the person you take care of. Love and support reduce stress, boost your immune system, help you enjoy and appreciate life more, and help prevent loneliness and depression.

Positive relationships give you strength and energy. Counselors call these healing relationships. They usually include trust, honesty, and compassion. If a relationship makes you feel exhausted, think about how to protect yourself. You might need to try some ways to take care of yourself and make the relationship better. Then, this can be a healing relationship for you, too. Your relationship with the person you take care of is a large part of your life. It might even seem like everything depends on it. If possible, this should be a healing relationship. This involves acknowledging how the relationship has changed; moving beyond the past; shifting roles, and responsibilities; reconnecting in love; looking forward to a different, joyful future, and keeping your sense of self.

Whether you are taking care of your spouse, child, friend, or neighbor, you had a relationship in the past. This can make it hard not to think too much about what things were like before they got sick or hurt. To heal yourself, it is important to acknowledge that what things were like before may no longer apply. But the after can be a happy one.

Thinking of what life was before the injury or illness might make you sad. Grief does not only happen when someone dies. You might grieve as you struggle with and accept the changes in your life. You might grieve for memories, dreams, or simply that the person you used to know is not the same person now. You might even grieve for your own old life and who you used to be. Grieving can help you understand who you are now and what your relationship is with the person you care for. Going through the grieving process might even help you heal.

"The five typical stages of grief are denial, anger, bargaining, depression, and acceptance. However, this is not a linear process. Not everyone experiences all five of these feelings, and they can occur in any order, in addition to other feelings. What's important is to acknowledge the role of grief in healing and know that it is normal and that there are resources to help. Community resource centers, your health care providers, and your chaplain can point you in the right direction." ~David Kessler and Elisabeth Kubler-Ross

When you take care of your adult child, your parent, or a partner who is an independent adult, the roles you play in your family and their lives change. Roles are the things you do and how you do them with one person in charge some or all of the time, one person acting like the strong protector or one person being the nurturing one. It can be very confusing and stressful when these roles change. You might have complicated emotions. Jobs and responsibilities change, and you and your loved one might not be sure what to do or who is responsible.

The person you take care of might be anxious, resentful, or angry if they could take care of themselves before but now cannot. These are natural reactions that you and your loved one can work through. You might need a professional helper, such as a counselor, or personal help, such as from friends or family. Eventually, with help, patience, and work, these intense emotions can lead you and the person you care for to feel like yourselves again. You might not be the old self, but you can be a new person who has a sense of peace.

Talk with the person you are taking care of about how roles can or have changed. Talking about your new relationship can relieve your stress. It can also help the person you are taking care of.

Being honest and understanding that you are still learning can help your relationship with that person. You might make mistakes along the way, and that's OK.

You might still need help even if you do everything "right." Ask people for help. You can ask doctors and other health care providers, counselors, and spiritual leaders. You can also ask family members, friends, and people in support groups or community groups, such as a neighborhood group or book club.

In your journal

5 roles you think define you. For example, you might be a mom, sister, daughter, or wife. Write just a one-word phrase or sentence for each one. They do not need to be in order of importance, and you do not need to list every role in your life. Just notice which ones you write down. Which ones seem most important right now? Then, write a couple of sentences about how each one is part of who you are. You can write down 5 roles every now and then to see how the list changes.

Write a letter to the person you are taking care of. What is on your mind and in your heart that is hard to say in real life? Writing it down might help you actually tell the person you care for about it. Or writing might help you understand your thoughts and feelings. This can help you feel better around your loved one and be a better caregiver.

In your journal

List 1 goal for today, 1 for this week, 1 for this month, and 1 for this year. Then, write a few sentences or a paragraph about each one. Write about the support you might need to reach those goals, ways to reach them, potential barriers, and how to overcome the barriers. Define your success. Don't let others define success for you. Paying attention to your goals and celebrating your achievements might help you as a caregiver. It is powerful to say, "We reached our goal today!" Goals might be small or step-by-step, but they give you pride and motivation for the next step.

Your medical team may provide advice about what is practical to make sure your expectations are realistic. A caregiver support group may also have ideas on what are appropriate milestones to work toward.

Some symptoms, conditions, and circumstances lessen with time and treatment. Others do not. You might be taking care of someone whose condition will get worse, not better. Learning to cope with reality is helpful in this case. When recovery isn't possible, shift your focus to discovery. You and your loved one may discover steps, self-care strategies, and behaviors that reduce daily challenges and improve the way your life feels to you.

As a caregiver, you learn to deal with someone else's moods and feelings of others. Taking good care of yourself is important because it can be easier to deal with other people's emotions when you are healthy and taking good care of yourself. Once you feel strong and healthy, you have a better chance of having a healthy relationship.

You might have to cope with two angry people if you are a caregiver. One might be you, and the other might be the person you are taking care of. Some people, such as armed services members and law enforcement or health care workers, might have learned some coping skills, such as self-regulating or self-relaxation skills and communication and problem-solving skills. Those same skills can help you cope, too.

When dealing with your loved one's anger, see if these strategies help:

- When a discussion starts to become a fight, stop talking. Agree to come back to the topic when you are both calm.

Make an appointment to talk. Say, "I'm getting upset. Can we talk about this in two hours when we have calmed down?"

- If your loved one starts getting louder, speak more quietly and slowly than usual. This allows you to hear and understand them better.
- Take 3 deep breaths. This will help you to calm down. It forces the other person to calm down because people copy each other's breathing unconsciously.
- Use non-threatening body language. Uncross your arms if you crossed them across your chest. Stand or sit at an angle so you are not directly confronting the other person.

You need outside help sometimes. That's when it's time to contact your support people. Also, professional counselors and many health care workers are well trained to help you deal with your anger and the anger of your loved one.

Somewhere on the journey of caring for their loved ones, many caregivers find that they have lost themselves. "Three years ago, I was someone else. Now I don't even know who I am." When so much of your time is focused on your loved one, it can be easy to forget who you are and what you enjoy.

When you are a caregiver, your own needs, wants, and thoughts don't disappear, but they can get lost. Being a caregiver is a role that you didn't plan for and have little or no training in, and that seems to change everything. But you are still a person, not just a caregiver. It's important to be aware of yourself, your interests, and your needs.

Keeping a journal is one way to get back to your sense of self by exploring your thoughts and feelings.

In your journal

Your thoughts, emotions, and behaviors are all related. Write down 2 examples of thoughts,

2 of emotions and 2 of your behaviors in the past month. What effect did they have on each other? How do you think your changes in each category affect the other two? For example, if your thoughts changed, how did that affect your feelings and emotions?

Keep from feeling lost by exploring your own interests when you have a moment. If you liked crafting before you became a caregiver, can you pick up a simple crochet or knitting project while in the doctor's waiting room? If you liked reading fiction, such as novels, before you were a caregiver, try reading again.

You may find that taking a moment each day to think about what makes you happy helps you remember who you really are. You might feel guilty if you think, "How can I feel happy when my loved one is in pain?" But it's OK to still feel happy during this time. Your happiness may also help your loved one feel better. Even wearing a top in your favorite color or taking time for a massage can brighten your spirits.

Moods and attitudes spread from person to person easily. So, it's important to acknowledge how you feel versus how the person you care for is feeling. Other people's moods spread as easily as the flu. You might hear that it is important to share someone else's feelings, but that is not always healthy. Sharing another person's pain or bad mood can leave you feeling tired. As a caregiver, it's important for you to be at your best, and that includes being aware of your mood and how other people's moods affect yours.

Here are some ways to protect yourself from someone else's negative feelings.

- Imagine a protective barrier around yourself. It could be a light or a warrior's shield that blocks negative emotions.
- Try to react positively instead of becoming negative when others are.

- Take a moment to pause, breathe, or walk away if a negative mood starts to affect you.
- Manage your stress level. This helps you react less and get less stressed when other people are negative.
- Spend time with a positive person to balance things out. Let their happiness spread to you and give you energy.
- Find a good place to let out your thoughts and feelings or "vent."

Letting your thoughts and emotions out is sometimes helpful and appropriate. It can help you release tension instead of keeping it inside. However, some ways and places to vent are more helpful than others. See if any of these work for you.

- Get out a piece of paper and write for 10 minutes without stopping. You can even pretend that you are talking with a person.
- When venting to a person, be sure to do so with someone you trust, are on good terms with, and are not upset with. Choose someone supportive and helpful but not someone who encourages you to have negative thoughts and feelings. Tell them you just need to vent and ask them to listen.
- Exercise. Physical activity can release certain chemicals in the brain. These chemicals relieve stress and tension. You can go for a walk or run, go to the gym, or do an exercise video at home. Consider yoga, qi gong, and tai chi because these can be calming.
- Breathe. It is impossible to be stressed and relaxed at the same time, so use breathing techniques to calm down. Taking 3 deep breaths in a row is one example of a breathing technique.

A boundary is how much you let other people affect your time, energy, feelings, and personal space. It is like an invisible fence you build around yourself, and it helps you control how much other people affect you. Having clear boundaries is an important part of taking care of yourself. If you do not have that "fence" to protect you, other people's comments, moods, and opinions can leave you feeling bruised and battered. On the other hand, staying closed up can leave you feeling alone and locked up inside yourself. Setting your boundaries where you need them is a process that happens with time. Counselors can help you set boundaries at your own pace. They can help you protect your feelings, stop needing to please other people all the time, and say "No" when you do not want to do something.

Learning to establish healthy boundaries can help you in all your relationships, including with the person you care for and your family, friends, neighbors, or coworkers. Developing a healing relationship with the person you take care of is important, but don't ignore the rest of the world. What is important to you may change with time, but it is important to build and maintain relationships that will support you over the years to come.

It is easy to feel alone with all your new responsibilities. Instead, think about bringing people who support you together. You can imagine a circle of people around you, holding hands around you and your loved one. Then, consider making that circle wider by adding new people.

Look at your community and think about who might join your circle. Consider family, friends, co-workers, neighbors, and people from community groups such as volunteer groups or places of worship.

It might help to create a written directory of your circle of support, including contact information and notes. You can put this on paper, on your phone, or the computer. Looking at it can make you feel better, and you can call these people for support if you need it. It can also help people who want to contact your other friends and family so they can support you.

Create a team of caregivers who can work together. Here are some tips:

- Develop a shared family calendar. You can use an app on your phone, an online calendar, or a paper calendar.

- Introduce people in your circle to the person you are caring for. That way, they know them when you need someone to help instead of you.

- Recognize who can give help and who cannot. Set limits on or let go of those who are not helpful. Some people might say they want to help, but their "help" causes problems, or they bother you with constant questions. Those people do not need to stay in your circle, at least not to help. Being independent is important, but being too independent can lead to burnout. Asking for help is a sign of strength, not weakness. Being a superhero can be isolating and lead to exhaustion.

There are things that people can do for you to lighten the load, such as getting the oil changed in your vehicle, doing laundry, or helping you with errands. When you see how wide your circle of support really is, it is easier to give people different jobs to do. That means no one is overwhelmed.

The following tips might also help:

- When asking for help from others, use "I" statements. Rather than saying "You never help!" try saying, "I feel burned out. I need help with the chores." (See Communication is Key.)

- Don't let small things become overwhelming. You might find yourself doing things that you have never done before now that you are a caregiver. Jobs like taking out the trash and maintaining the car. Think of one thing you need right now. Write out how you can tell a specific person about that need. Then, write out what you think that person's response will be.

  Consider asking someone in your circle to help. Although you can do these things, not doing them lets you spend more time doing what you value, such as spending time with family and taking care of yourself.

- Arrange regular breaks for yourself. This helps avoid "caregiver burnout." A break might be meeting a friend, taking a walk, or taking half a day, a weekend, or several days off while someone else takes care of your loved one.

- Say yes when people offer to do things for you. Give them the gift of accepting their help, even if you think you should do the job yourself.

- Ask your doctor about respite care programs. These are programs where someone else takes care of your loved one while you take a break. How do you take care of someone while keeping your own life together? How do you keep your spirits up for a long time without becoming emotionally, physically, and spiritually exhausted? At times, you need to ask other people for help.

Here are some signs it's time to do this:
- You begin feeling a lot of anger, fear, resentment, guilt, helplessness and grief. Talking about these difficult feelings can help you to deal with them.

- You show signs of depression or anxiety. These can include crying spells, loss of sleep and appetite, losing or gaining weight, irritability, restlessness, difficulty concentrating and making decisions, feeling sad much of the time, feeling anxious or empty, and thinking about suicide.
- You show signs of burnout. These can include feeling tired even after resting, increased feelings of resentment, new health problems or problems getting worse, difficulty concentrating, neglecting your responsibilities, and withdrawing from activities or people.
- You have difficulty maintaining balance in your life. You feel overwhelmed by caregiving and no longer do other activities that are important to you.
- You have difficulty sleeping.
- It seems difficult to take care of your own healthcare needs. For example, you put off regular checkups or visits to the dentist.
- You use alcohol and drugs to escape.
- You think about dying or hurting yourself.
- Get Help If You Are Dealing with Abuse

If you often feel frightened or threatened, don't feel like you have to stick it out. Learn the signs of abuse and get help. If you are like most family caregivers, you are not trained for the challenges you are facing now. You probably never thought you would be in this situation. But there are places you can turn to for support, including

- Family members or friends who will listen without judging you.
- Your church, temple, or other place of worship.
- Caregiver support groups at a local hospital or online.

- A therapist, social worker or counselor.
- National caregiver organizations.
- Organizations for your loved one's illness or disability. For example, if they have Alzheimer's disease, an organization for this illness probably has help and information for caregivers.

"The capacity to care is the thing that gives life its deepest significance and meaning." ~Pablo Casals

In order for you to maintain your capacity to care, it is essential for you to receive the support you need. If you do not take care of your own needs, you may begin to feel distracted, burned out, or overwhelmed by the daily routine of caregiving. Learning to manage your stress and responsibilities as a caregiver is the first step to taking care of you.

Think of a recent conversation with your loved one. First, write out the words that were said as much as you remember them. Then, describe what was communicated by facial expressions, body language, posture, and other non-verbal messages. What did you both "say" this way? Did your words and non-verbal messages match? Or were they different? Which was the true message?

Being aware of your communication style can lead to fewer misunderstandings among family members, healthcare providers, employers, friends, and the person you take care of. Also, honest and open communication is important to the healing relationships you are building. Although we all communicate daily, we rarely see that what we say and how we say it affects what people hear.

You probably already know that most communication has little to do with what you say. Your posture, breathing, and even your muscle tightness all send a message—as does the tone, speed, and volume of your voice. When you listen, focus on both verbal and nonverbal messages. Here are some tips for active listening:

- Maintain appropriate eye contact for your culture.
- Paraphrase to confirm you understand what the other person is saying. Don't jump to conclusions.
- Ask questions to clarify.
- Try not to think about what you are going to say next; it's more important to be attentive, even if it means there is a thoughtful pause before you talk.
- Affirm their comments and offer encouragement by nodding, saying yes, or saying things such as "Tell me more" or "I understand."
- Listen to disclaimers (maybe, but, mostly, usually, probably), as they are typically followed by new information.
- Give your care recipient time to form a response; try not to interrupt.
- Avoid distractions such as TV or pets so you don't have to compete for attention.

Especially in high-stress situations, the more you can encourage the other person to talk, the more you can understand what they are trying to share with you. Encourage conversation to continue through active listening.

Honest communication is vital. It can be important to talk about feelings or fears that may seem unthinkable. Keeping them inside can lead to angry outbursts, withdrawal or resentment, and guilt. These things can cause problems in your relationship.

Here are some tips for open communication:

- Relax and breathe.
- Go into difficult conversations with a goal. Example goals include Being honest and direct, expressing feelings and thoughts, and finding things in common. Do you need to

ask for help? Address the way they have been treating you or the person you provide care for. Raise a concern.

- Treat the person with dignity, respect and courtesy.
- When helping, do not insist or be offended if your offer is not accepted.
- Ask if it's a good time to talk. This can start the conversation off better.
- Make appointments to talk.

Think of two recent conversations—one that went well and one that didn't. In each one, explore the positive and negative aspects. What led to the outcome? Think about 2 group experiences—one that helped you and one that didn't. Write a few sentences about each one. Why was it helpful or not? Was there a specific incident that was especially helpful in the positive group? Did something specific happen in the group that did not help you?

- Don't be afraid to say, "I don't know," or "Let me check." You can be clear about how much you can respond to a person's needs or requests.
- Be mindful that symptoms of traumatic brain injury, or TBI, and post-traumatic stress may go up and down. Many things influence these symptoms. Your loved one might have times of ease and comfort as well as more challenging times.
- Support, patience, and understanding go a long way. Be generous with these.4

Focus on "I" Communication. Use sentences that start with "I" instead of "you." These types of sentences are called "I" messages.

"I" messages:

- Help you take charge of your own thoughts and feelings.

- Make you explore what you really think and feel.
- Increase your chances of being heard.
- Help keep conversations positive.

"You" messages may make a person feel uncomfortable and attacked. They may make a person stop listening, withdraw, or fight back. None of those answer your question or solve your concern.

Examples of "I" and "you" messages:

"I" message: I can take John to his appointment on Wednesday. Can we talk about Friday? I need help, then. "You" message: You need to take John to his appointment on Friday since you can't take him on Wednesday. Do you notice the difference? How do you think the person you are talking to might respond to each type of message? Good communication skills build strong relationships.

Whether it's a school, workplace, church, or community organization, you are part of many groups that impact your ability to care for yourself and others. Seeking out and being involved in groups that are healthy and have positive healing qualities supports your health and well-being.

Healing groups:
- Promote open and honest communication.
- Create a climate of trust and personal responsibility.
- Inspire a sense of belonging.
- Allow you to make decisions that affect you in a positive way.
- Focus on learning rather than blame.

Support Groups

The best emotional and practical support and advice often comes from others who have experienced something similar. That's why caregiver support groups provide such great help. They can speak to your fears, know what you need even before you do, help you find resources, and begin to see hope, joy, and potential in the new path. You might also find comfort in giving advice that helps another person or family in a similar situation. Being able to help someone else can give your caregiving

Think about a negative relationship that drains you. Write a few sentences about the reasons it makes you feel tired or discouraged. Next, answer these questions. Are these things that

1. You can accept?
2. You can work on?
3. Mean you should let this person or relationship go from your life?

You can find support online, in person, and even on Pinterest. Visit drwaynejonas.com/ caregiver for a list of resources. Family and friends want to provide comfort, but most people don't know what to say. During stressful times, you may be more vulnerable and sensitive to comments. Comments made with good intentions can hurt, minimize feelings, or underestimate the problem. Whether it's "I know how you feel" or "Everything happens for a reason," all caregivers have heard phrases that irritate or upset them.

Dealing with insensitive people or comments in a productive way is part of caring for yourself because it helps you manage your stress.

Here are 3 ways to handle insensitive comments:

- Remind yourself that people often mean well but make such comments out of ignorance and fear. When people can't relate, they may say things they have heard before. Or they might make comments that make your situation or feelings seem less serious.

- Tell them where to find information on your loved one's condition so they can learn about it. Tell them in a kind way why their comments hurt or bother you.

- Keep taking good care of yourself. When you feel well, rested, and calm, it's easier to handle insensitive comments.

Becoming a caregiver means experiencing surprise and shock. It is not a life you expected. Many days, it can feel like there is no plan or roadmap. Rather, it's a series of changes that can be painful and scary. You and your family would rather have a stable, predictable life again, but the healing process changes constantly. This can make you feel uncertain almost all the time.

You can compare caregiving to riding a roller coaster. One doctor's appointment may have you plunging into sadness. Two days later, better news may boost you to a false high. Your loved one may go to the hospital for a simple procedure and be back in the hospital for weeks. You may become depressed as your life is turned upside down once again.

Set a Self-Care Goal

What is one realistic goal that you can set today to improve your social connections?

"Each day is different, and you get up, put one foot in front of the other, and go—and love; just love." ~First Lady Nancy Reagan

When your focus is on caring for your loved one, the places where you live, care, work, and play may fade into the background. But what is around you affects your ability to find peace, rest, and strength. Your home and workplace, as well as the time spent at the doctor, in the car, outside, and in the community, can add or subtract from your stress levels.

Have you ever been somewhere that just makes you feel good? You might consider this a space where you can heal and feel better. These "healing spaces" minimize stress. They let you bring your family and friends together and feel your best. Many things are outside of your control, but your physical space is one thing you can control. You can try to create spaces at work or at home that add to your joy instead of your stress.

When you walk in the door after a stressful day at work or a medical appointment with your loved one, it can help if home is a place of peace. Your home's colors, organization, smell, and decorations all affect you. Here are some tips to make your home a place of healing and peace:

Surround yourself with nature. This can include Natural light

Write down the places you spend most of your time. In your car? At home, work, or school? Compare those places to the place that makes you feel good. This is the "healing space" you thought about earlier. What are some specific things about your healing place that make you feel better?

Now, write a few notes about each of the places you spend most of your time. What can you change in those places to make them more nurturing, safe, and peaceful? For example, if you spend a lot of time in the car, you might decide to add a soft seat cover or listen to podcasts while you drive. If you spend a lot of time at work, adding a green plant and some photos to your work area might make the space more pleasant.

- A view of nature through the window or art that shows nature scenes
- Nature sounds from an open window or recording
- Flowers

- Decorate with things that mean a lot to you. These can include
- Photographs of family and friends
- Religious symbols
- Objects that reflect your interests. For example, if you love traveling, a globe might make you feel happy.
- Furniture arranged to encourage people to enjoy being together. For example, a coffee table you and your family can enjoy snacks and board games on.
- Simplify your life. This can include
- Getting rid of clutter. This means things you no longer use, don't plan to use, don't like, or don't need. It also means garbage, such as wrappers, papers, boxes, and packages.
- Clean the space. Dust, vacuum, wash windows, clean furniture, and wash soft items such as throw rugs and cushions. This is healthier for you and your family and makes you feel better.
- Create quiet spaces where you can sit, think and rest. For example, you might put one chair in a quiet area.

Each change, like becoming a caregiver, is a chance to think about your own life. The need to be calm and have times of rest can encourage you to throw away old items and make your schedule simpler. Having an orderly, peaceful home helps you feel calmer.

You might want to ask for help doing things in your home. You can ask a friend, family member, or someone from one of your community groups, such as your church, temple, or book club. The people in your circle of support might be able to help you make small changes in your home that make a big difference in how you feel.

When your loved one returns home from a hospital stay, they might have physical challenges that require changes to your home. Their healthcare team can help you get your home ready. For example, you might need a hospital bed, a walker or wheelchair, a ramp instead of stairs, or a shower stool in the bathroom. You might also need to remove items that are easy to trip on, such as clutter, area rugs, and cords.

You might also want to replace some items because they bring up emotions. You and your loved one are both going through emotional changes that can affect how your home feels to you. Items that once brought you joy may now make you sad or angry. Recognize those items and consider replacing them with things that make you feel good. This will be different for each person.

Having a dark, clutter-free bedroom at night is a great way to sleep better. You can buy inexpensive blackout shades or curtains if streetlights keep your room too bright. Find comfortable bedding that feels good against your skin. Choose colors to suit your mood. Reds, oranges, and yellows can stimulate you and give you energy. Blue, green, and purple can make you feel rested and at peace. Think about how you want to feel in each room of your home.

Your sense of smell has a powerful connection to your brain. What you smell can give you a sense of feeling well, improve your mood, relieve stress, and clear your mind. Experiment with different scents in your home, whether from candles, natural herbs, or air fresheners. Only burn candles when someone is in the same room with them, and look for non-toxic or natural air fresheners. When you choose a scent, ask yourself what makes you and your loved one enter a room and breathe more deeply? That scent could be a good choice for you.

Describe your home before and after your loved one required care, identifying the changes you made. Determine whether those changes are truly serving you both and explore what further adjustments you might make to render the home environment more nurturing, safe, and peaceful.

Talk to your care provider about using aromatherapy. If you or someone in your home is pregnant or has asthma or a chronic lung disease, your doctor might want you to avoid certain essential oils. You should also check with your doctor about air fresheners and sprays to make sure they are OK.

Sounds can be stressful or soothing. Experiment with playing music to set a mood or block out disturbing noises like street traffic. Carpets, curtains, and soft fabrics absorb sound, so you might want to add more of these if your home has a lot of noise from outside. Hard surfaces, such as hard floors and furniture, make sounds seem louder. This might be fine if your home is in a quiet area or you do not mind noise.

Warm, natural light is soothing. At night or when you don't have much natural light, try light bulbs that are marked "neutral" or "warm." Some LED light bulbs, and most fluorescent bulbs give a harsh, bright light that is not relaxing. Using bulbs that give a warmer, less bright light can make you feel warm and cozy. Use a dimmer switch for overhead lights, especially over a table where you eat. You can also use lamps on side tables or have some lamps attached to the wall.

Taking care of a loved one can prevent you from keeping your home clean and clutter-free. Not being able to clean regularly can allow clutter to build up. This might make you anxious. Clutter around the house can also trip people who have difficulty walking or keeping their balance, so it is a good idea to get rid of it for their safety. You might feel ashamed of not being able to clean or stay organized, but you are a busy caregiver. Talk to your doctor, nurse, social worker, friend, or family member about getting help to clean and get rid of clutter.

If you feel like you live in your car, make it a positive place. Small changes like keeping the inside of your car clean and throwing trash away every night might make the traffic jam less stressful. Here are a few more ideas for making car rides more pleasant:

- Consider adding an air freshener or car diffuser. Smelling lavender or vanilla can relax you, while orange or eucalyptus can give you energy.
- Turn "wasted" car time into time to learn or relax. Play an interesting podcast or listen to an inspiring radio show.
- Take a few minutes to repeat a positive or motivating thought. This helps you focus your attention on something positive, interrupting your stress response. Your thought can be a religious or spiritual prayer or an affirmation. Affirmations are positive thoughts you can repeat every day, such as, "I'm doing the very best I can," or "We are creating a new life together." Affirmations help you change your mindset and stay positive during challenging times, even when things seem impossible.
- Play music to set your mood.

You might be a full-time caregiver or go back to work after taking time off to care for your loved one. You might be part-time or retired when you take care of someone. But if you work at least part-time, you have unique challenges. You play two roles in life: worker and caregiver.

Changing your workplace to be a positive place might take more than creating a pleasant, clutter-free area. Life as a caregiver can be unpredictable. You might have emergencies or other demands on your time, and these might take you away from the office more than your boss and coworkers would like. Even if they try to be sensitive, their sensitivity may run out over time.

In your journal

List 3 changes in your work situation since you started being a caregiver. Then, write a few sentences about how they affected you and how you handled them.

You might wonder how to manage the demands of work with the growing needs at home. A support group can help you answer the following questions:

- How can I talk about my caregiver experiences at work without seeming weak and vulnerable?
- How can I talk about the challenges of being a caregiver when I don't want them to think my productivity and performance will suffer?
- How much of what I'm going through should I tell people at work?
- How can I be a good worker and focus on my job while fulfilling my duties as a caregiver?
- How can I be a good caregiver and keep my business running if I work for myself or own a company?

You might need to ask for more time off, a more flexible schedule, or different work responsibilities when you are a caregiver. Asking for these things can be challenging. But you might be able to use some of the communication skills you have gained in communicating with the person you take care of.

Here are some tips for communicating in the workplace:

- Think about the message you want your boss to get. Write down what you want them to know before you talk so you feel ready for the conversation.

- Be clear about what you want or need from your boss. Be pleasant but firm. Avoid sounding demanding, angry, or upset.
- Practice what you want to say. You can do this alone or in front of a mirror if you want. Or you can practice with someone in your circle of support.
- Use "I," statements such as, "I need to leave at 5 o'clock to pick my child up," instead of "you" statements such as, "You always make me stay late."
- Communicate regularly with your boss to develop and maintain a comfortable relationship.

Being a caregiver might make you set work-related goals and dreams aside. You might also miss the sense of identity, purpose, or self-esteem you got from work. Now, you might feel a loss of meaning. Stress can build if you have to change or leave a job, face a loss of income, or have a tighter budget.

But the changes are not all bad. Recognize the new skills you have learned as a caregiver. The challenges you have overcome as a caregiver might make you more flexible at work. Little things might bother you less, and you might feel stronger or better able to set priorities. You might be proud of all you can get done during the day.

If you need to change jobs, give yourself credit for all the new skills you have gained as a caregiver and mention them in your job search. For example, if you have learned better communication skills, you can add "excellent communication skills" to your resume. If you have learned to read complicated records or use new apps or software, you might share that in an interview.

When dealing with the stresses of a busy life, it's easy to tune out the natural world of plants and animals around you. But spending time in nature can be good for your mind, body, and spirit.

Take time to watch the sunset or find a green space to eat lunch on a workday. Working in a garden can help you connect to the earth. If gardening is not an option for you, try walking in a local park.

What new skills have you learned as a caregiver that you can bring into your current workplace or a new career?

In your journal

Write down 5 important experiences in your life that you think define you. Write just one word, a phrase, or a sentence for each one. They do not have to be in order, and you do not need to write a summary of your whole life. Don't overthink. What is important now? You can even do this exercise again from time to time to see how the list changes. Then, write a few more sentences about these experiences, exploring the effect they had on who you are.

Whether you live in the city, country, or somewhere in between, be aware of the life around you. You can do this through artwork that shows nature scenes, a view of green grass and sky through a window, or an online video of waves crashing along the shore.

In your own life, find places that involve all of your senses and help you feel peaceful, safe, and connected to other people. You can also keep track of how changes in nature affect you, your mood, your weight, and your energy level.

Being aware of these things can help you to make the best decisions. You can even try to change the way you think about a situation. For example, if you find yourself becoming depressed or sad during rainy weekends, try to see the beauty in the raindrops or make something you love a rainy-day-only activity. You might even begin to look forward to rainy days!

Although bad weather can make you feel down, nature can also give you positive images for meditation. Just as winter turns to spring, your ability to heal yourself can come to life and grow. The way nature and your body both recover is an important image to hold onto throughout your journey.

Put on some comfortable shoes and go for a walk. Slow down from your normal pace and focus on each of your senses. Notice the colors of nature, hear how each bird's song or city noise is different, feel the air on your skin, and smell a flower or the other scents around you. As your mind begins to wander, gently but firmly return to experiencing the moment so that you can make the most of this healing time. As you start to look outside yourself and take in more and more, you become more aware of the life around you. By being aware, you might appreciate your surroundings more. You might feel more like a part of things than an outsider looking in.

Whether it's a school, workplace, place of worship, or community organization, you are part of many groups that affect your life. Being involved in groups that are healthy and have healing qualities supports your health and a general feeling of wellness. A healthy group allows you to participate in making decisions that affect you. It promotes open and honest communication, creates a feeling of trust and personal responsibility, and makes you feel that you belong.

Take part in groups that are specific to you or your loved one's experience. Some of these include

- Veterans' communities. Be aware that groups for Vietnam-era veterans might have a different culture than groups of veterans who served in Iraq and Afghanistan.
- Groups of people with your condition. There are groups for people with traumatic brain injuries, post-traumatic stress, heart failure, and more.
- Caregiver groups. You can find groups for spouses and partners, parents, friends, and other caregivers of people with your

loved one's condition. Connecting with people who share your experience can provide practical tips and a lot of emotional support.

Describe your current medical care. When was the last time you got a checkup? Do you have any long-term health problems that need care? List the things you think are keeping you from getting regular checkups. For each one, write down the support you need or the changes you could make to overcome these barriers.

- Survivors. If you lost a loved one, you might find comfort with other spouses of people who had cancer or Alzheimer's disease or with Gold Star Wives, mothers, and fathers. Survivors of suicide might find help in connecting with others who lost a loved one this way.
- Volunteer groups. Joining a group that helps others can be rewarding. You will expand your social circle and enjoy a sense of being useful.

Making the most of your experience with the medical system is important. This includes taking care of your own health, communicating with your loved one about appointments, feeling less anxious during appointments, and finding integrative care. Without proper care, a cough can become pneumonia, and a strain can become a broken bone. Keeping up your own medical care is important to prevent long-term problems and keep your body, mind, and spirit as healthy as possible.

Regular dental and medical care are more important now that you're a caregiver. Finding out what is keeping you from getting any needed care can be helpful. Certain beliefs can get in the way of taking care of yourself. For example, it might seem easier to care for someone else than for yourself. You might have a lifelong habit of not taking care of your health. Or you feel guilty going to a doctor or dentist appointment when you feel your loved one needs you. Finding the thoughts that keep you from getting the care you need can help you decide to get it.

You might also want to learn certain caregiving skills. For example, learning how to lift your loved one or move them on a bed or chair can protect you from getting hurt when you do it. Ask your loved one's doctor or nurse where you can learn this or other skills.

Depending on your loved one's healing process, you might spend a lot of time in the hospital or doctor's office. Talking with your loved one before, during, and after a healthcare appointment can help decrease tension and conflict. This is especially true when you and your loved one have different ideas about what you want to discuss. Consider the following:

- Prepare for the visit—Write down what you need to talk about during the appointment to make sure you don't forget something important. Bring a list of their medicines and the doses they are taking. You can find forms online to write this information down. Also, bring notes about symptoms or problems your loved one has had.

- Consider talking with the doctor separately sometimes. This can help with sensitive topics such as memory loss or anger. Ask your loved one ahead of time how they want to handle sensitive topics or if they want you to leave the room at any time. Would they like you to sit in the waiting room or go get coffee during their appointment? Would they like you to go into the exam room but stay silent? Or would they like you to ask questions or lead the conversation?

  Talking about this with your loved one makes it easier for you to talk with healthcare providers in an appropriate way. If you bring up a problem your loved one was not ready to talk about, they might feel betrayed. You might benefit from having your loved one sign a form that says you may talk about health concerns with healthcare providers.

- During the visit—You might want to record the appointment on your phone or computer. Ask the doctor or other health care provider first because not every hospital or clinic allows this. You can also take notes on paper to remember what the doctor or other health care provider said. If you are confused, ask them to repeat or explain. Make another appointment if you need more time or want to talk more about the problem.

  Speak up for your loved one and yourself when you think you need to. Tell the doctor or other health care provider what you need. If they do not seem to understand, it is OK to ask more questions or explain your needs in a different way.

- After the Visit—Ask your loved one how they think the appointment was. Do they wish anything had been different?

You might not be able to control the things that stress you, but you can learn to keep the stress from controlling you. First, check your breathing. Are you taking short, shallow breaths that only reach as far as your upper chest? This is a sign of stress. Take 30 seconds to do a deep breathing exercise. This will cause your body to relax naturally.

Take a "4 X 4"

Pause and breathe in for a count of 4. Count slowly, "One, two, three, four." Then, let the breath out, counting slowly to 4 as you do. Exhale. You can also try doing things to distract yourself from what stresses you. For example, if the sounds of medical equipment make you anxious, try listening to music or a book or podcast.

Take a moment to be mindful of how these things make you feel. How does listening to music, a book, or a podcast change the way you react to your environment?

You might have heard the term "integrative care" before. Other names are "alternative medicine" and "complementary medicine." This type of care combines conventional medicine and other treatments such as acupuncture, massage, chiropractic care, and more. You might hear that you should use these treatments instead of regular medical care, along with other treatments such as energy medicine, homeopathy, or mind and body medicine. But integrative treatments work best when you use them with conventional care. When you do this, you get the best of modern medicine and science, plus care that helps your mind, body, and spirit heal naturally.

If you are confused by all the terms for types of health care, keep reading to learn more. You can also decide which term describes this type of health care best for you. According to the National Center for Complementary and Alternative Medicine at the National Institutes of Health

- "Complementary" generally refers to using a non-mainstream approach together with conventional medicine. This means using regular medical treatment, plus other treatments such as massage or acupuncture.

- "Alternative" refers to using a non-mainstream approach in place of conventional medicine. This means not using regular medical treatments but only using other treatments.

- "Integrative" means using both. You receive mainstream medical therapies and complementary and alternative therapies for which there is high-quality scientific evidence of safety and effectiveness. These are the other treatments that researchers have studied and found to be effective for certain conditions. Integrative care is important for you and the person you care for because it acknowledges the whole person in mind, body, and spirit. You can do some types of integrative care by yourself, so it can be useful for taking care of yourself. You can learn some things from a healthcare provider and then do them at home without more help.

When your loved one is receiving care, ask yourself, "What is it about this place that bothers me? What sights, sounds, smells, and touch sensations do I have control over? How could this be a better experience for me and my loved one?"

1. You matter. You play a major role in your own care, especially treatment decisions. This is commonly called "patient-centered care" or "person-centered care."

2. It is the care of the whole person. Exploring more than just one part of a person or one issue works to solve issues at the core and acknowledges the effect of many factors, including your mind, spirit, and environment, on your body. It also acknowledges how your body can affect your mind and spirit.

3. Your doctor is your partner. The doctor-patient relationship is important, and you and your doctor develop it in a way that helps you receive all the care you need for as long as you need it.

4. The body is a self-healing machine. Integrative care recognizes that the body heals itself, so helping you make the most of this ability is a top priority.

5. You get the best of both worlds. Integrative care includes the best of conventional and complementary medicine.

6. Learn more about the evidence behind integrative care, including fact sheets on acupuncture, yoga, and art therapy, at drwaynejonas.com/caregiver.

Proper health care requires teamwork with the patient in the center. You, the caregiver, are in the center too. The health care providers for your loved one should communicate with each other. Ask if they are doing this, and if they are not, ask them to start. They should have your loved one's best interest and your best interest as the top priority. Your healthcare providers should work together to set goals and expectations for your loved one's care.

Spending time in places you enjoy is one way of taking care of yourself. A comfortable couch, a clean bedroom, or colorful towels in the bathroom can comfort you and cheer you up.

Wherever you spend your time, make sure that the spaces around you don't add unnecessary stress to your days and nights. Ask a friend or neighbor to help you clean up, or take a break to go shopping for new sheets, towels, or something else to freshen your space. Start with the spaces where you spend the most time first, and then move on to make the others more pleasant.

What is one improvement that you can make at home, work, or at the doctor's? Take a moment to reflect on these 3 pieces of advice for being a healthy caregiver:

1. Being a caregiver is like running a marathon, not a sprint. This means taking care of yourself is extremely important for your mind, body, and spirit.
2. Focus on your breathing at different times during the day. Taking just 5 seconds to feel thankful for something or to focus your mind on what you are doing right now helps lower your stress back to normal levels.
3. Ask for help. Accept it when you get it. You do not have to be alone. Friends, family, respite care, nonprofit

groups, your doctor or hospital, your church or temple, and your military organizations if your loved one is a service member can all help. You can also look at the resources on drwaynejonas.com/caregiver.

You have seen that self-care means the following:

- Getting back a sense of who you are
- Building strong social connections
- Making healthy life choices

In your journal

Write a letter to yourself. What advice would you give yourself if you were just starting out as a caregiver? What would you say to reassure yourself that you did not know when you started?

Surrounding yourself with healing where you live, care, work and play

You are on your own unique place on your journey. To make progress, you might need to take some steps that feel like you are going sideways before you go forward. When you are ready, take your next step to improve your own situation.

Too often, we tell ourselves and others that we aren't caregivers because we feel caregivers have special training and fancy titles after their names. In reality, few people choose to be an informal caregiver—it's simply what happens when you are drafted to care for those you love while also trying to negotiate the countless other responsibilities in your life. ~Zachary White, PhD, Author Of The Unprepared Caregiver Blog

What does a caregiver do? 🔍

1. PERSONAL ASSISTANT
2. ADVOCATE
3. PHARMACIST
4. CHAUFFEUR
5. CHEF
6. HEALTHCARE COORDINATOR
7. FINANCIAL ADVISOR
8. SOCIAL COORDINATOR
9. TECH SUPPORT
10. NURSE
11. HOUSEKEEPER
12. BODY GUARD
13. INTERPRETER
14. THERAPIST
15. STYLIST
16. MIND READER
17. ENTERTAINER
18. ACTIVITY DIRECTOR
19. RECEPTIONIST
20. FITNESS COACH
21. NUTRITIONIST

and more...

@dementiadarling

CHAPTER 23

The Sine Wave Continues

♦ ♦ ♦

"Life itself is a privilege, but to live life to the fullest—well, that is a choice." ~Andy Andrews

When asked how Cat is doing, I always reply she is like a sine wave in a slight decline. Some days are better than others. Rarely do I see sharp declines, but in every case, I will see within a month or two an uptick in what she can still do or in regards to her behavior.

Unfortunately, about 3 months ago, the downward turn of the sine wave began and continued until about two weeks ago. From time to time, I would record how she was doing daily, but after a while, I would find it depressing, so I would delete the document. So that is why I can only give an approximation. As you know, I do post to my blog from time to time on her condition, but usually, I am talking about something positive like this one.

There are two different scales they use to track the progress of the disease. One is 4 stages and the other is 7. I use the seven stages. 1 and 4/7 are the same on each. 1 is when the person actually has the disease but does not know what it is or, in some cases, has not shown any signs of ALZ. 4/7 is when the person is basically bedridden. For Cat, she has been bouncing back and forth between 5 and 6. Before 6 months ago, mostly 5, and within the last 3 months, mostly 6. I will not go into detail what that all entails.

As you know, I am always looking for ways to hold off stage 7 as long as possible and to continue to enjoy life as much as we can. I have mentioned in an earlier chapter that we are doing the Doctor Dale Bredesen protocol. Many of his recommendations we were already doing, and our lifestyle revolved around his suggestions.

In Atlanta, we were able to find a practice that follows his protocol, and we had plenty of blood, urine, etc., taken and analyzed. As best as possible, I gave her the recommended supplements but did not see any improvement over time. In some cases, it can take 6 months or more and usually works best for folks early on.

Two weeks ago, I met up with my sister, Gwen, my sister-in-law, Joan, my son, Shawn, my daughter-in-law, Cassie, and my two grands, Luca, who just turned 7 months, and his older sister Lily, clocking in at 2 1/2 years old. We spent a lovely week in Washington, Virginia, aka, Little Washington. While there, we also were able to have lunch with Karen and Aprille, who are from previous Marathon Tours and Travel trips. They live nearby in Sterling, Virginia.

I gave everyone the heads up on the recent decline of Cat so they would know what to expect. I was also looking forward to the help that each could provide me since, by this point, I was worn out. I have written about the importance of taking care of oneself in a previous chapter and later in this book.

Not unexpectedly, I saw an immediate uptick in Cat's cognition and behavior. I often talk about the role socialization plays and the benefits for folks with ALZ. The negative effects of isolation due to COVID-19 have been well documented.

Thinking there might be more to this event rise on the sine wave roller coaster I observed her and my family members very closely. I also took a hard look at the past two weeks and noticed that our typical exercise routine had been taking a backseat to the cold weather we had been experiencing. We did do a 10k back on February 12, 2022, in Mesa, Arizona, but besides that, nada.

The winter months are tough for us, especially the last two years since we usually cruise the Caribbean on and off during the winter months before Covid and have not done so since. No one likes to bundle up to go for a run, and it is especially tough for me since I now have to dress and undress Cat.

My observations of Cat with family also brought an awareness of how we have typically been spending our days and the comparison of how our days were spent with family. One thing I did notice was the lack of TV. It is not recommended that folks with ALZ in the later stages watch large quantities of TV, especially the news. They are overly sensitive to negative stories and tend to think that these things are happening to either themselves or their family members. Unfortunately, I have not been very diligent in that regard. In contrast, when the TV was on in VA, it was mostly kid shows with a lot of singing, and Lily was always trying to get everyone to join in with her.

As my search continued to find what is best for Cat I ran across an article on music and its benefits for people with ALZ. The brain is powerful; the soul is even more so. The combination of the two is the beginning of wisdom.

Music and the creative arts have a way of mending minds—mind to soul.

In Alzheimer's disease and other forms of dementia, music, and the creative arts can often keep people whole as they grip life, tantamount at times to a terrifying ride on the Coney Island Cyclone.

Take the case of Glen Campbell, an icon in music and life, who ultimately succumbed to Alzheimer's after a long, bruising battle—buttressed by the love and support of his wife Kim and children. On the heels of his Alzheimer's diagnosis, Campbell embarked on a celebrated "Goodbye Tour" with three of his children in the backup band. His farewell was the focus of an award-winning 2014 film, Glen Campbell: I'll Be Me, produced by Trevor Albert and directed by James Keach.

"Some inside this disease can talk about it," notes George Vradenburg, co-founder of UsAgainstAlzheimer's. "Few, probably a handful, can talk about it in ways that inspire…It is remarkable to see, and it says something about how we know or does not know how the brain works…There is something about training one's brain for a singular moment in life. I saw this with Glen Campbell. In what was to be the final tour, he had scheduled three to five concerts—150 concerts later, Campbell would be on stage, playing music he had played all his life, yet when he got off stage, he often didn't know where he was."

Campbell's innate genius was the kind of musical memory that the remarkable non-profit program Music Mends Minds seeks to nurture. And then there's the legendary Tony Bennett, with the same gift of muscle memory in music. Bennett, now in the throes of Alzheimer's, was the subject of a recent "60 Minutes" segment hosted by Anderson Cooper.

"On any given day, the 95-year-old may forget a lot about his past life," writes Brit McCandless Farmer for CBS News. "He (Bennett) likely won't recall the stories behind the photos that fill his New York City apartment, not the ones with Frank Sinatra or Rosemary Clooney, not even the one with Bob Hope—the man who gave Anthony Dominick Benedetto his stage name: Tony

Bennett. But when Bennett hears that music, the soundtrack that has accompanied more than seven decades of American life, the singer that millions have come to know returns."

Like Campbell, Bennett's brain "is built around his music." Such also is the case with the late Irwin Rosenstein, the inspiration for Music Mends Minds, the creation of his wife Carol, who has offered a ray of sunshine for those suffering from Alzheimer's and other forms of dementia.

Music Mends Minds was founded in 2014. It fashions musical support groups nationally and internationally for individuals with Alzheimer's, dementia, Parkinson's, traumatic brain injury, PTSD, and other neurological disorders. The vision of Music Mends Minds, now working closely with Rotary International Clubs, is to give hope to and encourage afflicted individuals around the world and their families, friends, volunteers, and caregivers.

Irwin had a great ear for music throughout his life, Carol says, noting he was a marching band member at the University of Pennsylvania and enjoyed playing saxophone and the piano. Professionally, he worked in real estate law for the Federal National Mortgage Association (Fannie Mae). Irwin passed away in 2021, having been diagnosed with Parkinson's disease, an advancing form of dementia, on his 70th birthday in 2006, and later with dementia in 2015.

"Our home in Los Angeles was always filled with music," Carol says. "We became volunteers for the Los Angeles Philharmonic. And we spent time together at the Hollywood Bowl, the Dorothy Chandler Pavilion, and the Walt Disney Concert Hall." Then came the diagnosis. "This was shocking to me, especially having spent my life in healthcare and knowing a little bit about the challenging journey ahead," she notes. After several years. Irwin's prescribed Parkinson's medication brought on hallucinations and agitation, as he believed there were other people living in his home.

Carol immediately called Irwin's neurologist, who advised reducing the dosage of Irwin's medication, the cause of the hallucinations. "Then one day," Carol recalls, "when Irwin was feeling very low from reducing his medication, he chose to play his piano... and it became clear to me that something extraordinary had just happened. I called his neurologist again, who told me that I was witnessing the power of music changing brain chemistry."

Carol was advised that playing the piano had such a complex neurological demand on Irwin that his brain pushed harder and harder for more natural dopamine (a neurotransmitter in the brain that sends messages between nerve cells). "It became clear that the music empowered Irwin; he became more aware, responsive, confident, energetic, talkative, and hopeful," she recalls.

Carol asked Irwin's doctor if this process meant "we could find some like-minded souls who had a similar diagnosis so that we could all gather in a social setting to make music together—thereby changing everyone's darkness into light."

The rest is history. After witnessing this dramatic transformation in Irwin's condition, Carol was inspired to start a band to help others with neurodegenerative diseases, and The 5th Dementia Flagship Band was born. Since then, Music Mends Minds has grown to 20 bands nationally and has hosted 24 concerts.

Research shows that music can improve speech, attention, executive functioning, orientation, and memory and reduce anxiety, agitation, and depression. The same is true for those blessed with other creative talents, as I've found it to be the case in my writing as my journey continues down this twisted dementia path that has taken several family members.

In 2018, Carol was nominated for a "CNN Heroes Award," which honors everyday individuals who do extraordinary things to change the world. Carol made it to the top 20 out of thousands of nominees. Then in 2020, "CNN Heroes" returned to document Carol's pivot to Zoom sessions during the pandemic.

"We were featured in a story about the universal role music plays in changing brain chemistry and in helping to combat depression and isolation among seniors with cognitive issues," she proudly says. Music, indeed, has mended minds—yet another pushback on the oftentimes and sadly inaccurate stereotypes of Alzheimer's and other dementias.

Elsewhere, I have read that grooving to the oldies helps people with dementia tap into their memories—and studies show it eases agitation caused by changes in routine. While other cognitive functions and memories fade away with dementia, musical memories are the last to go. Music transports patients to a comfortable moment in the past. As a result, familiar music eases agitation and other psychiatric symptoms.

Alzheimer's disease damages the areas of the brain involved in processing memory. Why do musical memories stay? Concetta Tomaino, executive director (and co-founder) of the Institute for Music and Neurologic Function and board member of the Music & Memory. Dementia damages the parts of the brain that process environmental information. Tomaino explained in a Being Patient LiveTalk that this causes a lot of agitation and confusion. "However, familiar music initially gets processed in deeper areas of the brain, more resilient networks in the brain that are connected to long-term memory retrieval," Tomaino told Being Patient. "Emotional responses don't get as damaged because of chemical changes in the brain [during dementia]." These areas still recognize the music, stimulating the brain from the inside.

These articles brought back memories of taking care of my mother. My sister, Gwen, would always bring an updated playlist for her to listen to when she visited. I would make sure she listened to it also during my visits. It also reminded me of Cat and I's Motor

Home trips when we would always have the radio playing the old-ies.

So, with all this new information in hand, I made a new plan of action moving forward. Now, we have the TV on sparingly, with comedy shows being the dominant format to watch. In the car, hotel, during runs and walks, and even on airplanes, music will always be playing. Mostly music from the 70's and 80's.

I am also experimenting with 40Hz gamma tones with music when Cat gets somewhat agitated. Here is something I found on the subject.

An MIT team and other researchers have gone on to show that sensory stimulation of 40Hz rhythm power also appears to help people with Alzheimer's disease retain brain volume and cognitive ability.

How does it work? In their ongoing investigations of the underlying mechanisms, Tsai's lab became the first to show that increasing gamma promotes improved neural network connectivity, widens brain blood and lymphatic system vessels to increase waste clearance, and causes an improved disease response by brain immune cells called microglia, for instance by reducing their inflammatory state. These differences were reflected in substantial changes in gene expression in neurons and microglia that the team measured in mice exposed to 40Hz sensory stimulation. These findings are the first to directly link brain wave changes with differences in cellular and molecular activity in neurons and their supporting cells, or glia.

So far, I have not seen any adverse reactions in response to this type of music, and in some cases, it does settle her down. Right now, I limit it to 30 minutes a day.

We now dress every morning, except for travel days by plane, for exercise. We throw sweatpants over top of our running shorts or tights, thus always ready to go for a run or long walk. That does require me to change our clothes three times a day, but it is worth it if I can keep the lines of communication open between her mind and body and thus keep her mobile as long as possible.

Lastly, for me to seek warm climates as much as possible. Right now, we are in Tallahassee, Florida, on what will be our first-ever month-long road trip, by car. The plan is to stay here for a week, then move over to Pensacola, FL for a few days, then on to Gulfport, MS for state 42 for half marathons.

This one with Mainly Marathons is our first in 4 months. Then, head back north to make it to Bluefield, WV, by the end of the month. Half Marathon number 43, once again with Mainly. Unlike us, only doing two races with them, we have a friend, Ernst, who will do 11 Marathons in 11 days. That will be 4 states with the Gulf Coast Series and another 7 with the Appalachian Series.

Plan B will be for us to bail out when we head back north and drop the car in ATL. Then fly to Richmond and pick up Mainly in Bluefield. I can only drive the equivalent of 4 hours a day, which takes me 6 hours when you add the stops about every hour to stretch my legs and get some air and, of course, some Starbucks. From the quote above, you can see that no matter the circumstances, our choice is to live life to the fullest.

Washington, Virgina
March 3, 2022

CHAPTER 24
What People With Early-Onset Dementia Want You to Know
◆　◆　◆

dementia, noun
de· men· tia di-ˈmen-chə
"Medical Definition: a usually progressive condition (as Alzheimer's disease) marked by the development of multiple cognitive deficits (as memory impairment, aphasia, and inability to plan
and initiate complex behavior)." ~Merriam Webster

An elevator encounter that happened to Laurie Waters
highlights the daily plight faced by early-onset
Alzheimer's patients like her.

Waters, 57, was stuck in an elevator at an Alzheimer's con-
vention with other folks who were growing loud and excited—and
the situation was getting to her. "I was starting to get panic-
stricken, being in that enclosed space. And one gentleman was like,
'Well, what's the matter with you?'" Waters recalled. "I said, 'I'm
actually living with Alzheimer's.' And this woman next to him said,
'You know, that's really mean to say that.'"

June is Alzheimer's & Brain Awareness Month, and people like Waters are taking the opportunity to share what they'd like others to know about what it's like to live with dementia.

Her elevator tale illustrates two important lessons—younger people can have dementia, and people with this disease would really rather not debate their diagnosis or be told they don't look like they have Alzheimer's.

"I look young, and people even in the Alzheimer's community who are around it still don't recognize younger-onset," said Waters, who lives in Clover, S.C. "It's everywhere. I've had doctors who have sat there, who haven't met me before, just look at me and be like, 'Are you sure you're diagnosed with Alzheimer's?"

The frustration for Deborah Jobe comes from folks who talk about her as though she isn't there. "My husband and I will be in a room, and people will ask him, you know, 'She looks pretty good; how is she doing?" said Jobe, 55, of St. Louis, who has an early-onset form of dementia called posterior cortical atrophy.

"I'm like, 'Hello! Right here! You can ask me. It's OK. I don't mind," Jobe said, laughing. "I'm still here. I'm still human. Please address to me, and if I can't answer, I'm sure he'll step in and help." The upshot from Waters and Jobe—people with Alzheimer's are still people.

"One of the common themes I hear over and over again is that how the diagnosis does not define who they are," said Monica Moreno, senior director of care and support with the Alzheimer's Association, who works with early-stage families in the wake of their diagnosis.

"It's not uncommon that when people hear that someone has been diagnosed, they immediately think about the end stage of the disease, where an individual may not be communicative and may not necessarily be aware of their surroundings," Moreno said.

"And while we know that that may be that's where the disease leads to, in the early stage of the disease, individuals still want to live a meaningful life, and they know that they still have things to contribute to society," she said.

Waters received her diagnosis in 2017 when her husband noticed that she wouldn't quit working. "I wouldn't leave my office. I used to work for a pharmaceutical company, and I used three computers in my office going through patient records," Waters recalled. "And I could fly through a patient's record in, like, five to 15 minutes."

"All of a sudden, it was taking me a half-hour, 45 minutes to an hour just to get through one record," Waters continued. "My husband noticed I wasn't even coming out of my office for coffee or lunch or dinner. I was working eight to 12 hours a day just to get work done. And when I had to go into the office to train people, I couldn't even remember some of the people's names that I knew for years. It was horrible."

Jobe had to walk away from a high-powered career as a customer success manager for global companies following her own diagnosis two years ago. "I would be in front of governance boards, executive management, to do a presentation and just find myself stopping," Jobe said. "Literally, the words were in my head, but I couldn't get them out, or the wrong words would come out. And so I would joke, and I would say, 'You know, I'm sorry, let me take a step back, I haven't had enough coffee today."

She also found herself struggling to keep up with new product updates, never mind explaining them to clients. "I just couldn't grasp it," Jobe said. "I've been in this industry for over 30 years, and I just couldn't grasp it. I would have to ask questions over and over."

Both women's lives are different now as they've adapted to their illnesses. For example, Jobe's husband uses laminated cards to help her around the house—"The dishes are clean" or "The stove is hot." Jobe can't drive or cook or ride a bike and often forgets to eat.

But she still loves new technology, word games, and creating art. She's still living her life. "So don't treat me differently unless I ask you to in some way—meaning like, OK, you know, slow down a little bit more," Jobe said. "I'm still me. I'm still who I was before. Some days, maybe it doesn't show. But the heart of me, and the soul of me is."

Jobe and Waters and other Alzheimer's and dementia patients have a few other things they would like others to know to help make their lives less frustrating. Dementia sometimes leads Jobe to act in ways that don't reflect her true self, for example.

"I do have bad days where I'm maybe more agitated or defensive or confused," Jobe said. "My husband sees these days coming up before I do. I get what he calls crazy eyes, and it starts before I realize that it's happening.

So maybe I'm doing something that's out of character for me, but it's not because I want to do it to hurt somebody or get mad at somebody," Jobe continued. "Sometimes I can't help it."

People dealing with a person with Alzheimer's or dementia also can help by being very patient with them. Waters recalled a day recently when she couldn't for the life of her figure out how to scan a document.

"Now you're talking about somebody who used to work with three computer screens," Waters said. "I sat in my office for almost an hour and a half trying to figure out how to scan this document into my computer. Couldn't do it."

"People are looking at me and I'm like, I have to now explain to all these people who are looking at me like, 'What do you mean you can't scan a document? What's wrong with you? You don't look like you have anything wrong with you. You don't look like you have Alzheimer's. Are you crazy?" Waters continued.

Jobe agrees. "I don't think as fast as I did before, which really frustrates me," Jobe said. "I'm like, give me a minute. Let me try to process it first, and then I can answer it. Or maybe I'll need you to break it down into something a little simpler."

The very best way that a person can help someone with Alzheimer's or dementia is by staying in touch and learning all you can about the illness, Moreno said. "When the diagnosis is shared with others, it really does test relationships," Moreno said. "And it's not uncommon for friends to kind of step back and really not engage with the person living with the disease in the family anymore. And there really isn't a reason for that."

"A lot of times, it's just because they don't understand the disease. They don't understand the progression," Moreno continued. "And if they just took some time to educate themselves, they can get a better understanding of the disease and how to support that individual—to stay friends with them and engage with them and help them live the best life they can for as long as they can."

For Cat, like many, it was her job performance that caught her attention. I remember the fitful day when she tried to balance her checking account. The once-a-month activity usually took minutes; this time, it took around the entire day. It was a year before her diagnosis, but it was not until she feared losing her job that she agreed to get the required neurological testing to find out the root cause of the current problem.

Cat's folks referred to her as "Chatty Cathy," and there are no strangers in her book. Since we were always together, after the diagnosis, I was there to help her with the details. She was always chatting up someone we had just met. Her go-to line, when details of her many stories were asked, was for her to simply reply, "You have to ask Tony; he is my brain."

Early on, no one was the wiser. No matter what I was doing, if she was talking, my ear was always tuned in, ready to fill in the requested details of our grand adventures. A few times, I was asked to let her talk, and then either Cat or I would divulge her diagnosis. With tour groups that we often use, I would advise the tour coordinator of her condition. Also, as we became friends with many of the other participants, we would advise them to help me keep an eye out for her.

Most were unaware of her condition. For the majority of the time, we were nomads. Since we were bouncing from place to place every four to five days, many had limited exposure to us on a strictly one-on-one basis. I cannot exactly say when the tide turned, but now it is very obvious that there is a problem as I gently guide Cat through the maze of life. It probably is her sometimes blank stare towards the ground.

Everyone lends a hand, offers a seat or hand, and most don't stare but simply have a welcoming glance. As time moved on, a few would comment on what a wonderful job I was doing and how lucky she was to have me by her side. Most times, I have to fight back the tears, knowing that I am truly the lucky one.

When Cat was first diagnosed, and I told her about my writings about us, she often told me to make sure I documented every detail in hopes that it would help someone else who might be as unfortunate as her. Back then, she would sometimes, out of the blue, tell a stranger of her predicament. I would joke that she would bring home what I referred to as "strays." These were women traveling by themselves with Cat's thought that I would protect them in any far-flung lands. The three of us would stay together during the tours, and they were more than willing to lend a helping hand. In all cases, those folks and many others would become members of the ever-growing list of our "new best friends."

I stay in communication with many, and it always makes my heart sing when they ask about her. I, in turn, give my standard answer, "Some days are better than others." That is always true as her sine wave is in decline. I always seem to find a way to adjust to the new normal. Most times, my research would give me the answer to how to handle the ever-changing landscape. Sometimes, I simply follow what I would want her to do if the tables were turned.

CHAPTER 25
The "Cat" Mobile
♦ ♦ ♦

"When you've met one person with dementia, you've met one person with dementia." ~Professor Tom Kitwood

No two people with the disease are alike, and life expectancy after diagnosis is 2 to 20 years, with the average being 8 years. That, in itself, is a very wide range. The only thing we can do is to enjoy life as best as we can along the way. We believe in the additive model. What more can we do and not concentrate on what we can no longer do?

If I have learned anything about early-onset Alzheimer's, it is that you have to be flexible. After 8 years of navigating this twisting and winding road, I have learned a great deal along the way. When my now-grown kids were growing up, I learned flexibility was extremely important. Just because these three very talented and active youths had the day planned out, rarely did the day go as planned. As a pilot, for over 37 years, we always had contingency plans, and being in management for most of my career, I kept coming back to that principal day in and day out.

As the disease progresses, it becomes more and more difficult for the brain to talk to other body parts regularly. I try my best not to dwell on what Cat can no longer do but, by contrast, concentrate on what she can still do and try my best every single day to support those accomplishments. I have written about the critical role exercise plays in keeping this disease at bay, so I am always thinking of ways to keep the brain talking to the body.

As running becomes more difficult, especially long-distance runs of 4 miles or more, I have devised a workaround. That is where the "Cat" mobile comes into play. Unfortunately, back in April of 2022, while on the West Coast, Cat had two seizures within 4 hours that landed her in the hospital for her first overnight stay. She was there for two nights, and I had to beg and plead to get her out of there. It was not that they did not have her best interest in mind, but it was more that the environment was not conducive for someone with Alzheimer's. Many get much worse over time while in the hospital.

With that said, she is now on anti-seizure medications, and even though it is great at keeping them from recurring, they do have some side effects. Mostly, she becomes extremely tired, especially right after taking the medication, which she now has to take twice a day. The evening dosage has its challenges, but the one in the morning makes it very hard to get her to exercise at the intensity she once did.

My new workaround is to break up our exercise routine to several times a day. However, it is now very difficult to get her to run at all. It was hard enough in the recent past since her coordination is now compromised. So she now has to be very careful with foot placement to prevent trips and falls. Instead of trying to get 6 or more miles done several times a week, we now break it up into vigorous walks of a few miles each, several times a day. One of them might simply be walking the halls of the hotel. Down the hall, down the stairs, and then down the hall and back up the stairs.

The other thing we now do is to go for longer walks with short sporadic runs until she tires and then give her a ride in the Cat-mobile. That gives her some time to recuperate and then out she goes to continue the walk/run. Cat enjoys the breaks, and I still get my exercise of running while pushing her along.

We have even done two races with her new ride, and it breaks down so I can put it in a bag, and it will fit in the trunk of some cars. The back seat of all cars and with the wheels on right in the back of an SUV. I do have to take it to the oversized baggage area, but Delta does a great job transporting it for us.

It is not perfect, but it works well for us as we adjust to the new normal. I have vivid memories of Dick Hoyt as he did Marathons and sometimes even Iron Man Competitions while pushing his adult son. He has since passed away, but I remember the statue of him along the Boston Marathon route, which I ran back in 2016. I have been a firm believer that if someone else can do it and I want to do it, then I can also do it. Maybe not a marathon right now, but since I have 2 more to get 70 marathons done by the time I turn 70 in three years. You never know with me.

The first race we did to try out the Cat-mobile was in New York with our dear friends with Mainly Marathons in Port Jervis in June 2022. I did the half marathon to get me one step closer to getting a half marathon in all 50 states. That being number 44. We started out walking together for the first out and back, then transitioned to the Cat-mobile while I did 4 out and backs. Cat got out and did another out and back and then back in her ride while she cheered on the true die-hards that were doing the marathon and other various distance races.

Once again she got out for the final lap together as we once again finished up hand in hand. The second race was in nearby Roswell, Georgia, along the Chattahoochee River. This time, I pushed her for the first five miles in the 10K, and she walked with me for the final 1.2 miles, and we both had a great time. There was one rather steep hill, and I kept telling myself what goes up must go down, and we kept yelling wheeeee all the way back down. It does have a strap that goes around the runner's wrist just in case you trip and fall and don't have a runaway, Catherine Popp.

We are now in St. Kitts for at least a month. We got stuck here 2 years ago for a month when COVID-19 hit, so fingers crossed, nothing like Monkey Pox prevents us from getting back to the States this time around. My sister and sister-in-law have a condo there and found someone to help out several times a week for several hours a day while there. I must admit this will be hard for me since I tend to just do everything myself and rarely ask for help.

I say at least a month, but it might turn into two months, depending on how things go. Nonstops back to ATL come to an end after Sept 3rd, but then there is always winter for a return trip. The way we left Atlanta was a first for me. Usually, we just catch the sky train from the Renaissance Hotel to the airport in ATL, but with the Cat-mobile and Cat's 50 state marathon quilt and various other items for an extended stay was a bit much, so I opted for an Uber for the 3-minute ride to the airport.

At the skycap stand, the guy there loaded up our bags on his cart and bypassed the mass of humanity to the front of the Delta Sky Priority lane. It does help to both be Diamond Medallion and Million Milers. My motto is, "Don't leave home without her." He then called for a wheelchair and took the oversized bags to the oversized belt, and even though he was wearing a mask, I could tell he was very pleased with my generous tip and heartfelt "THANK YOU." A very nice lady showed up with the Wheel Chair and swiftly took us past the very long lines to the Wheel Chair Security lanes, along with about 50 others.

A mere 45 minutes from the time we were dropped off at the curb, we were in the Sky Lounge enjoying juice, fruit, and one of the best machine-made cappuccinos known to man. I gave myself 2 plus 30 for this flight and wondered without their help if we would have made the flight on time. I have not seen crowds like that at the airport since Mother's Day and made a note to myself that few there were worried about gas prices or inflation. They simply wanted to get away to far-flung places like Punta Cana and Cancun. Unfortunately, the Customer Service line was extremely long for people needing to rebook their flights, but our flight was right on time, so no worries for us.

For me to fully unpack our bags and finally have a meal out on a patio overlooking the water instead of cooped up in our hotel room, as we have for the last two years, was what I was looking forward to. There is a golf course across the street from the Condo with our names on it for morning and afternoon walks/runs along the cart path, and too many beaches to mention for us to walk hand in hand. There is a Marriott right down the street, and we will make sure to frequent it often as we sip soft drinks by the pool. We do have two friends coming down for a week each to enjoy the fun and sun, and we have booked a morning sail with Miles. Instead of rental cars, Mr. Mack, a personal taxi service, will be our new mode of transportation while there.

Fingers crossed that all goes well, but as I started this Chapter off, you have to be flexible in life in general and especially when caring for someone with Early Onset Alzheimer's. Don't get me wrong. I don't have all the answers, and it has not been a bed of roses by any stretch of the imagination, but that is how life is. Very few go through it without obstacles along the way, and we all know how it ends, so we might as well make the best of it.

Port Jervis, New York
June 6, 2022

Royal St. Kitts Golf Club
June 20, 2022

CHAPTER 26

Loving Someone Who Has Dementia
How to Find Hope While Coping with Stress and Grief

♦ ♦ ♦

"The test of first-rate intelligence is the ability to hold two opposed ideas in the mind at the same time and still retain the ability to function" ~F. Scott Fitzgerald

This is the third book that I have recommended. The first one was This Naked Mind, and the second was Younger Next Year. As the other two have done, this book has helped me a lot. This one in particular, when it comes to caring for Catherine. The first chapter set the tone for me and answered a question I have had for years. The writer puts her finger on the issue of ambiguous loss. How absence and presence can coexist. Having a loved one that is here and not here at the same time. It also covers in great detail how to take care of oneself while taking care of someone else.

The Caregiver's Companion, caring for Your Mind, Body, and Spirit handbook that I included in an earlier chapter was more of a practical guide, whereas this book comes at this topic from more of a mental standpoint. A striking statistic is that a person caring for someone with dementia is 63% more likely to die from stress than someone of the same age who is not caring for someone with dementia. The author does give more insight by demographics, broken down by race and age. This is not something I particularly need to be worried about. But the bottom line is that taking care of someone with dementia is dangerous if you do not take precautions.

I am the type that likes to control situations, and this book teaches the reader how to perceive and manage the situation. To control my frustration towards them, I have named the disease Allie. When I would get upset, I would direct my frustration towards Allie, the disease, and not Cat. I learned in this book that folks with dementia are still very perceptive, so they pick up on the stress, and it literally stresses them out. I have always told myself that I am doing the best that I can. I now include that thought process for Cat. She is also doing the best that she can at that moment in time.

Just because she was able to do something one day or a minute does not mean she will be able to do that same task right now. The opposite is also true. I try to allow her to do as much as she can, but since those abilities vary, I just need to learn to go with the flow. It sounds simple enough but it is critical to only speak in loving terms and praise her accomplishments.

It teaches you to find meaning in what she calls "Delicious Ambiguities." That phrase came from Gilda Radner, of Saturday Night Live fame, only months before her death. Our brains have problems dealing with ambiguities. I want to find answers and solve problems. My flying career taught me to always do what is necessary to land the plane safely at its destination. In this case, even though the outcome will be the same for all of us. I need to focus on doing all that is possible, to have the smoothest of flights along the way.

She also discusses in detail what is known as the Psychological Family. Since it is critical for the caregiver to have a support system, she suggests that you find friends and neighbors to be part of that psychological family. This is very important if your actual family members are unable or unwilling to provide the support that you need.

I have a group of folks I can reach out to via email, text, and occasional phone calls. My sister, Gwen, has been right by my side throughout, and we figured she has joined us on over 20 different excursions over the years. My grown kids have also been there for moral support.

I make sure we make it back to see Cat's family every three months, just like clockwork.

There were so many hidden gems in this book, so if you are caring for someone with dementia, I highly recommend you read this book, most likely several times, as I have. The best part of the book was chapter 7, where she went over her 7 guidelines for the Journey.

"There is only one way, go within", Letters to a Young Poet' by Rainer Maria Rilke

1. Find meaning
2. Balance and Control with Acceptance
3. Broaden Your Identity
4. Manage Your Mixed Emotions
5. Hold On and Let Go
6. Imagine New Hopes and Dreams
7. Take the Time to Mind Yourself, mind your step, as said at the end of the moving walkways at the Amsterdam Airport.

I find significant importance to the mind-your-step emphasis. I have had to catch myself to be sure to pay particular attention to the little details that could have tripped us up. We often simply go through the motions when, in actuality, our heads should be on a continuous swivel. Some parts of this book would be helpful in theory but, in practice, did not work for me. Unlike the guidebook in a previous chapter that was backed up with years of research, this was just one person's opinion. I believe after reading it and comparing it with your personality and values, everyone will find some things that apply to their situation.

CHAPTER 27

Running Around the World with Alzheimer's, Tony & Catherine's Story by Bianca Ansbro-Elliott

♦ ♦ ♦

I would like to share with you in this chapter one of the few articles that were written about us over the years. The interview was done while Cat and I were enjoying the fun and sun on the Island of St. Kitts in July of 2022.

Like the love stories that you read about or in the movies that you see, Tony and Catherine have a love for each other and life that has not let the challenge of Alzheimer's stop them from experiencing new countries or creating beautiful memories together.

Catherine was diagnosed with early-onset dementia in her early fifties. A year before her diagnosis Tony had the realization that Catherine was becoming very repetitive in speech, and simple tasks were becoming more difficult. This then began to seep into her work life where Tony became more involved as they were discussing letting her go – Tony wanted an answer, so he took her to a neurologist. Tony was a Pilot and was used to problem-solving and looking for the best course of action in difficult moments. Once they had received the news of Catherine's dementia, they did not want to wait as they knew that the time horizon was unclear, and Tony had recently been told that he needed a heart valve replacement.

Tony and Catherine looked for activities that they enjoyed doing together and decided to take early retirement, sell their home, and travel the world whilst taking part in various marathons. "We didn't set out to be nomads, but it just happened," said Tony. Crossing the finish line hand in hand, Tony and Catherine had run 55 marathons before her diagnosis, and since then, they have continued to add to that astonishing number. They are now on stop 681 and have been traveling for the past 8 years, only staying in one place for 3-4 days. During 2020 with traveling being quite different, they stayed in St Kitts for 6 weeks but were still planning on what would be their next race and where they would go next. They return home to the US every 3 months to see their four children and six grandchildren. Although it was difficult for the children to understand why they were going traveling after the diagnosis, Catherine and Tony were adamant that this was how they wanted to spend their time together. Catherine, being an extremely strong woman who had once walked a half marathon in the Australian Outback just weeks after breaking her ankle, knew that she had the inner strength to push herself mentally and physically over the next challenge.

Since their journey began, they have traveled to eighty-two different countries and have run at least a half-marathon in thirty-five countries on all seven continents. Tony shares, "Over the last year, it is getting harder for her, and she has less stamina, but we just take it easy, walking more, and we use her 'Cat Mobile,' but we will always cross the finishing line together hand in hand as we have always done." As they set off on their travels, Tony started writing a blog so that he could share the stories with their family and friends but also to share with Catherine as her memory faded. The book has now been published and provides first-hand accounts of their travels and journeys until now.

What is it like to travel with someone who has dementia?

The traveling industry is very accommodating and is part of their training to assist people. I would tell people to try it. It was daunting at the beginning, but if you explain your situation, people are very helpful. There have been many times when we have been brought to the front of the queue, had help with our luggage, and let off the plane first. It is doable so give it a go!

Our traveling days are Catherine's favorite now; it has become the norm, and she looks forward to the routine of them. She does have what is known as 'sundowning,' so we must ensure that we are settled at that time and usually travel early in the morning.

Would you have done anything differently?

At the beginning of the journey, I wanted to find a cure for Catherine. That became all-encompassing. I have always been a problem solver, so I wanted to find a solution. In hindsight, I wish that I had just spent the time with Catherine more. I only gave up a year ago, so it had delayed the grieving process.

What has been your biggest lesson that you would like to share?

Do not get caught up in the disease; there is still so much life to live. Find something you love with your loved one and explore it; just be together. It has been amazing creating these memories and how we have shaped a whole new life for ourselves, even throughout the challenges that we face.

What is your advice for being a caregiver?

Find things that bring you joy; you need to keep yourself happy too! I enjoy running so that is something that I do to bring me happiness.

What brings Catherine and you joy?

I love making travel plans, but we enjoy our walks or runs together every day, seeing our friends, meeting new people, and finding new places to eat!

Tony and Catherine are currently heading back to the US to run all the half marathons in each state; Catherine has already accomplished this and has run a marathon in all 50 states!

We would like to share our gratitude for the time that Tony took with us to share his story as he sat in the beautiful St Kitts; it was inspiring to hear of their beautiful love story and how life can continue after diagnosis, but just with a little more planning and patience.

CHAPTER 28
Deep Sleep May 'Clean' Away Alzheimer's Risk
♦ ♦ ♦

"Sleep is the golden chain that ties health and our bodies together." ~Thomas Dekker, American Actor

What does your brain do while you sleep? According to a new study, deep sleep is when your brain gets a scrub down, washing away the toxic waste that contributes to diseases like Alzheimer's. The brain also processes memories and thoughts from the day, and because Alzheimer's is a memory-loss disease, one can see how the lack of quality sleep might affect your brain negatively.

Researchers at the University of Rochester Medical Center in New York led the study, which was conducted using mice and published in the journal Science Advances. They looked at the efficiency of the lymphatic system—essentially, the brain's waste management system that gets rid of waste and cycles nutrients like glucose, lipids, and amino acids through the brain. The catch: The lymphatic system largely operates when we're in a deep sleep and is inactive when we're awake. Scientists have theorized that it's why mammals operate on the sleep schedule that they do. So the researchers decided to test how deep sleep might affect how efficient the lymphatic system is in clearing proteins like beta-amyloid and tau, both of which are associated with Alzheimer's disease.

For the study, scientists tested six different drug cocktails that put the mice in a sleeping state. They then tracked cerebrospinal fluid as it traveled through the brain. They also tracked the animals' blood pressure, heart rate, and respiratory rate, along with watching their brain activity on an electroencephalograph or EEG.

A combination of two of the drugs, ketamine, and xylazine, put the mice in the deepest sleep and most closely mimicked non-REM deep sleep according to the brain activity, heart rate, and breathing monitors. That sleep appeared to allow the lymphatic system to work the best.

"The synchronized waves of neural activity during deep slow-wave sleep, specifically firing patterns that move from the front of the brain to the back, coincide with what we know about the flow of CSF in the lymphatic system," said Lauren Hablitz, Ph.D., a postdoctoral associate and first author of the study. "It appears that the chemicals involved in the firing of neurons, namely ions, drive a process of osmosis which helps pull the fluid through brain tissue."

The study findings highlight that sleep is not just necessary to feel alert—it appears to keep your brain healthy over the long term. "Sleep is critical to the function of the brain's waste removal system, and this study shows that the deeper the sleep, the better," said Maiken Nedergaard, M.D., D.M.Sc., co-director of the Center for Translational Neuro-medicine at the University of Rochester Medical Center and lead author of the study. "These findings also add to the increasingly clear evidence that quality of sleep or sleep deprivation can predict the onset of Alzheimer's and dementia."

Previous research shows that adults who sleep poorly early in life have a greater risk of Alzheimer's as they age. In fact, a study in 2017 showed that poor sleepers had an approximately 68% higher risk of developing Alzheimer's in comparison to those who were well-rested. One study found that people who experience disrupted sleep also showed abnormal levels of beta-amyloid plaque, the protein that many scientists believe drives Alzheimer's. Other studies have shown that those who wake up feeling unrested or engage in daytime naps also have more tau in their brains. Years before a diagnosis, the effects of restless sleep showed up in participants' brains. It is not only the amount of sleep one gets that is important but the quality of sleep as well. Sleep that is interrupted throughout the night can be just as harmful to the brain as not getting enough sleep.

The study also shed light on the link between anesthesia and memory loss. Many patients report a lasting fog after coming out of surgery that results in cognitive problems. The drugs used on the mice were similar to those that might be used during surgery. Mice in the study who were given anesthetics that did not cause slower brain activity didn't see the same efficiency in their lymphatic systems. If doctors switched to a drug that induced deep sleep, they may be able to avoid the memory loss that can accompany anesthesia.

"Cognitive impairment after anesthesia and surgery is a major problem," said Tuomas Lilius, M.D., Ph.D., with the Center for Translational Neuro-medicine at the University of Copenhagen in Denmark and co-author of the study. "A significant percentage of elderly patients that undergo surgery experience a postoperative period of delirium or have a new or worsened cognitive impairment at discharge."

Sleep patterns change in older adults, but the following tips can help ensure good, restful sleep:

- Go to bed and get up at the same time each day, even on the weekends.
- Do not take naps longer than about 20 minutes.
- Do not read, watch TV, or eat in bed.

- Avoid screen time before bed.
- A warm shower before turning in for the night.
- Use your bedroom for sleep only.
- Create a cool and dark sleep environment
- Avoid caffeine for about eight hours before bedtime.
- Avoid nicotine and alcohol in the evening. Alcohol might help you fall asleep, but it can cause you to wake up in the middle of the night.
- Do not lie in bed for a long time trying to go to sleep. After 30 minutes of trying to sleep, get up and go to a different room. Do something quiet, such as reading or listening to music. Do not do anything that stimulates your brain. Then, go back to bed and try to fall asleep.
- Try to be active each day. Exercise can help you sleep better.
- Ask your doctor if any of your medicines could be keeping you awake at night. Medicines that can disrupt sleep include antidepressants, beta-blockers, and cardiovascular drugs.

Here is another study that stresses the importance of deep sleep, even for folks in the advanced stages of dementia.

Dreaming Away Dementia: Berkeley Research Shows Deep Sleep Alleviates Alzheimer's Memory Loss By UNIVERSITY OF CALIFORNIA - BERKELEY MAY 7, 2023

UC Berkeley sleep scientists have found that deep sleep, also known as non-REM slow-wave sleep, may protect against memory decline in older adults with high amounts of Alzheimer's disease pathology. Disrupted sleep has been associated with a faster accumulation of beta-amyloid protein in the brain, which is linked to memory loss caused by dementia. However, this new research suggests that higher levels of deep sleep can act as a cognitive reserve factor, increasing resilience against the effects of beta-amyloid protein. By practicing good sleep hygiene, older adults may be able to benefit from this compensatory function against Alzheimer's pathology.

A deep slumber might help buffer against memory loss for older adults facing a heightened burden of Alzheimer's disease, new research from the University of California, Berkeley, suggests.

Deep sleep, also known as non-REM slow-wave sleep, can act as a "cognitive reserve factor" that may increase resilience against a protein in the brain called beta-amyloid that is linked to memory loss caused by dementia. Disrupted sleep has previously been associated with a faster accumulation of beta-amyloid protein in the brain. However, the new research from a team at UC Berkeley reveals that superior amounts of deep, slow-wave sleep can act as a protective factor against memory decline in those with existing high amounts of Alzheimer's disease pathology—a potentially significant advance that experts say could help alleviate some of dementia's most devastating outcomes.

"With a certain level of brain pathology, you're not destined for cognitive symptoms or memory issues," said Zsófia Zavecz, a postdoctoral researcher at UC Berkeley's Center for Human Sleep Science. "People should be aware that, despite having a certain level of pathology, there are certain lifestyle factors that will help moderate and decrease the effects. One of those factors is sleep and, specifically, deep sleep."

As the most prevalent form of dementia, Alzheimer's disease destroys memory pathways and, in advanced forms, interferes with a person's ability to perform basic daily tasks. Roughly one in nine people over age 65 have the progressive disease—a proportion that is expected to grow rapidly as the baby boomer generation ages. In people with similar amounts of beta-amyloid protein deposits, more deep sleep corresponded with improved memory function.

In recent years, scientists have probed the ways that deposits of beta-amyloid associate with Alzheimer's disease and how such deposits also affect memory more generally. In addition to sleep being a foundational part of memory retention, the team at UC Berkeley previously discovered that the declining amount of a person's deep sleep could act as a "crystal ball" to forecast a faster rate of future beta-amyloid buildup in the brain, after which dementia is more likely set in.

Years of education, physical activity, and social engagement are widely believed to shore up a person's resilience to severe brain pathology—essentially keeping the mind sharp, despite the decreased brain health. These are called cognitive reserve factors. However, most of them, such as past years of education or the size of one's social network, cannot be easily changed or modified retroactively.

That idea of cognitive reserve became a compelling target for sleep researchers, said Matthew Walker, a UC Berkeley professor of neuroscience and psychology and senior author of the study.

"If we believe that sleep is so critical for memory," Walker said, "could sleep be one of those missing pieces in the explanatory puzzle that would tell us exactly why two people with the same amounts of vicious, severe amyloid pathology have very different memory?"

"If the findings supported the hypothesis, it would be thrilling because sleep is something we can change," he added. "It is a modifiable factor."

To test that question, the researchers recruited 62 older adults from the Berkeley Aging Cohort Study. Participants, who were healthy adults and not diagnosed with dementia, slept in a lab while researchers monitored their sleep waves with an electroencephalography (EEG) machine. Researchers also used a positron emission tomography (PET) scan to measure the amount of beta-amyloid deposits in the participants' brains. Half of the participants had high amounts of amyloid deposits; the other half did not.

After they slept, the participants completed a memory task involving matching names to faces.

Those with high amounts of beta-amyloid deposits in their brain who also experienced higher levels of deep sleep performed better on the memory test than those with the same amount of deposits but who slept worse. This compensatory boost was limited to the group with amyloid deposits. In the group without pathology, deep sleep had no additional supportive effect on memory, which was understandable as there was no demand for resilience factors in otherwise intact cognitive function. In other words, deep sleep bent the arrow of cognition upward, blunting the otherwise detrimental effects of beta-amyloid pathology on memory.

In their analysis, the researchers went on to control for other cognitive reserve factors, including education and physical activity, and sleep demonstrated a marked benefit. This suggests that sleep, independent of these other factors, contributes to salvaging memory function in the face of brain pathology. These new discoveries, they said, indicate the importance of non-REM slow-wave sleep in counteracting some of the memory-impairing effects of beta-amyloid deposits. Walker likened deep sleep to a rescue effort.

"Think of deep sleep almost like a life raft that keeps memory afloat, rather than memory getting dragged down by the weight of Alzheimer's disease pathology," Walker said. "It now seems that deep NREM sleep may be a new, missing piece in the explanatory puzzle of cognitive reserve. This is especially exciting because we can do something about it. With a small sample size of healthy participants, the study is simply an early step in understanding the precise ways sleep may forestall memory loss and the advance of Alzheimer's, Zavecz said. Still, it opens the door for potential longer-term experiments examining sleep-enhancement treatments that could have far-reaching implications.

"One of the advantages of this result is the application to a huge population right above the age of 65," Zavecz said. "By sleeping better and doing your best to practice good sleep hygiene, which is easy to research online, you can gain the benefit of this compensatory function against this type of Alzheimer's pathology.

I have often written about the importance of quality, restorative sleep. As we bounced around time zones with our nomadic lifestyle, sleep was always paramount in our travel plans.

After the diagnosis, I always set aside 8-9 hours for Cat to get the deep sleep required. Things don't always work out as planned, but as said by Benjamin Franklin, "If You Fail to Plan, You Are Planning to Fail."

Knowing that pharmaceutical medications can accelerate the disease progression, in some cases, I have always used supplements to aid in helping her fall and stay asleep as long as possible. However, research is underway on a medication called Suvorexant, which belongs to a class of insomnia medications known as dual orexin receptor antagonists. Orexin is a natural biomolecule that promotes wakefulness. When orexin is blocked, people fall asleep. Three orexin inhibitors have been approved by the FDA, and more are in the pipeline.

Unfortunately, looking back in time to right before she was diagnosed, I do worry that her sleep patterns were not as regimented. Back then, she was up at the crack of dawn corralling our two 90-pound dogs, and I am not sure she ever got more than 6 hours of sleep a night. At one point, she juggled two jobs. One during the day and one at night for a short period. You hear many folks touting the fact that they only need 4-6 hours of sleep a night. They wear that fact as a badge of honor, but I caution all to rethink that philosophy as it might bite them where the sun doesn't shine later in life.

Our society tends to reward people with that character trait. I saw that with my career path as I was willing to take a job at night, with long hours, for some time. In turn, I was rewarded with a promotion. As Cat recalled her past to me, I was in awe as to how she was able to throw packages at night at UPS and take classes during the day, all while raising a daughter pretty much on her own.

Research has shown that lack of sleep in the past also is a harbinger of Alzheimer's disease progression in the future. I caution all reading this to reconsider their priorities when it comes to sleep. Burning the candle at both ends is looked at as a good thing, but it does not pay dividends later in life.

There is not much we can do if we have to have surgery. Cat was not unlike many, having one surgery to remove a benign lump from her breast and two Colonoscopies. We all know about the brain fog mentioned above and have been cautioned against further surgeries in the future. It is just one more thing to consider as you guide your loved one and yourself down this path.

"Slumber is the main course in life's feast." ~William Shakespeare

CHAPTER 29
The Start of a New Chapter in Our Lives
♦ ♦ ♦

"When one door closes, another opens; but we often look so long and so regretfully upon the closed door that we do not see the one which has opened for us." ~Alexander Graham Bell

In this case, since Catherine can no longer run, our chapter of running all over the world is now behind us, and a new chapter has begun. She is still very active, walking 6-8 miles a day, and with the use of the "CatMobile" when she gets tired, I can get my much-needed runs in while pushing her. We have even done some races and still cross the finish line hand in hand, as always.

Since far-flung destinations are now in our rearview mirror, it was time for me to look into an alternative living arrangement. Typically, at this stage of the disease progression, the care partner, as I like to be referred to, looks for a memory care facility for their loved one.

Since my approach towards this terrible disease has been counterintuitive, I could not see myself doing such. I promised Cat that we would always be together and tackle this disease as a team effort. My mom instilled in me the golden rule. Do on to others as you would want them to do on to you. Knowing that if the tables were turned, Cat would also be by my side. With that being my guiding light, the selection process began back in July of 2022.

I had several different options to vet, and the process took about 3 months. When buying a house, they say location, location, location; the same is true in this case. Our doctors recommended Atlanta since they are all here, but I did look into Bloomington, Indiana, where Cat's daughter and grandkids live. It is also close to the rest of her family in Jeffersonville, Indiana. I was not impressed with the facilities there, with the majority of the good ones being of the assisted living variety.

These are facilities that offer 24/7 care and 3 meals a day. They are usually rather small and are not cheap. We stayed at one in Alpharetta, Georgia, about 30 miles north of downtown Atlanta, but since I do everything Cat needs to be done for her, it was over-kill. Why pay for something we don't need?

Another option was Harrisonburg, Virginia, where one of my two sons, Shawn, lives. He and his wife have two small children, so it would be great to see these grandkids grow up daily. It had the same drawbacks with the facilities and was even more expensive than Bloomington. State laws require that they charge for all the extra services, even if you only need some of them. The extra twist is that after a few more years there, they might have to once again relocate.

My other son, Aaron, lives with his wife in San Diego, California, and even though we love the city, it is simply too far away for us now. My daughter, Mariah, her husband, and my grandson recently moved from Athens, Georgia, to downtown Atlanta, so that was a plus. We also have some friends in the Atlanta area, so we were pretty sure Atlanta would work.

My thoughts were that we would not stop traveling but just not at the every 3-4 day rate we enjoyed for nearly 8 years. More like a 3-4 day trip somewhere once or twice a month. With that in mind, Atlanta was now the most logical choice for the same reasons we chose it when we first became nomads. With Delta nonstops to just about everywhere, it is becoming a no-brainer. Easy for us to visit others, and the same is true for others to come visit us. Now that the location of the Atlanta area was decided upon, all that was left was the location geographically and, finally, the physical location of the facility.

As an alternative, I could have looked into a retirement community or an Apartment and augmented it with an Adult daycare program. However, the social services folks at the Integrated Memory Center reminded me that I would not have the as-needed 24/7 oversight I now need. Let alone I would have to fend for myself when it comes to meals. More about that later.

Even though the assisted living facility in Alpharetta had its drawbacks, I did like the area. We did look closer to downtown and my daughter and also south near the airport. One of the caregivers I used, while trying out the Alpharetta facility, recommended a place called, Brookdale in nearby Roswell. They are a national chain and my mom stayed at one similar called Atria. They have all three levels of facilities, starting with Independent Living, Assisted Living, and Memory Care. After touring the facility, it was suggested that we try out one of their furnished apartments for what they refer to as a respite stay. They use these apartments for when someone has a home but wants a bit of a rest from the day-to-day chores or, in our case, just want to try it out.

I was not sold on the idea since Catherine and I were going to be the youngsters at the place. Mentally, it was going to take me a while to adjust to all the canes, walkers, and motorized scooters. It took me back to the nine years when my mom was at Atria and tried to compensate with something else she instilled in me. Do something for someone else every day. I found that to be easy to accomplish and, in turn, very fulfilling.

After the 30 day, respite stay, it was mutually decided that we give the place a try for 90 days. I say mutually, since management was a bit leery, their words, on my idea of us both living in an independent environment. As I said earlier, most at this stage have their loved one placed in memory care, and the partner either lives independently, stays at home, or moves into the assisted living facility.

Management can ask anyone there to leave for 8 listed reasons in the lease agreement, with 60 days' notice, or immediately for 3 listed reasons. In the 7 stages of Alzheimer's, Cat has now stabilized in stage 6, and unfortunately, with that stage, some individuals can become uncooperative and, in some cases, combative. Memory care facilities usually handle this by medically or physically restraining their residents.

The actual Brookdale property, they like to be referred to as the Senior Living Solutions, has a rich history. The original owner of the property was Chambrel, and the land was bought from the Mansell family back in the 80's. The original farmhouse is now home to the Alpharetta & Old Milton County Historical Society and is also used for weddings and special events.

Chambrel sold the property to Brookdale in 2002, and the actual name is Brookdale Chambrel, Roswell. Despite the age of the property, it is very well-kept, and you can't beat the location. They have a 1/2 mile sidewalk/path around the facility lined with gorgeous trees and landscaping. There are also several garden areas and an outdoor pool.

The main tri-level building can house around 300 folks with various-sized apartments. The total carpeted corridors are about 2 miles in length, so it is great to get our daily walks in. This is particularly important since folks at this stage of the disease tend to simply pace. Many decorate their doorways, so it is fun to see what they all have displayed, and we jazzed up ours. The walls of the halls and lobby area are filled with outstanding artwork, and there are lovely plants and plenty of chairs along the way for some to rest as they make their way to the main lobby and dining area. So walking amongst the beautiful scenery outdoors and the comfortable settings inside makes her walks more meaningful.

There are several quiet neighborhoods nearby, so I can easily get in a 6-mile run/walk without ever needing a car. Speaking of which, there is a Hertz facility within walking distance, so when one is needed, getting and dropping off one is a breeze, and they don't gouge me if I pick up or drop one off at the airport.

In the main building, they also have the Assisted Living Facility, which I was not impressed with. Once again, it was rather small and more expensive than the independent living apartments. There are also several detached 2 bedroom cottages which did look very inviting but larger than we would need. One feature all of the apartments have which I have not seen anywhere else is that they all have screened-in porches/balconies. We often keep that door open for a little extra space and fresh air as we watch the leaves change colors and the gorgeous sunsets through the trees. We did clear out our storage unit, so it will also be perfect to put Cat's bike up on a stand for her to ride. One of the staff members, Charlene, lent us two fabulous rocking chairs and a nice dining table with two chairs.

In a separate, adjacent building, there is a rather new building where the Memory Care facility is located. We were offered a two-bedroom apartment there, but after visiting several before, I knew I did not need to see theirs to know that it was not for us. When I contacted Brookdale Corporate offices, they told me that even though they do allow couples to stay together there, it was discouraged.

I did have to agree to a concession for us to stay at Brookdale. That being for us to eat all of our meals in our room. It seems some here are not comfortable watching me feed Cat. It is not that she can no longer feed herself, but she did lose weight since she would get frustrated and would simply stop eating the meal provided. She was able to put back on the lost weight, and since we had been eating in our hotel rooms due to Covid over the last two years, it was not a big deal. I guess some people are more comfortable with physical disabilities versus mental disabilities.

It ended up being a plus since I order and pick up our meals and can use the leftovers for lunch the next day and wait and enjoy our desserts later that evening. Let alone we can watch TV or listen to our favorite tunes while enjoying the outstanding meals. I must say the food here is exceptional. This is from a guy who has eaten out all over the world for the last 8 years and did not ever actually cook myself.

The people here are very nice. However, many do not even come out of their apartments regularly. Brookdale offers meal delivery for an extra fee. For those that do, I try my best to remember them by name and have been keeping a list in the note section of my phone so I can greet them by name in the hallways.

All of the staff members are extremely nice and very helpful. They are all well-trained and properly staffed. They even have their in-house caregiving team called Brookdale at home. So far, I have used them several times; however, they are somewhat reluctant to care for someone like Cat. I think they would rather have an assignment to watch someone watch TV versus having to keep up with Cat as she gets in her multiple miles an hour. As a welcome gift, I get 10 hours free.

Even though I am in pretty good shape, I did have to take into consideration what if something were to happen to me. A while back, I signed up with Life Alert; we have all heard the commercials, "I have fallen, and I can't get up." It was more for Cat than me. Her entire health history is included in my profile, so if alerted, they know to send someone to also attend to Cat's needs. At Brookdale, not only do they have emergency pull cords in the bathroom, but they also issue pendants to alert staff members 24/7. Because of the mobile alert unit I have with Life Alert, they are not needed by us. Lastly, they have a call sheet they go through every day to check in on everyone. To alleviate the call to us we stop by the front desk every morning on our way to pick up our breakfast items.

For the monthly lease payment, you get two meals a day. That includes breakfast and either lunch or dinner. Weekly apartment cleaning, which includes washing your towels and sheets, and they will even change your bed. Each corridor has free washers and dryers, plus in the same area, there are garbage shoots and recycling bins. There are plenty of various types of activities, transportation, an exercise area, and in-house physical therapy. There are weekly outings, last week to a nearby orchard, and we never miss the singers they bring in for weekly entertainment. In the area, there are plenty of grocery stores and a multitude of great restaurants.

This decision was harder than us becoming nomads in the first place. I believe that is because the plan was not for us to be nomads this long. We were supposed to just find someplace else to live. I guess it just took us 8 years. I have always joked that we were like Goldilocks looking for that perfect porridge. While trying to decide where would be best for us now, I realized that nothing in life is perfect. For now, Brookdale Chambrel, Roswell is where I plan for us to "age in place." That is a new term I learned through this process.

The folks here are very nice, especially to Cat. I have given our book to some who befriended us when we first arrived. Cat is a rock star here since she is the main character in the book. They have been passing the book around to their friends here, and most greet Cat with a warm smile and a motherly-like hug from time to time.

We are once again very unique here for several reasons, including being the youngest here and also being one of the 10 percent of couples here. I had one gentleman tell me that I was a very interesting experience. I did chuckle, but I will always take that as a compliment.

As we bring 8 years and 750 stops as Nomads running all over the world to a close. The picture on the previous page is our King-size quilt on our bed at "The Brook." It is made of the 50 states plus DC, T-Shirts Cat got for doing a marathon in each of them. The one on above is another king-size quilt for our couch of the 30 out of the 35 countries T-shirts we have run at least a half marathon out of the 82 countries we have visited.

Nomads

Why nomads, you might ask?
It is impossible to make it last.
She has Alzheimer's, so let her be
She needs routine, can't you see
I like to explore, manage, and travel, so what about me?
Nomad is a noun with no fixed residence
Whereas I am somewhat hesitant.
I like Peregrinate, which is a verb since we did most by foot
Over the last 8 years, it took all of our loot
If you were to ask me, I don't give a hoot.
Marathons were mostly our fair
But none were ever done on a dare.
It was ours to spend as we saw fit
I would do it again, since some were spent on beautiful Islands,
such as St. Kitts.
Alzheimer's really does not care
It is not something you would want to share.
Everyone's experience is somewhat different
But I can now assure you, that the damage is permanent.
I once thought I was going to find the allusive cure
Many companies use that hope as their lure.
As the disease progresses, we will have to settle down
But not until sundown.
We used to run when the sun would rise
Now, it is slow walks, hand in hand, to no one's surprise.
We saw and did so many things she will not always remember
I would not trade away those memories since they now define
her.
Her beautiful smile and baby blue eyes sparkle remain
We all now know it will never be the same.
They say Alzheimer's cruel joke is called the long goodbye

However, my "Cat" will always know that I will never leave her side.

CHAPTER 30

How can you live well after being diagnosed with dementia?

♦ ♦ ♦

The Alzheimer's Association in California estimates that 690,000 people aged 65 and older are living with Alzheimer's, and almost 12 percent of those aged 45 and over report worsening confusion or memory loss, known as "subjective cognitive decline."

By TANYA WARD GOODMAN | Orange County Register

Bonnie Erickson is an avid hiker who enjoys camping with her extended family. She hunts for petrified wood and Montana Agate along the Yellowstone River near her home in Billings, Mont., often incorporating her found specimens into handcrafted jewelry. These relaxing activities supply a counterpoint to a schedule of speaking and advocacy that defines her role as founder and board president of the National Council of Dementia Minds. It's been five years since she was diagnosed with vascular dementia.

"Once I came out of the darkness," Erickson says, she had one question: "Do I embrace this and live well with it, or do I let it consume me and drag me down?" And every day, more people find themselves at a similar crossroads.

According to 2020 statistics used by the Alzheimer's Association, in California, 690,000 people aged 65 and older are living with Alzheimer's, and 11.7 percent of those aged 45 and over report worsening confusion or memory loss, known as "subjective cognitive decline." More than half of these individuals have not voiced their concerns to a doctor. In Orange County alone, Alzheimer's disease is the third cause of death, with nearly 12 percent of older adults aged 65 and older reporting a diagnosis of Alzheimer's disease or dementia.

While it may be difficult to move forward, it can be helpful to know that many of those living with and around the disease are working hard to light the way.

"When you hear the word dementia," says Brenda Roberts, co-founder and executive director of The National Council of Dementia Minds, "you go into end-stage thinking right away." After her husband, Mark was diagnosed with early-onset vascular dementia, Roberts turned to social media for support. "There were all these people talking about how horrible their person was, and I thought, 'Wow, is nobody living well with dementia? Is nobody happy?'"

More than 40 years of experience in the human service field working with older adults with disabilities and a position as director of Quality assurance and education for Michigan Assisted Living Association had not prepared Roberts for encountering her own husband's diagnosis. Undaunted, she enrolled in caregiving training seminars and certificate programs.

"I still wasn't getting what I wanted," she says. "So I started talking to people with dementia, and then I got it." Inspired by these conversations, she created a conference for healthcare providers featuring a panel of those living with progressive neurocognitive disorders. "It's too easy for professionals and caregivers to take over," she said.

In 2019, she recruited a group of eight volunteers, including Bonnie Erickson, to create the first of what would become an ongoing series of educational panels. By 2021, this group, known as "The Originals," had presented to over 3,000 people in four countries and formed a nonprofit organization. Currently, members from 18 states, ranging in age from 45 to 85, participate in a growing number of support groups. Together, they've produced video presentations on a variety of topics, including diet and exercise, how to talk with your doctor, and living well.

"A diagnosis doesn't signal the end of life, but signals a change of life," Steven Barbieri says. "You need to find new normals." Barbieri, board treasurer and founding member of Dementia Minds has been living with chronic traumatic encephalopathy (CTE) for over 10 years. He explained that when dressed for work as a Wells Fargo district manager, injuries sustained during a lifelong martial arts practice were invisible to physicians. It took what he calls "a life conversation" with an attentive doctor before he was seen as more than a suit.

Like Erikson, he's found meaning and purpose in education and advocacy for person-centered dementia services. "Nothing about me, without me," he says.

Alzheimer's Orange County attempts to take this philosophy into account in all aspects of programming. As the independent nonprofit celebrates its 40th anniversary, it continually works to connect with individuals and their loved ones on a dynamic and personal level.

"We want to keep celebrating people for all of their lifetime achievements and not focus on the losses of the disease," says Kim Bailey, programs and education specialist. Support groups, educational opportunities, and social activities, such as outings at Bolsa Chica Wetlands or the Memories in the Making art series, serve people with dementia and their care partners.

"I love having meetings with other people in the same situation," says Kathy S., who has a diagnosis of Lewy body dementia. Kathy, who prefers to remain anonymous, describes Alzheimer's Orange County support groups as a place to "cry together and laugh together" but also a space to explore life in the present. For Kathy, this means connecting more deeply with family. When an Ancestry.com profile turned up previously unknown relations, she traveled to meet them. She found more in common than expected.

"My uncle's wife has dementia," she says. "I saw her in the kitchen going around in circles, not being able to function, so I went and said, OK, you do this, I'm going to do that. We helped each other, and it was great."

Kathy's visual-spatial issues have increased her anxiety and often make it difficult for her to use escalators and moving sidewalks. Her husband, Sam, takes advantage of elevators and makes a point of arranging to preboard, helping to limit overwhelming sensory input. Both he and Kathy have found the world to be a welcoming one.

"You hear all the bad things in the news," Kathy says, "But I'm not afraid to go places because I know if I say I need help, someone will come and help me whether they know me or not."

Anthony Copeland-Parker, author of "Running All Over the World: Our Race Against Early-Onset Alzheimer's" (Morgan James Publishing, 2023), finds that travel not only cultivates optimism about his fellow humans but is also a daily practice in socialization and problem-solving.

When his partner, Catherine, was diagnosed with younger-onset Alzheimer's disease, they decided together to focus on a mutual passion for long-distance running. Taking an early retirement, they sold their house and set out. Over the last eight years, the two have traveled to 82 countries on all seven continents and participated in at least one half-marathon in thirty-five countries.

"They talk about the importance of routine," Copeland-Parker says. "Well, our routine is travel." His book began as a blog he used to update family and friends. "'She's OK,'" he says, "is not a good enough answer."

Later, this narrative became an external memory for Catherine. "Now," he explains, "we listen to the audiobook, and she gets a smile on her face because it's a familiar experience. You might forget a dinner, but you're less likely to forget dinner at the Eiffel Tower."

Picking up and moving every four or five days takes planning and organization, Copeland-Parker admits. "I'm a pilot," he says, "trained to expect the unexpected and figure things out on the fly." This means relying on Uber or Lyft and finding local help to give him a little break. He's become adept at "MacGyvering" hotel rooms to keep Catherine safe and comfortable and has purchased an adult stroller they've dubbed "The Cat Mobile." She might walk a bit and rest a bit. "We like to cross the finish line hand in hand," Copeland-Parker says. "Cat started out being a lot faster than me, but she always waited, and now, I wait for her."

Flexibility and unwavering curiosity nudged Gus Rogerson to move virtually beyond the walls of his home when he opened a Facebook account. In his first post, the poet and former artistic director of The 52nd Street Project, a New York nonprofit, quoted a line from E.M. Forster's "Howards End." "Only connect," he wrote, wishing that "all of my family and friends understand what is happening to me with kindness and witness."

Since his diagnosis with younger-onset Logopenic variant Alzheimer's and aphasia, Rogerson has been collaborating with filmmaker Michelle Memran, whose 2018 documentary, "The Rest I Make Up," chronicled her friendship with playwright Maria Irene Fornes. The two meet and write together over Zoom. In prose and poetry, Rogerson has described the feeling of being on stage, the birth of his daughter, things he has lost, and things he has found. Memran provides prompts that often arise organically from her own questions, their previous conversations, and shared situations. Rogerson's succinct reasoning for wearing bright clothing has sparked an ongoing dialogue. "Diagnosis dark," he said. "So color."

The only constant is change, but for those living with dementia, this process occurs more rapidly. Understanding limitations and developing "workarounds" become part of living well.

Steven Barbieri wears sunglasses to disguise the fact that he often closes his eyes to limit distractions and make it easier to find words. He's helped his wife to understand that, in a restaurant, sitting with his back to the wall improves his concentration. When Kathy S. gets discouraged, she finds comfort in coloring or pulling weeds in the backyard. "Don't waste your time," she says. Bonnie Erikson has dropped the phrase "I forget," preferring instead "a glitch in the Matrix." Choosing her own definition allows her to move on.

"I just make light of it and start over," she says. "I'm not one to give up."

For information about online support groups or to schedule a presentation, contact National Council of Dementia at dementiaminds.org

There are many different types of dementia, including Alzheimer's, Vascular dementia, and Lewy Body dementia. An accurate diagnosis can help those living with dementia and their care partners come up with personalized strategies and accommodations.

Tanya Ward Goodman is the author of the award-winning memoir "Leaving Tinkertown," which chronicles her father's struggle with early-onset Alzheimers'. She lives in Los Angeles with her husband, a daughter and a son.

CHAPTER 31
Why Do a 5K Race When Catherine Does Not Run Anymore?

♦　♦　♦

"Forever is composed of nows." ~Emily Dickinson

Now that we have settled down somewhat, it would make much more sense not to incur additional expenses of race registration, hotel, rental car, airfare, and meals when we pay for room and board at Brookdale Senior Living Solutions. My plan all along was to still travel once or twice a month for 2-4 days, so if we can fit in a race along the way, why not? Catherine and I very much enjoy doing things together, so for us to bundle up and walk along the Chattahoochee River in Columbus, Georgia, sounded like a solid plan.

We were going to see Cat's folks for Thanksgiving a few days later, so off to Columbus we went. The Marriott hotel was the race, Hero's of America Marathon, Half Marathon, and 5K designated hotel, so the rate fitted right into my new and revised budget. Also, the packet pickup was right in the hotel, and the start/finish was right out the front door.

With hundreds of races under our feet, I am pretty good at picking the right clothes for the current weather conditions. I always figure you can always take off clothes if you get too hot but can't put on clothes you left behind if you get cold. So layers and plenty of them was the plan for the day. The feels like temperature was 32 degrees, and with light winds, we were both not too cold or hot. It was funny lining up for the start as others were clearly dressed to run, whereas we were more suited for a stroll in the park, and that is pretty much what we did.

It has been over 6 months since Cat has run, and unfortunately, that ability has been taken away from her as the disease has progressed. I must admit that that fact is rather sad since, in actuality, running is what brought us together in the first place. My goal for us was to keep a steady pace and enjoy the scenery and our company for the entire 3.1 miles. Of course, as we always do, cross the finish hand in hand. I can proudly say we did achieve all of those goals.

Back in the heyday of our running and racing exploits, we were doing about 16-20 races a year. This being the last one planned, we will clock in right at 10, with me pushing Cat in the CatMobile during a few of them. We have on the schedule to do the Key West Half Marathon in the middle of January 2023. I will be, once again, pushing Cat most of the way in the CatMobile, however, I am unsure if we will be able to pull that off. I have done a few Half Marathons already with Cat, usually walking alongside for 3 or so miles.

That is the only race I have planned right now, but I have decided to complete the 7 half marathons needed to complete one in all 50 states plus DC next year. Maybe I will also pick off one or two marathons out of the 8 needed to get them all done in that category. That is going to take a bit more training than I have done recently to get myself in shape enough to push Cat that far. Only time will tell.

As always, I figure if anyone else can do it and I want to do it myself, then it is in the realm of possibility. I will just need to find races that have a very lenient time policy, like Mainly Marathons. Another problem is that Cat is not going to want to sit for 6 plus hours, and I don't blame her, so I will have to schedule walk breaks for her.

From Columbus, we were off to visit Catherine's family for the Thanksgiving holiday and back to " The Brook," which I am affectionately calling it now. Much better than the Old Folks Home. It is always interesting to observe folks react and interact with Cat when they have not seen her for a while. The last time she was with her family was back in August. I try my best to make the pilgrimage every 3 months.

Unfortunately, she now has Aphasia, which is an inability to comprehend or formulate language because of damage to specific brain regions. She still has rather good comprehension, but she often speaks in the form of word salad, commonly referred to as gibberish. I try to find a word or phrase that she might be repeating and engage her in a short conversation. For example, if she repeats the word "Mom", I might remind her when we will see her next, and she might say something like, "That would be nice."

It reminds me of when we were touring Egypt in 2019, and Cat suggested we use our own language consisting of gibberish to get the constant street sale folks to leave us alone. While at "The Brook", we were sitting next to a lady, and Cat chimed in during our conversation with some of her own word salad. I mentioned to the lady that sometimes Catherine only knows what she is truly saying, and the lady grabbed Cat's hand and said, "I hear her in my heart." I could not have said it better myself.

I cherish those brief times when, out of the blue, she will tell me she loves me, thank me, or simply show her appreciation with an unprovoked hug. Occasionally we can participate in a normal conversation for a brief period. It is still unclear why however they call that paradoxical lucidity, which refers to an episode of unexpected, spontaneous, meaningful, and relevant communication or connectedness in a person who is assumed to have permanently lost the capacity for coherent verbal or behavioral interaction due to a progressive and pathophysiologic dementing process.

Returning to my original question in the title, I am reminded of the following quote found at, ThePurpleSherpa.Org. Caring for someone who's living with dementia is like running a marathon across the shifting sands of a desert. It's hard; it can be lonely, and it requires you to develop skills you never imagined. And, if you keep your eyes open, you'll find a certain beauty in the experiences you share.

It reminded me of the Australian Outback Marathon and Half Marathon we did back in 2015. Cat had broken her ankle 6 weeks prior but was not to be outdone. So with a boot and a cane, she walked the half marathon in the desert sand. I did the full where we could both see the famous Uluru (Ayers Rock) and Kata Tjuta (the Olgas) and even though we did it separately, we both came away with the same impression, which was that it was a very spiritual experience.

As time goes on with this disease, my goal now is to keep her brain talking to her body as long as possible. The amount of determination it took for her to complete the race in the shifting sand tells me that if we need to make side trips to a race as motivation for her to walk 3.1 miles, so be it. We do walk 6-8 miles throughout the day. "The Brook" has a half-mile path around its wonderfully wooded and landscaped facility, with another 2 miles of carpeted corridors indoors. Maybe I will chart out an indoor 5K one day.

No one will win this race we call life, but Catherine and I will continue to compete one footstep at a time as long as possible. Right now, we are concentrating on quality versus quantity. At "The Brook", there are many here in their 80's and 90s with the same philosophy, and it is very enlightening and inspirational to experience.

Columbus, Georgia
November 21, 2022

CHAPTER 32

New Year's Resolution

♦ ♦ ♦

"You Go One Day at a Time" ~Maureen McGovern

A friend of mine stated that they always took one day at a time. I was working on my New Year's resolution for the coming year, 2023, so I gave, take one day at a time, some thought. I ran across this article and started giving taking one day at a time a more serious consideration.

Singer Maureen McGovern says her mantra is "don't give up"

Celebrated singer Maureen McGovern has spread a message of hope amid darkness for almost 50 years with her signature song, "The Morning After." But now the anthem also tells McGovern's story—an expression of her own sense of hope as she learns to live with Alzheimer's disease.

Though the progressive and incurable disease has begun to rob the 73-year-old artist of her everyday vocabulary, she still effortlessly recites the lyrics to the 1973 chart-topper: "It's not too late, we should be giving / Only with love can we climb / It's not too late, not while we're living / Let's put our hands out in time." "It's not too late," McGovern tells PEOPLE, emphasizing the line.

"There's hope. Don't give up. That's my mantra. Don't give up."

McGovern shared her diagnosis and announced her retirement from the stage this past August with a poignant website post and Facebook video, admitting she at first "struggled with the inevitable shock with fear and, frankly, hopelessness."

But today, she keeps those fears at bay with an active life and an intense sense of purpose. An Ohio native, she resides in a Columbus retirement community that offers her both independence and security, and she has surrounded herself with a tight-knit circle of family and devoted friends. "I truly, truly do believe I've been blessed with so many things," she says.

Her younger sister, Patt Sweeney, lives nearby, making sure the details of her life are in order. And she's relying on longtime associates, including arranger and accompanist Michael Shirtz, to lay the groundwork for a recording project of children's songs, among her many musical passions. Sweeney and Shirtz both offer assurance that McGovern's famously nicknamed "Stradivarius voice" remains clear and vibrant, and she keeps it that way with regular warmups in the shower.

Shirtz recalls that, when McGovern came to him with news of her diagnosis, "there was never an 'oh woe is me,' or 'how sad is this.'" He says she also didn't linger on the doors that were closing: "There was a conversation and an excitement about, 'OK, so we can't do this, but here's what we're going to do, and let's figure it out.' That just comes from her spirit."

Maureen McGovern Reveals Symptoms of Alzheimer's Disease: 'My Inner Life Has Not Changed'

It's the same spirit that has sustained a rich five-decade career. McGovern was an unknown folk singer, just 23 when her demo caught the attention of a record exec looking for someone to sing "The Morning After" for the credits of The Poseidon Adventure, a 1972 blockbuster disaster film. After the song won an Oscar, McGovern's version was released as a single. After it took off, she soon made a splash with more movie and TV theme songs, as well as a tour de force spoof as a singing nun in the hit film comedies Airplane! and Airplane II: the Sequel.

In the 1980s, McGovern reinvented herself, going on to star in such Broadway shows as Pirates of Penzance, Nine, and Little Women, as well as establishing herself as an in-demand touring artist. She became renowned not only for her voice but also for her wide-ranging repertoire, holding hundreds of complicated songs in her memory.

But about five years ago, Shirtz recalls, McGovern began struggling with familiar lyrics. She compensated with more rehearsal and using a notebook onstage while she pursued medical opinions. Batteries of tests finally offered a conclusive diagnosis in 2021, about a year after she'd performed her last concert right before the COVID-19 lockdown.

Alzheimer's Patients and Their Caregivers Find Solace and Socialization in 'Memory Cafes'

Today, music still remains at the center of her life. At home, she listens to a constant rotation from her vast collection of recorded music. "Sometimes classical, sometimes jazz, sometimes I'll pull out the old records and sing with myself," she says with a chuckle.

Though her days of public concerts are over, McGovern has still been entertaining her fellow retirement community residents, joining one who is a jazz pianist in occasional recitals. "You just go one day at a time," she says. "Every day is a day to make it better."

Her joy, she says, also comes from her family—she's close to her sister's three children and seven grandchildren—and a large circle of friends who have rallied to her side. And there's joy, she says, "that I'm still here, frankly."

That sentiment, of course, echoes in her signature song: Wherever there is life—and love—there is hope. "I don't fear dying, particularly," McGovern says. "I just want to make sure I get all of what I can out of living. Whatever's out there, we don't know. So you just have to start singing."

What it means to me.

I am a planner at heart, setting short and long-term goals, so this is a new way to approach tackling this goal. Most times, they were exercise-related, like the time I exercised 30 minutes every day for the entire year. I have also done the traditional vision boards, which are more suited for long-term goals.

Consciously invest a small amount of time into what you love every day, one day at a time, and the cumulative effect of those days will naturally lead you where you want to be. Here's how you do it: Choose one area of your life you want to excel in.

"Every day is a day to make it better," as McGovern said. I believe in the additive model; what more can we do? What has yet to be done and try our best to do each. That way, we don't dwell on what Cat can no longer do.

As a care partner for Cat, my goal is for her to have the absolute best quality of life for as long as possible. So I will be focusing each day on what I can do that day to achieve that goal. On the exercise front. I am planning on getting in as many Half and Full marathons done, this coming year. My goal over the next two years is to get one done in each category in all 50. I have 8 marathons and 6 half marathons left.

This means each day; I need to focus on what I need to do to prepare my body to accomplish them. I will also need to incorporate the CatMobile, an adult-size stroller, so Cat can join me. I am sure she will want to also walk a portion of each race.

CHAPTER 33

Seizures and Proper Hydration

♦ ♦ ♦

I should've known better, "Better late than never"—Idiom. It is better for someone to arrive or do something late than not to arrive or do it at all.

As an endurance athlete for nearly 25 years, you would think I would know the importance of proper hydration, but what I have learned is that it is even more critical when it comes to folks with Alzheimer's. It never occurred to me since Cat has not been running since April of 2022. However, she is still very active and walks 6-8 miles a day.

Cat started having seizures over a year ago this past October. First time at this, we ended up calling 911 and spent several hours in the hospital while they ran a battery of tests.

Over the next 16 months, she has had a total of 13 seizures. Most of them happen first thing in the morning, with a few occurring later the same day. Most seizures last anywhere from 30 seconds to two minutes. A seizure lasting longer than five minutes is referred to as status epilepticus and is considered a medical emergency. Her's lasted about 1 minute, so there was no need to go back to the hospital, so I thought at the time.

While we were in California, visiting my son, Aaron, it was the first time that she had two in one day, so off to the hospital we went. That time she spent 2 nights. She had not been out of bed anytime during those two days, and she was now having serious problems eating.

A percentage of folks with Early Onset Alzheimer's (EOA) get seizures, but in some cases, they only have one in a lifetime. People with Alzheimer's disease are estimated to have anywhere from a two to six-fold increase in the risk of seizures compared to the general population. Over the course of the disease, anywhere from 10 percent to 26 percent will experience some form of seizure, both apparent and non-apparent, according to research from the Baylor College School of Medicine. While it is still unclear which mechanisms trigger seizures, there are certain characteristics that can place an individual at higher risk.

She was having what is known as awakening tonic-clonic seizures: A seizure that occurs upon waking from sleep and causes uncontrolled jerking, all-body convulsions, and stiffness of the arms, legs, or body. They are often accompanied by the abrupt loss of consciousness and/or bladder control.

A seizure is a sudden, uncontrolled electrical disturbance in the brain. While we tend to associate them with convulsions, seizures can sometimes manifest with subtle symptoms, such as changes in behavior, movement, feelings, or levels of consciousness. Another type of seizure is a partial complex seizure, in which you become unaware of your surroundings and engage in unconscious actions such as fumbling, lip-smacking, wandering, or picking at clothes. Another type, an absence seizure, is sometimes misdiagnosed as early-stage Alzheimer's. An absence seizure is one in which an individual will suddenly "blank out" and wander aimlessly, a behavior referred to as amnestic wandering.

While it may seem reasonable to assume that the degeneration of the brain triggers seizures, evidence strongly suggests that it is related more to beta-amyloid itself. Beta-amyloid is actually a fragment of a larger compound known as an amyloid precursor protein (APP). As APP is broken down, certain byproducts are released into the brain, which can overexcite—and effectively overload—nerve pathways.

As the disease progresses, the accumulation of these byproducts can cause nerve cells to fire abnormally, triggering seizures. Individuals like Cat who have been diagnosed with Early-onset Alzheimer's are associated with an increased likelihood of seizures, although the seizures themselves tend to develop in later stages of the disease progression.

It was decided that she be put on anti-seizure medication, Levetiracetam better known as Keppra. They started with 1000mg twice a day. There is even some evidence that the anticonvulsant Keppra is approved for the treatment of epilepsy and can help reverse some of the memory loss in people with Alzheimer's disease. So, at this point, we were very hopeful, but that was short-lived.

The Common side effects of Keppra include drowsiness, nervousness, abnormal behavior, aggressive behavior, agitation, anxiety, fatigue, hyperkinetic muscle activity, irritability, and mood changes.

Other side effects include change in personality, combativeness, difficult urination, quick to react or overreact emotionally, rapidly changing moods, restlessness, sleepiness or unusual drowsiness, unusual tiredness or weakness, itching feeling, clumsiness or unsteadiness, increase in body movements, loss of bladder control, mood or mental changes, outburst of anger, shakiness and unsteady walk, or other problems with muscle control or coordination.

Incidence not known: constipation, difficulty with moving, general feeling of tiredness or weakness, increased thirst, large, hive-like swelling on the face, pains in the stomach, side, or abdomen, possibly radiating to the back, pinpoint red spots on the skin, skin rash, encrusted, scaly, and oozing, twitching, twisting, or uncontrolled repetitive movements or jerking of the arms, loss of strength or energy.

That was the partial list, but all the ones Cat experienced while on Keppra. We tried lesser dosages, but either she would have a seizure or the side effects were intolerable. Listening to a podcast by the renowned Teepa Snow on the topic of medications for seizures within the Alzheimer's community, she said, "Darn if you do, Darn if you don't."

After 6 months, we took her off of Keppra, and like clockwork, the seizures returned within 5 days. I looked into other medications, but they all had far worse side effects, including possible Kidney damage.

The diagnosis of Alzheimer's-related seizures is often an inexact science and one that may require input from a specialist known as an epileptologist. While an imaging study known as an electroencephalogram (EEG) can be used to confirm seizure activity, it has its limitations. An EEG measures electrical activity in the brain and, as such, can only definitively diagnose seizures if abnormalities occur during the test. As a result, only between 3 percent and 10 percent of Alzheimer's-related seizures are diagnosed with EEG alone.

With that being said, an EEG can sometimes detect abnormal electrical activity, known as epileptiform discharges, 24 to 48 hours after a seizure. While neuroimaging studies, such as computed tomography (CT) and magnetic resonance imaging (MRI), can detect changes in the brain consistent with Alzheimer's, they cannot tell us whether those changes are consistent with seizures. The same applies to genetic blood tests, which are more useful in supporting a diagnosis rather than making one.

We thought about going to a seizure clinic, but we had an EEG done while in San Diego, and they needed her to be sleep-deprived to ensure an accurate result. The one done in San Diego did not show any brain bleeds or evidence of a stroke, so I decided not to put Cat through that again.

After Keppra, I did some research and thought that CBD might help prevent them or at least lessen their frequency of them. CBD is short for cannabidiol, which is a chemical found in marijuana. It is not the same as tetrahydrocannabinol (THC), the chemical in cannabis that is responsible for the "high" feeling people get from marijuana. The Endocannabinoid system, ECS, regulates the sleep/wake cycle. "Cannabinoid" comes from "cannabis," and "endo" is short for "endogenous," which means that it is produced naturally inside of your body. So, Endocannabinoid simply means cannabis-like substances that naturally occur inside us.
Because cannabis products can stimulate the activity of the ECS, they're obvious targets for potential treatments, and a ton of research is going on around the world. Cannabinoids are being researched as potential treatments for all kinds of conditions, not just those involving endocannabinoid deficiency.

Some of the illnesses they're being researched for include:
- Alzheimer's disease
- Cardiovascular disease
- Neurological, neurodegenerative, neurodevelopmental, and psychiatric illnesses
- Acute and chronic kidney disease
- Autoimmune diseases
- Chronic inflammatory diseases
- Chronic pain conditions

With all this research in hand, I thought I had found a possible answer. Unfortunately, Cat only went a month without a seizure, and the downside was it did make her a bit more agitated.

With that rabbit hole dug up and found to be empty, the research continued. This time, in the direction of starting a Keto diet. Research has shown to decrease the frequency of epilepsy, but if not done correctly, it could cause more complications and possible Kidney damage. I did run across a statement about how a Keto diet can cause dehydration. Following the rabbit, this time about dehydration, I ran across this article.

Can dehydration impair cognitive function? January 10, 2020, Betsy Mills, PhD

We often hear the adage about the importance of drinking eight glasses of water a day to keep our bodies healthy, but how about our brains? The adult human body contains around 60% water. All the cells in the body, including our brain cells, depend on this water to carry out essential functions. Therefore, if water levels are too low, our brain cells cannot function properly, leading to cognitive problems.

The brains of dehydrated adults show signs of increased neuronal activation when performing cognitively engaging tasks, indicating that their brains are working harder than normal to complete the task. In healthy young adults, this additional effort typically manifests as fatigue and changes in mood, but in populations with less cognitive reserve, such as the elderly, this can lead to a decline in cognitive performance. Performance on complex cognitive tasks that require high levels of brain power is most likely to decline due to the strain of dehydration. A meta-analysis of 33 studies, including a total of 413 participants, found that dehydration corresponding to more than a 2% reduction in body mass (e.g.

3 lbs. of fluid loss in a 150 lb. person) was associated with significant impairments in attention, executive function, and motor coordination.

Women of all ages are more sensitive to the effects of dehydration, but elderly women are especially vulnerable. A study examining the hydration status of 2,506 adults over age 60 found that women with inadequate levels of hydration showed worse performance on cognitive tasks related to attention and processing speed. The performance of dehydrated men also declined but to a lesser degree.

In young women, cognitive deficits can be readily reversed by replenishing fluids, while in the elderly, the prolonged cellular stress of dehydration may promote brain pathology and continued cognitive decline. A study assessing the cognitive function and hydration status of 1,091 people over age 65 found that dehydrated individuals were at higher risk for dementia, while individuals with dementia were at higher risk for dehydration. Additional studies indicate that dehydration can accelerate cognitive decline in people with dementia.

Decreased water levels in cells can cause proteins to misfold and prevent the clearance of these toxic proteins, causing them to build up in the brain. While it is clear that dehydrated cells are associated with brain dysfunction, it is not yet known whether dehydration is a cause or an effect of dementia.

In addition to being most vulnerable to dehydration-related cognitive decline, the elderly are also at higher risk for dehydration. The levels of water stored in the body decline with age due to changes in body composition, namely the loss of muscle and gain of fat. Muscle tissue provides a large reservoir of water since it is made up of nearly 80% water, while fat tissue has a much lower water content of around 10%. The lower percentage of muscle mass in women may contribute to their increased sensitivity to dehydration.

The elderly are also less likely to notice they are dehydrated. The brain becomes less sensitive to the thirst sensor with age, so thirst is a less reliable indicator of hydration status in this population. Due to changes in kidney function with age, the elderly are less able to concentrate urine to conserve water and regulate sodium levels, putting them at higher risk for complications related to dehydration or overhydration. Furthermore, it is more difficult to accurately diagnose dehydration in older adults. Traditional physical signs of dehydration, saliva tests, and urine tests are often inaccurate or misleading due to the presence of other chronic conditions. Blood tests are the only reliable indicators of dehydration in the elderly.

There is also a higher risk for urinary tract infections (UTIs). UTIs are more common in people with Alzheimer's disease. Dehydration makes them even more likely to occur. UTIs are caused by bacteria entering the urinary tract. It is a common condition, but it requires treatment. Staying well hydrated is crucial in preventing these infections. A person with Alzheimer's disease may not know they have a UTI, or they may not be able to communicate their symptoms with you. A common first sign of a UTI in someone with Alzheimer's disease is a sudden change in mental state – confusion, agitation, or disorientation. Dehydration can result in headaches, constipation, and other health problems. It can also lead to more serious complications, such as kidney issues and low blood pressure, which are especially concerning for older people.

To keep your brain adequately hydrated, it is recommended that women consume 2 to 2.7 liters (8 to 11 cups) and men consume 2.5 to 3.7 liters (10 to 15 cups) of fluids per day, though individual needs may vary depending on activity level and medication use. It can help to develop a schedule to keep track of daily fluid intake. It is important to keep in mind that cognitive function can also be impaired by over-hydration. Overhydration can lead to a drop in sodium levels that can induce delirium and other neurological complications, so fluid consumption should not vastly exceed medically recommended guidelines.

Diet and exercise are also important components to remaining hydrated. The hydration guidelines refer to the consumption of all fluids, not simply how many glasses of plain water we drink per day. However, it is counterproductive to start drinking more beverages laden with sugar or artificial sweeteners since they have their own health risks. Our bodies obtain water from multiple nutritional sources, including many healthy, mineral-rich foods, so it is possible to get adequate levels of hydration by incorporating more water-rich foods into your diet. Some nutritious water-rich foods include melon, oranges, berries, lettuce, cucumbers, and tomatoes. You can also preserve your body's stored water content through strength conditioning exercises, which build muscle.

Being dehydrated is one possible cause of electrolyte imbalances. This refers to changes in the balance of minerals known as "electrolytes" in your body. Electrolytes have many important roles and contribute to nutrition, waste management, and organ function. Due to this, electrolyte imbalances can significantly impact health, including the function of the brain. As a result, sometimes severe dehydration leading to electrolyte imbalances may cause a provoked seizure as a symptom.

With all this information in hand, I went to dig up yet another rabbit hole. But first, I had to put a detailed plan together. That is the pilot mentality shining through. The easy part was during the day, but since her seizures were when she first woke up, what to do overnight and first thing in the morning?

During our marathon days, we were mostly Gatorade-type folks with the occasional off-brand that was being handed out at the marathon expos. Just like anything else, I had to do my research on what drink mix would work best. It had to be something Cat would not hesitate to drink.

I found a product called Liquid IV. It turns out my daughter, Mariah, used it when she was pregnant to keep hydrated. It touts that it has twice the hydration power of water alone. It also has several electrolytes crucial to keep seizures at bay.

On the electrolyte front, I also found a product in gummy form, Olly, Post-Game Recover, that I could get her to chew as soon as she woke up to immediately boost the electrolytes. Of course, I had to go buy a humidifier since it was winter here in Atlanta, and with the heat running overnight, it would add to keeping us both hydrated.

Early on, I could get Cat to drink during the day with no problem, but first thing in the morning was becoming an issue. More research showed the benefits of Green tea, so decaffeinated Green tea and Chamomile tea were added about 50/50 with some honey. I then had no problem getting her to stay hydrated all during the day and night. Between this and a fruit smoothie poured over her granola and drinking the rest with her breakfast, she is getting about 1.5-2 liters of liquids a day.

I don't use just any water. However, we have been using Fiji water since it contains Silica, which also promotes brain health. It also has a PH of 7.7, which aids in water absorption to all your cells. As they say, so far so good. It has been over three months since her last seizure, but I do realize there are two possible flaws in my plan of action.

The first one is that I have to be awake before she wakes up so I can start having her drink before the tremors, which turn into a seizure, take hold. Secondly, not every morning, Cat is in the mood to drink as much as she should. So far, I have been able to stay ahead of the curve, but I resolved myself to the fact that it is not if she will have another seizure, but when.

I am okay with that eventuality as long as I can push each of them off as long as possible. They kick us both in the gut. As I mentioned previously Cat disease progression is like a sine wave. Some days are much better than others, but for several weeks after a seizure, we have to climb back out of the deep hold it puts us in.

I realize this chapter was a bit lengthy, but I wanted to give each of you as much background and context as possible. I am sure that this will not work for everyone facing seizures in general or those with Alzheimer's in particular. I must say, aside from the possible anti-seizure benefits, keeping Cat hydrated has shown some improvements in her overall cognition. Just the other day, she walked up to me, and in a voice as clear as a bell, she said, "you are really pretty." Those are the moments I live for.

CHAPTER 34
Run At Least One Mile a Day

♦ ♦ ♦

Find the thing you do well and do it again and again for the rest of your life. ~Jóhann Jóhannsson

It all started on a nice, warm, late winter day, the 5th of March 2023, at Willis Park in Roswell, Georgia. It is the home to the renowned equestrian complex. I am not sure exactly why, but after that unimpressive 2-mile run, I decided to run at least 1 mile a day. I am undecided as to how long I will keep this going or if I will try more mileage a day. I know there are plenty of people out there who have run a lot more miles a day for a much longer stretch, but you have to start somewhere. Looking back at my stats over the last 12 months I have walked or run over 6 miles a day.

Over 20 years ago, for no particular reason, I then decided to exercise at least 30 minutes a day for the entire year. Back then, I was only a few years into running marathons, so I figured the cross-training would be good for my body. Little did I know how hard it would be to carve out 30 minutes every single day. Back then all three of my highly competitive kids were deep into all sorts of sports. I was right alongside them, either helping out with the coaching or managing their teams. I remember one occasion where

I started my exercise routine at 11:30 pm one night and finished at 12:30 am the next morning to get both days accomplished.

Back in 2014, I participated in a 100-day challenge to either walk or run 3 miles a day. That led right up to my open heart surgery that June. I follow a lot of weekend warriors on social media, and I think reading about all their race accomplishments is part of my motivation. Unfortunately, Catherine lost her ability to run about a year ago, so now we do a lot of walking. She walks 6-8 miles a day. Now, not always together since I have found two fantastic ladies that come for 3-4 hours, mostly in the morning, 3-4 days a week. Finding them was not an easy task since I needed someone to walk around 2 miles an hour the entire time they would be with her. Most folks wanted to sit and watch whomever, watch TV, do a puzzle or card game. The other rub is that most wanted 30-40 hours a week, which I did not need. Also, the biggest thing was I needed someone Cat felt comfortable being with.

In retrospect, I think the desire to do any running every single day was taking me back to my after-heart surgery days. Back then, walking was all I could do for six weeks while my body healed, and in my mind, I could not wait to be completely airborne again, even for a fraction of a second. Secondarily, maybe it went back to my 37 years of gently pulling back on the yoke of an airplane and the rush I felt every time the main gear struts decompressed as we went airborne and hearing the words "positive rate" from the pilot not flying and my response, "gear up."

Who knows, but the 12-13 minutes are both like heaven and hell. The hell being the fact that I no longer run with Cat by my side. Yes, that is the slow pace I now run, one mile a day. They are usually done on days when no one is scheduled to be with Cat. Sometimes, they are done 1/2 mile at a time when I take the long way around the building to pick up breakfast for the next day or dinner. When it is too cold or rainy, I do it on the treadmill at the gym.

Other times, when someone is with Cat, the pace is even slower when I can do more miles at various locations near and around "The Brook," as I affectionately call where we have lighted since September. I say lighted since we still go on short trips about every two weeks. I still can't bring myself to stay put for very long. My running pace is never slower than 15 minutes per mile since I can race walk faster than that. It might be in the 15-minute range when I am running/walking while pushing Cat in the CatMobile. I will be getting some of those daily miles done while pushing her. In those cases, since I use a 30-second run and 30-second walk regime, I will have to do two miles or a combination to make it count towards my goal.

In a way, I think having a sense of control in my life has something to do with it. We can't control how much sleep we are going to get each night or the quality of sleep, for example. This is one thing I can accomplish every day, no matter the external influences. I get to decide when and how it will be checked off my list each day. Some days will be much easier than others, but at the end of the day, I know it will be done.

It is much like those who pray or meditate each day. It is something just for them, and at the same time, they are the only one who knows that it was done. This is especially true while caring for someone with Early Onset Alzheimer's, where I often have so little control over how each day will go.

I often listen to a meditation during a portion of my daily runs on gratitude. This one can be done anywhere and anytime and have you look at 5 different aspects of your daily life you are grateful for. They are something about your day that you are grateful for. A person, a place, and what about yourself you are grateful for. The hard one is to be grateful for something that did not go right either today or yesterday, and what did you learn from it, and what did it keep you from doing that would have been even worse. The last one is to be grateful for something you are looking forward to in the future.

Turns out, I connected with a lady who pushes her adult son during half marathons. She did a race with Mainly Marathons a day before we met up with the group last year. She told me about the group, AINSLEY'S ANGELS OF AMERICA, Which provides support to folks in similar situations as us. Their mission is, Together, We Shall educate, advocate, and celebrate inclusive communities while connecting everyone through empowerment and belonging.

I had my first support team effort by "The Angels" on Saturday with a 5K in Suwanee Town Center. I was a bit apprehensive about having someone help me during a race, but it turned out very well. Three, "Guardian Angels," as they call themselves, showed up to help me, especially with the uphill portion back to the finish line. Cat got out near the finish, and we once again crossed the finish line hand in hand. I am looking forward to working with the folks here in the Northern Georgia chapter of the Angels and also nationwide as I attempt to get my last half and full marathon states done while pushing Cat and the Cat mobile. This was only our 2nd race this year, both being of the 5K variety. Last year, we did 4 races, 3 half marathons, and 1 10k. However, 2021 was one of our best years with 25 total races, 18 half marathons, 6 10k's, and 1 8K.

For May 2023, I entered an Alzheimer's challenge of 60 miles your way, so I set out to run at least 2 miles a day. I was able to run 85 miles that month and walked or ran a total of 226 miles. I also was able to raise $3500 and came in as one of their top 5 in terms of donations. I think I will drop back down to at least a mile or two a day and see how long that lasts.

At some point, Cat will inevitably lose her ability to walk. I have decided that when that dreadful day comes, I will pick up my quest to run my last 8 states to get a marathon done in all 50 states plus DC while pushing Cat. She accomplished that back in 2020. For me to pull that off I will have to be in much better shape than I am in now and will need a chair more suitable for going the distance.

I guess that might be another reason for a mile a day. I don't think much about how much longer I can keep her brain talking to her legs, but I know for sure that won't stop any time soon. With all of that in mind, there is no time like the present to prepare myself for the over 209 miles necessary to complete 8 marathons one completely airborne, footstep at a time.

CHAPTER 35

If I Get Dementia

◆ ◆ ◆

"Every minute with your loved one is precious because every minute keeps getting smaller" ~Ashley Campbell

Recently, I have seen something posted on social media called If I Get Dementia. It was over 10 years ago that I first noticed something was just not right with Cat, and because of our due diligence, it was only a year later that Cat was diagnosed with Early Onset Alzheimer's, EOA.

They also added the caveat of, or like, condition. The reason is that it actually can not be confirmed until after the autopsy when the person's brain can be observed. Cat has asked that her brain and all other body parts be donated to science. There are several different terms used for EOA. Them being Younger Onset Alzheimer's/Dementia or Early Onset Alzheimer's/Dementia.

Here is the list of different types of Dementia. Dementia is a general term for loss of memory and other mental abilities severe enough to interfere with daily life. Physical changes in the brain cause it. Alzheimer's is the most common type of dementia.

Alzheimer's disease, Vascular dementia, Lewy Body disease, Frontotemporal dementia, Alcohol-related dementia, Down syndrome, Alzheimer's disease, HIV-associated dementia, Chronic Traumatic Encephalopathy (CTE) dementia, and Childhood dementia.

The typical life span after diagnosis for Early Onset Alzheimer's is 2-20 years, with the average being 8 years. Everyone's journey varies for many factors. I look at it as a life lesson, not a death sentence. Here are the stages of Alzheimer's using the 7-stage scale I use. There is also a 4 stage scale.

Stage 1: Before memory loss

Alzheimer's disease begins in the brain before a person starts showing symptoms. This is called pre-clinical Alzheimer's disease. Stage 1 can start 10 to 15 years before any symptoms appear. There is no treatment for pre-clinical Alzheimer's disease right now, but doctors hope that in the future, there will be drugs to stop the progress of the disease at stage 1. The risk of Alzheimer's disease increases with age. Be sure to visit your primary care doctor regularly as you age so they can screen you for Alzheimer's.

Stage 2: Forgetfulness

Everyone can forget things from time to time. And forgetting things can happen more often as people get older. People in the earliest stages of Alzheimer's might forget things like people's names or where they left their keys. The person with stage 2 Alzheimer's can still do things like drive and work. But memory problems will happen more often. You might notice these problems before your loved one does. If you do, you can suggest they get treatment sooner to slow the progression of Alzheimer's. This stage is also commonly referred to as Mild Cognitive Impairment, MCI.

Stage 3: Noticeable memory problems

This stage can bring changes that are noticeable to many people. Diagnosis is common at stage 3 because the person's daily routine becomes disrupted. In this stage, people commonly have problems with forgetting names and misplaced objects.

Symptoms might include:

- Forgetting recently read material, like news articles or books
- Problems finding and speaking common words
- Forgetting plans
- Difficulty staying organized in daily tasks
- Social or work problems

This may be a difficult time for your loved one. They may deny that anything is wrong. That is normal. But talk to your loved one's doctor early, before symptoms get worse. Your loved one's doctor can help guide treatment options, including medicine and care planning.

Stage 4: Major memory loss

In this stage, damage to the brain often affects things other than memory. Language, organization, and calculation skills may all be impacted. Because of this, completing everyday tasks can be difficult. Stage 4 can last many years. Major memory problems occur in this stage. People usually remember important details from their life better than everyday details. For example, they might be able to recall the state where they live or their spouses's names. But their memory of the distant past will usually be worse than their memory of things from today.

Other challenges in stage 4 include:

- Being confused about where they are or what day it is
- Getting lost or wandering off
- Sleep problems, like sleeping more during the day and trouble sleeping at night
- Problems choosing the right clothing for the weather
- Your loved one might have a tough time with situations that require a lot of thinking. Social gatherings might be especially frustrating. Those in this stage might be:
- Moody
- Withdrawn
- On edge

Stage 5: Decreased independence

Until this stage, your loved one may have been able to live on their own with no regular help. Checking in on them might have been enough. But by stage 5, your loved one might not remember the people who used to be most important to them. Learning new things is now hard or impossible. Also, basic tasks like grooming and getting dressed may be too hard.

Common symptoms in this stage include:

- Paranoia – Feeling like others are out to get them
- Hallucinations – Seeing, hearing, touching, tasting, or smelling things that are not there
- Delusions – Believing in something that is not true, for example, that an imposter has replaced a family member

Stage 6: Severe symptoms

In stage 6, people with Alzheimer's will have symptoms that will impact their ability to manage their care. They will be more dependent on others for help. It can be difficult to communicate with your loved one at this stage. They may still use words and phrases, but it can be hard for them to express specific thoughts. For example, they may be unable to tell you where exactly they are feeling pain. Your loved one's personality may significantly change in stage 6.

They might have more:

- Anxiety
- Hallucinations or delusions
- Paranoia
- Frustration with you or those around them

Not everyone with Alzheimer's disease will have severe behavioral changes. But if your loved one is experiencing such changes, try not to take it personally. Their frustrations are part of the disease's progress and not a reflection on you.

Stage 7: Decreased or inability to control bodily functions

As Alzheimer's progresses, it destroys brain cells. This can lead to severe mental and physical impairment. Your loved one may start to have problems with their body shutting down. This happens when their mind can no longer process, communicate, or delegate tasks effectively.

Your loved one's needs will increase a lot now. They will need help walking, sitting, and even swallowing. Because they are not as mobile, they can get infections more easily. At this point, your loved one will need full-time care.

Cat has settled in with Stage 6, and this stage can last several years. I have found that this stage has subtle differences that can last a few days to weeks so I must draw upon patience and understanding daily. Luckily, her kind and loving personality, which was dominant throughout her life, still shines through.

My additional comments are annotated by a *. First and foremost, please have a lengthy discussion with your loved one about how they would like this uncharted journey to end. This would include a last will and testament, living will, health care directive, and establishment of who will be the power of attorney. The most difficult discussion revolves around Do Not Resuscitate, DNR, and Do Not Incubate, DNI, which would include the use of feeding tubes.

If I get dementia, I want my friends and family to embrace my reality. If I think my spouse is still alive, or if I think we're visiting my parents for dinner, let me believe those things. I'll be much happier for it.

*Please try your best to have me visit with them as often as possible. Also encourage them to come visit me when it becomes difficult for me to travel. Try your best to explain to the children in my life the changes I am going through. If you find that difficult, there are plenty of books that can be read to them.

If I get dementia, don't argue with me about what is true for me versus what is true for you.

* You might have to demand certain things of me to keep me safe but don't sweat the small stuff.

If I get dementia, and I am not sure who you are, do not take it personally. My timeline is confusing to me.

* Please keep telling me and showing me how much you love me.

If I get dementia and can no longer use utensils, do not start feeding me. Instead, switch me to a finger-food diet and see if I can still feed myself.

* However, if I start to lose weight or struggle to eat, it is okay to feed me. No feeding tubes for me, and if I refuse to eat, please understand that is my way of letting you know I am ready to go.

If I get dementia, and I am sad or anxious, hold my hand and listen. Do not tell me that my feelings are unfounded.

* There are supplements that can help with that, and in gummy form, they taste really good. However, understand that prescribed medications might accelerate the progression of the disease.

If I get dementia, I don't want to be treated like a child. Talk to me like the adult that I am.

* However, that might only work for a while since as the disease progresses, my level of understanding will decrease, and you might have to repeat yourself several times. Please do so only with a loving tone of voice.

If I get dementia, I still want to enjoy the things that I've always enjoyed. Help me find a way to exercise, read, and visit with friends.

* Draw on activities I did most of my life, which include those you enjoy doing with me. If at first you don't succeed, please keep trying and understand that what might worked today might not work tomorrow. Take me to parks and botanical gardens so I can have meaningful walks instead of simply pacing in our home or apartment.

If I get dementia, ask me to tell you a story from my past.

* As my communication skills dwindle, you will have to take up the slack by telling me stories and showing me pictures of our past.

If I get dementia and become agitated, take the time to figure out what is bothering me.

* Pay particular attention to if I might be dehydrated. Make sure there is always something to drink readily available. Especially when I first wake up, and as time goes on, you might have to remind me yourself.

If I get dementia, treat me the way that you would want to be treated.

* That is the golden rule. However, our discussions when I was first diagnosed might need you to modify this rule to honor my wishes.

If I get dementia, make sure that there are plenty of snacks for me in the house. Even now, if I don't eat, I get angry, and if I have dementia, I may have trouble explaining what I need.

* Please make sure they are of a healthy variety. Apple slices with peanut butter are my favorite.

If I get dementia, don't talk about me as if I'm not in the room.

* I might try to join in with my form of gibberish, which is okay. Find a word or phrase that can be drawn upon to include me.

If I get dementia, don't feel guilty if you cannot care for me 24 hours a day, 7 days a week. It's not your fault, and you've done your best. Find someone who can help you, or choose a great new place for me to live.

* Cat witnessed the deterioration of her dad from Vascular Dementia. First at the VA hospital and then where he passed away at a nursing home. This was devastating to her, so I promised her after she was diagnosed that I would not put her away. I understand the need, in her father's case, since he was aggressive and difficult for her mom to handle. The majority of the time, we have been tied to each other's hip 24/7. It was decided that we would

handle this as a team effort. I have realized that I also need to take care of myself. We are still able to live together in a senior living facility. I do now have someone come help me a few days a week. I know a gentleman in his mid-seventies doing the same, and he said that his dad took care of his mom until she passed when his dad was 89 years old. I figure if someone else can do it, and I am relatively young and in good shape, I should be able to do it myself. As for me, I have a plan of action if I can no longer take care of myself.

If I get dementia and I live in a dementia care community, please visit me often.

* I hope this not to be necessary since I plan to stop eating or taking a one-way trip to Switzerland, this time not for a race when I can no longer take care of myself.

If I get dementia, don't act frustrated if I mix up names, events, or places. Take a deep breath. It's not my fault.

* Cherish those moments since, as time goes on, I will tell you the same story over and over and talk constantly. At some point, I might not be able to talk at all.

If I get dementia, make sure I always have my favorite music playing within earshot.

* Tunes that I grew up on are the best. You will be amazed to find all sorts of soothing tunes on YouTube.

If I get dementia, and I like to pick up items and carry them around, help me return those items to their original place.

* Leave out items that you don't mind me moving around, and please remove any items you are afraid I might break or hide.

If I get dementia, don't exclude me from parties and family gatherings.

* I realize that some folks will withdraw due to lack of understanding, but don't give up trying to include me. Sundowning is a real condition, so I might not be able to be out past sundown or

with large crowds since the noise of multiple conversations might agitate me. I also might not want to be among others for long periods of time.

If I get dementia, know that I still like receiving hugs or handshakes.

* My disease is not contagious.

If I get dementia, remember that I am still the person you know and love.

* I am still here and will always love hearing the words, I love you, often.

CHAPTER 36

Birthday Road Trip

♦ ♦ ♦

Things have a marvelous way of working out. Trust that.
~Adel Ahmed

It has been quite a while since Cat and I went on a 10-day 7-leg road trip, and it felt great to get back out there. We have been doing mostly local 5 and 10K's with the occasional overnight. It was my birthday on July 6th, 2023, so what better way than to spend it with my son, Shawn, and his family? I turned 68 and feel better than I did in my 50's. About the same physically but much better mentally. It might have to do with the fact that back then, I was still working.

Since I don't drive more than about 4 hours a day, we stopped outside Knoxville, Tennessee, for the night on our way to Cincinnati, Ohio, where they now live. My mother started a tradition of having Lobster for dinner when I was a kid, so my son had to scramble to make that possible. The two Grands were happy to see us, but unfortunately, Cat had her 18th seizure in that many months a few days before us starting the trip. It was over 2 months since her last one and she seemed to be bouncing back quicker than usual, which was a good thing. Unfortunately, she could not interact with them as she had previously. The seizures took a lot out of her, and I did consider canceling the trip. She had a really good month of June, so since we were doing this trip by car, I decided to give it a go and thought I could always change our plans if necessary.

There was another reason for this trip, and that was for us to continue checking half-marathon states off our list. We only need 6 to get one done in all 50 states. Cat accomplished getting all the marathons done back in 2020. Even though the seizures have taken away her ability to run over a year ago, I came up with a workaround. She still walks 6-8 miles a day, so I figured she could walk a 5K interspersed with me pushing her in the CatMobile.

What better way to get two states done than with Mainly Marathons during the first two days of the Heartland Series? These states were Ohio and Michigan, but the only trick was that they had to be done back to back. Unlike the Mainly Loonies, who will do Marathons each day during this 7-day series, it has been many years, 12 to be exact, since I had done that. A few times, I have done 2 races in three days, so we shall see how this works out. Lucky for me, back in March, I started running at least a mile every day, so after 4 months of that, I feel pretty confident I can pull it off. The month of May I did an Alzheimer's challenge where I raised $3,500 and ran 85 miles.

Turns out Henry, who is in his 70's, will accomplish his 1900th Marathon during this series. We met up with him back in Guymon, Oklahoma, 2 years ago. Back then, he got his 1600th marathon. You do the math. Needless to say, these people are serious about staying in shape. Some walk the entire race, but most do a variation of run/walk, and a few run the entire time, no matter the distance, for a 5K up to a 50K each day.

Our first day was in Hicksville, Ohio, at the Defiance County Fairgrounds. The park lives up to the name of the city, and the nearest hotel was 30 minutes away in Fort Wayne, Indiana. At first glance, I was glad it was going to mostly be in the 70's, but the rain gods had other plans. That was rain and wind most of the 4 hours we were there. I had Cat wait in the car for about 30 minutes during the heaviest portion of rain while I continued running. She got her 5K at .75 of a mile at a time, so she was in and out of the CatMobile multiple times.

To add a wrinkle to my master plan, she decided that she only needed 6 hours of sleep instead of the 9 hours planned for her. So, I did not get much sleep either. We got it done, so back to the hotel, lunch, shower, and off we were for the 2-hour drive to the next race in Niles, Michigan. There, I did laundry and dried out the CatMobile. We had dinner and went to bed, with the hopes she would need only 9 hours of sleep instead of the 10 hours she sometimes requires after a short night of sleep the night before.

Like clockwork, she woke up right on time for us to make it to the start line at Riverfront Park with a few minutes to spare. This time, Cat got her 5K done .60 of a mile at a time with us crossing the finish once again, upright, hand in hand, with our dignity intact, as always. This time it was a beautiful sunny day, and we got it done before it got in the 80's, even though there were portions that were shaded.

I have concluded that one of the things I like about our travels is all the logistics required to get us from place to place on time. What is the best location for the hotel, where to eat, and what supplies will I need along the way? It reminds me of my flying days, with my desire for on-time departures and as early as possible to arrive safely and on time.

Both days, it was great to see all the smiling faces encouraging us. Some that I knew or had met before, but there were a few I had never seen before but would smile and wave every time we passed each other. There were a lot of opportunities during both races since the courses with Mainly are set up with multiple outs and backs. It is amazing how much that kept me going. Especially during the periods when I thought that maybe I had bit off more than I could chew.

I ran for 1 tenth of a mile and walked for a tenth the entire time I pushed Cat in the CatMobile, and that gave me a very respectable overall time each day. My time was only 6 minutes slower on the second day, which I attribute to running some of the first race by myself.

After another night here outside of Niles in Mishawaka, Indiana, then we have a 4-hour drive back to Cincinnati for two more days with the Grands. Hopefully, Cat will be able to enjoy their laughter and shenanigans when we get back to see them. Shawn and Cassie both have new jobs with this relocation from Harrisonburg, Virginia, so hopefully, I will be able to check out their new digs.

My plan now is to get three more states done in October and November, with the last one being in Wisconsin around this time next year, all with Mainly Marathons. The Heartland series goes there later this week, but I just could not figure out a way to make it happen this time around.

We had an uneventful drive back to Cincinnati, with only one stop to get Cat, her favorite Pumpkin Loaf, from Starbucks. Thinking back over the last two days with the Mainly Family, I hope to one day do an entire series. That is now being added to my Life List, as I call it.

The Grands did not disappoint on our stop back in Cincinnati. Hide and seek plus hallway races were all the rage. They even made me a birthday day poster, glitter and all. Once again, we stopped north of Knoxville on our final leg back to Roswell, Georgia. Traffic has been manageable, probably because we have been driving between the hours of 10 am and 2 pm. There were numerous construction sites along the way, but nothing major.

We listened to some of our favorite tunes of Hotel California, Free Bird, and Jimi Hendrix. We also listened to our book, Running All Over the World, Our Race Against Early Onset Alzheimer's, on Audible. Cat still responds with smiles when hearing about shenanigans of our own. We also listened to 80's music on XM radio. and some of this book, which was in the works, that I can listen to on a Speechify application that I use often.

We have another trip scheduled at the end of August to visit Cat's family in Indiana, but I am undecided if we will drive or fly as we usually do. Cars darting in and out from lane to lane at top speed is in no way my cup of tea. If we drive, it will again add 2 days to that trip since we will once again have to stop somewhere overnight to and from Indiana.

The half marathons in October and November are in Montana, Nevada, and Utah, which are way too far for me to drive, so I will have to plan since I will have to negotiate the CatMobile and Cat at the same time. I have done it before, but I must admit Cat's abilities are on a continual slide with each seizure. That, in turn, requires extra effort on my part.

Well, as the quote suggests, I did trust that, and in fact, it did once again work out.

Niles, Michigan, July 2023

CHAPTER 37

It's About Time

♦ ♦ ♦

Idiom: It is past time when something should have happened.
~Cambridge Dictionary

This chapter will talk about when it is time for family members to look at alternative living situations for someone with dementia. Cat and I found our home at Brookdale Chambrel, Roswell Senior Living Solutions in Roswell, Georgia. The time was right for us, but many wait too long to start thinking about where their loved one's needs would be best served. This is not my first experience with a facility like where we are currently living. More about that later.

First, I would like to take the time to talk about the different living facilities available for someone like us. There are 5 types of living facilities that I will reference here. The first is the typical retirement community. Most folks are familiar with these types of communities, and they are dotted all over the US. Most are stand-alone condos, and they have many activities for active seniors. Some have a pool, golf course, tennis courts, and main activity building for card games and the like. The condo is self-contained, and you do your own laundry and cooking. The benefit is that you have activities with people your own age.

Next, I will talk about what is known as Independent Living Facilities. They can be small and self-contained like most, 20 to 30 apartments under one roof with some of the activities mentioned above but with the added amenity of having a place you can go to for your meals. Usually 2 meals are provided and in most facilities you get to pick which two you would like each day. They also clean your apartment and do some laundry, like towels and bed sheets, once a week. There are extras you can pay for on top of your monthly rent which would include help with medications, help dressing and bathing including toileting. These services are provided by in house caregivers. Or you can hire from an outside agency or privately yourself.

I found a place like that for my mom. At the time she had just turned 80 and had gone from a world traveler to a home body and the decline was becoming very evident. I had her come visit me in Louisville, Kentucky and after a few tries I was able to find the perfect place for her, near my home. I had her furniture moved into her new apartment so she then had all the comforts of home. She was surrounded by like minded individuals that made her feel welcomed.

It did not take long for her to fit right in, and she even became an Ambassador for the facility. In other words any one interested in living there would come by to ask her questions about her experience with the facility. She wore that like a badge of honor and took great pride in that role. If she was not in her apartment all I had to do was look at the activity board to figure out where to find her. Needless to say, she loved the place. I used an agency call, A Place for Mom. It is a free service and I am sure most of you have seen their commercials on TV.

It is important that you take the time to figure out which child is best suited for this responsibility. It has to be someone they not only get a long with, since they love all their offsprings, but also someone they can depend on when the eventual decline starts. For my family I took it upon myself to be that person. Through her life all three of us took our turns, when it was appropriate and for the last 9 years of her life it was my turn.

Cat and I are in the independent section of the facility here at Brookdale since I can provide all the assistance she now needs. I will talk later about, what if she did not have someone like me by her side and where most folks like Cat usually go. While we have been here for nearly 1 year, I have asked many here why they chose this facility. Most start out with the fact that they are near one of their children. Many had lost their spouse and the family did not feel it was appropriate for them to continue to live alone. Most couples also added that one was starting to have either physical or mental difficulties and they needed more support than they were getting living on their own.

The next level is what is known as an, Assisted Living Facility. There are many other names used from company to company. That environment is much more structured. We did spend a week in a facility like that, but the level of care was more than we needed, and of course, the cost was much higher. They have staff on site, 24/7, monitoring everyone and no one is allowed to leave without an escort. That being a family member or another staff member for an organized outing, which includes trips to the store or doctor appointments.

These facilities are usually very small, 20 apartments or so, and everything is very structured behind the locked doors of the facility. The part I did not like was the constant checking in on us in our apartment at all hours of the day and night.

There, too, you pay for the extras needed, and some state laws require them to charge you for all of them whether you need them or not. Some larger companies like Brookdale will have both types of facilities under one roof. The activities and meals are more structured and there you are provided 3 meals a day.

I am sure all have heard of the dreaded term, Memory Care. These type facilities are no joke and for obvious reasons are very regimented. Once again, you can only leave if signed out and back in by a loved one or staff member. Many times they have doctors and nurses that visit the facility and everything is controlled by the staff members to how many times a day a person is taken to the bathroom.

I have had two occasions to visit inside these types of facilities and it quickly took a toll on me, emotionally. Some living there are either chemically or physically restrained so not to do harm to themselves or others. When we first looked into Brookdale it was suggested that Cat reside in Memory Care, since they do have all three type of facilities on property, with me living in the Independent building.

Here Memory care is in a separate building and as an alternative they were willing to provide a two bedroom in Memory Care since I insisted that I was going to always be by Cat's side. I knew that I was not going to be able to handle, emotionally, living with her there. I, instead was able to convince management to allow us to stay together in the independent section of Brookdale.

I do know of a few folks who are living with us independently and visit their loved ones regularly as they reside in the Memory Care building. In discussions with some women here they tried their best to take care of their loved one with dementia, as I am with Cat, but as time went on they were just unable. I am still young by comparison so I truly understand also as the disease progresses some become uncooperative or downright abusive. So far, for me, sometimes Cat needs some coaxing but is usually very cooperative and pleasant to be around.

The last one I would like to discuss is Nursing Homes. I only have limited exposure to them. My mom was able to live independently until her diagnosis of Pancreatic Cancer, where she went from the hospital to a nursing home, for the last 2 weeks of her life. She then had standing orders for no operations, feeding tubes, resuscitation, or incubation. We moved some items from where she had been staying to the nursing home and I gave the rest away to a church agency.

I felt it was a quick, peaceful, and pain-free transition, but I could not imagine staying there more than we had to. All the care there is done by nurses or nurse aids with the rounds by the doctor to update the time horizon to expect. Visiting her there was very depressing but it was what was needed at the time. Since then, I have learned there was another alternative, and that was Hospice care. That could have been done either where she was living or at my home or at the Nursing Home. Payment for that level of care comes out of the persons, Medicare Hospital, Part A, since it is agreed upon that they will no longer be going to the hospital.

In April 2023 I enrolled Cat in hospice care. The requirements are that you first have to have a life-threatening diagnosis, which she does, and a time horizon of 6 months or less. Medicare agreed that her seizures fit her into that category. My research showed that folks live a longer, much better life when this level of care is added. It also does wonders for the folks taking care of her since I will have them by my side to help me navigate the final stage of this disease.

It has been over a year since she was enrolled and I can not say enough great things about this level of care. I have a nurse come out once a week to check her vitals and bring needed supplies. Also, a great lady that comes and sings to us while playing the guitar every other week for what is called Music Therapy. I also have at my disposal a Chaplin, a social worker, and if needed someone to come out once a week to help me with basic needs. I can also reach out to them by phone as the need arises 24/7.

Since our campus has over 300 folks under the roof in all three facilities, people do come and go from time to time. For some, it just did not work out for various reasons. Others moved to other facilities here at Brookdale as their needs changed, and for some, their time had come to leave their earthly body.

When I would sometimes visit my mom, she would greet me with as an example, "Martha passed away the other day." I would, in turn, joke that she would have someone else to make friends within a few days. I must admit for those who left us for the last reason, it is still taking me a while to get used to.

Most facilities have a table near reception where they put up pictures of those who had passed with a lovely arrangement of flowers. Some I did not recognize, possibly because they seldom came out of their apartments or a few I saw every single day as they walked the corridors, like us.

Cat and I are the youngsters here at 62 and 68, respectively; however, our neighbor is 103, dresses like she is going to the ballet, and her mind is sharp as a tack. It is always sad to see them go for whatever reason, but as I told my mom. Someone new to make friends with will be moving in the next few days. Everyone has been so gracious to Cat and me, and I am sure the same will be true for you when the time is right.

I believe it is important that each family try to stay ahead of the decision of where to go next for their loved one with dementia. Like me, the one best suited for that task needs to take action sooner rather than later. Your loved one is not going to like the change. Some have lived in the same house for 50 years or more. Some have been together for 60 years or more, and the thought of being separated would be devastating. I know of a few here who cherish their visits with their loved ones in the Memory Care facility. Bringing them flowers and singing old songs with them.

If you can find a facility that has Independent, Assisted, and Memory Care like Brookdale on the same campus, there are definite advantages. That being if, as a couple, you can both live Independently and one has a slip and fall. Then, after the hospital and rehabilitation, you could go to the Assisted living facility until you are once again able to live independently. The same is true as dementia progresses; that individual can move into the Memory Care Facility, which would facilitate regular visits from the other partner who is still able to live independently.

It is going to be a difficult discussion to have with your family members, but I hope that they understand that you have their best interest in mind. Some might outright say no, but with this information at hand, you can circle back at a later time when the situations have changed, and you can approach it once again. It is not only a benefit to them but stress upon them that it is also a benefit to you as well when it comes to peace of mind, knowing that you don't have to worry about them daily from afar.

I would caution everyone thinking about moving into a facility like ours to be sure they do their due diligence. Since they are all run by major corporations, there will be a few issues you might have to contend with. They all have an average of 20% profit margins, and quite a bit comes from add-ons. The list is too numerous to include here. Since I do the bulk of care for Cat and hire outside the facility for extra help, that has not been an issue.

Rent increases were a bit of a surprise to me. I am sure in previous years, COVID-19 demanded a higher-than-expected increase, but I was shocked by the increase proposed for 2024. I say proposed because it turns out the actual increase can be and was, by me, negotiated to a much lower increase. It concerns me that those who did not have the where with all to even try to negotiate get stuck with helping these facilities achieve those 20% profit margins they tout. These types of facilities do cater to the middle and upper class, so I expect it is not an issue for most. They also charge a nonrefundable Residence Fee to lock you in and or to cover the cost of new paint, etc, when you move out.

I hope this gets the wheels turning in the right direction, whichever direction that might be. I wish you much success and hope that this has given you options that are germane to your particular circumstance.

CHAPTER 38

Forty Nine States Down, One to Go

♦   ♦   ♦

"Ain't nothing to it but to do it." Statement of the raw simplicity of a task, implying that all it takes is hard, not necessarily intelligent, work, and effort. ~Ronnie Coleman

As you might know, I am very goal-oriented. I love setting goals for myself. It takes my mind off the daily tasks and keeps me focused on the future. I have completed many goals during my life, both career-wise and on the exercise front. Right now, my focus is to get a half marathon done in all 50 states. Cat got them done as marathons back in 2020, and I still have 8 left. More about that later.

The plan is to fly to Albuquerque, New Mexico, and drive two days to Bluff, Utah to complete state number 48. Then, drive two days to Laughlin, Nevada, for state number 49. During the half marathons, Cat walks a 5k, about 1 mile at a time, while I push her in an adult-size stroller, I call the CatMobile, the rest of the way.

During our last trip in October, which lasted 8 days, I was able to get a 10k done in North Dakota, state number 12 in that category, and a half marathon done in Montana. North Dakota was no joke with temperatures in the 30's with wind blowing 25 miles an hour off the beautiful nearby lake. Luckily, a friend lent Cat a heated jacket so she was toasty. Me, not so much since I elected to run while pushing her into the wind.

Once again, these and those races were with our Mainly Marathon family. Our plan now is to get our final state of Wisconsin done in Milwaukee in April of next year. That will be only fitting since Cat was diagnosed with Early Onset Alzheimer's in the same month, 10 years prior. For that race, Cat will only get to walk about a mile since they have a three-hour and 30-minute cutoff. She will accomplish that at 1/4 mile at a time. That will leave me only 3 hours to get the other 12 miles done. You know what Benjamin Franklin said about plans. "If you fail to plan you are planning to fail."

If all goes well my next goal will be to finish getting my 50 state marathons done starting in July of 24, shortly after I turn 69. No coincidence that will be my 69th marathon. Just think, I had planned on only doing one marathon 23 years ago. Cat and I did a 50 miler when I turned 50. We ran 27.5 miles to a hotel one day and then ran back to our Condo for a total of 55 miles when I turned 55. I accomplished 60 marathons by 60 and 65 by 65.

Well, Allie, which is what I call ALZ, decided Cat and I only needed five hours of sleep on departure day. We both got 8 hours of sleep the night before, so no big deal. On a positive note, at least I did not have to rush to catch our 8 am ride to the airport for our flight to Albuquerque. We will spend the night at a nearby Marriott then take two days to get to Bluff for the first half marathon. It is only a 5-hour drive nonstop, but for us, breaking it up with a stop in Gallop, New Mexico is more our speed. That, of course, is assuming that all goes well.

Transporting the CatMobile will be a bit tricky this time around. In Albuquerque, Hertz is located at the rental car center, and buses to them are notorious for being overcrowded with standing room only. It's not the best situation when trying to move a backpack, a suitcase, and a 50-pound stroller in a bag. That does not include the fact that I must be in constant contact with Cat these days. I am sure I will figure something out. That being going to the rental car center without the CatMobile and coming back around to pick it up before going to the hotel. What can possibly go wrong?

Well, the folks there did not want me to leave the car for even a minute to get the CatMobile from baggage claim. Our back and forth discussion, including a call to their operation center, took much longer than me going to get it. When the gentleman walked off to hassle someone else, I, of course, went in to get it. I had to laugh when loading it into the rental car since there were no other cars curbside.

The 3-plus hour flight once again went well. Cat was not fond of sitting still for that long but I have found that keeping food and drink headed her way helps a lot. This will be our last week long trip with the CatMobile for awhile. I am thinking that I might want to consider hiring a Travel Companion to help me with Cat. I actually posted a job on Craig's list to see the level of interest and I got about a dozen folks that were interested. I narrowed the list down to 3, and I will start interviewing when we get back from this trip. It would probably be more like 3 to 4-day trips once a month to start working on my 10k states list. Right now, I am keeping my options open.

Two of the folks who now help me with Cat are also interested in traveling with us. One of them, happens to also be a runner. Tammy has signed up to help me run the final half marathon in Milwaukee. She ran two half marathons several years ago, so the training will start in earnest in about a month. I am sure I can do it by myself, but I will take all the help I can get. I did my fastest 5k while pushing Cat, all by myself, last week in the little-known town of Flowery Branch, Georgia. That was a real morale booster. I ran across this quote the other day, which pretty much sums up my way of thinking. "Set a goal so big that you can't achieve it until you grow into the person that can." Dokeshi no Michi.

I try to have stretch goals but usually don't set a deadline for when they need to be accomplished. The first race went well, but once again, it was a bit chilly, and unfortunately, about half the course was on crushed gravel and somewhat hard-packed dirt. To keep it interesting, there was also a pretty steep hill I had to figure out how to tackle 8 times. Since Cat needed to get her walk on for a 5k, I had her walk that hill 3 times while I left the CatMobile at the bottom and picked it up on the way back to the start/finish. Two other times, I did that entire section by myself, pushing and grunting the entire way. I did have some help the other three times up the hill with Dave, who was doing the 50K, and Elizabeth, whom we had seen on various races with Mainly. The last time up, Clyde and Dave joined in and made the climb a piece of Cake.

Clyde is a legend amongst marathoners. At 76 years young, he has run over 600 marathons in all 50 states and all 7 continents and is one of only three who has also run a marathon on the North Pole. It was very inspiring to witness firsthand his dedication to the sport. The views of the rock formations were spectacular, which helped pass the time since it took me over four hours to get it done. They say all that does not kill you makes you stronger, but I had to repeatedly remind myself you could still kill yourself.

The next leg of this 7-day, 900-car mile trip was the worst. After all that huffing and puffing we had to drive about 4 hours to our next stop in Flagstaff, Arizona. The group was doing a race there, but since I already had the state, I did not see the need to stick a needle in my eye. We did come out to cheer them on, but only after the temperatures rose from the high 20s to a more respectable 50 degrees.

From there, we were off to Laughlin to meet up with my sister, Gwen, and sister-in-law, Joan. They have been on many a trip with us in the past, but now I think I have them hooked since they both wanted to check Nevada off their list of states they had done a 10k. I decided that on these trips where there are multiple time zone changes, it would be best for us to keep our body clocks on East Coast time. That way, I would not have to rush to get Cat to the start line for the 7 am and in Nevada, 6 am starts. It made for a lot of mental gymnastics to keep track of when to eat and to go to bed.

The race in Nevada had its own wrinkles I had to figure out on the fly. The little over 2 miles out and back had to be done 6 times, but the out part was downhill with a tailwind, and the back part, yep, you guessed it, was uphill in 20 MPH winds with gusts to 35. I had Cat walk her half a mile during the steepest part while I also navigated the CatMobile with one hand. So basically, I ran downhill and did my best to walk uphill without coming to a complete stop.

Well, with these two states behind us, there is nothing left to do but drive over the river to Arizona and find a park for Gwen and Joan to walk 6.2 miles so they could add another state to their 10K list. Cat rode some in the CatMobile, and we walked a bit with them. There was a Starbucks nearby, so I had to get Cat her beloved Pumpkin Loaf while they finished making the rounds in the park.

We then drove to Las Vegas for an overnight prior to our flight back to Atlanta. Overall I thought the trip went well, but you can be sure I had to do some MacGyvering to keep Cat safe as we stayed in a wide variety of hotels, with some having very limited amenities. With only one state left to check off our half marathon list, it is time for me to figure out what other goals to set for the future.

My plan now is to do one marathon a year so that I will have 70 done by the time I turn 70, 75 by 75, and all 50 states by the time I turn 76. All while getting as many 10k's done in as many states as possible. Even though Cat and I are both Million Milers with Delta, it does get harder and harder for her to make these multi-hour flights with us picking up and moving on to another hotel just about every day. Back in March, I set a goal for myself to run at least a mile every day. I have done so for over 8 months and now plan on doing so for the rest of my life.

I said harder but not impossible with another goal of mine for us to keep traveling as long as humanly possible, even if I have to hire someone to help me. I did some math the other day, and I figured I have been pretty much on the road for close to 46 years, which is 2/3rds of my life. I tried staying put when we first moved into our apartment at Brookdale Senior Living Solutions a year ago in September, but that only lasted about 3 months.

I keep asking myself why I do the things that I do. The road less traveled comes to mind. The Road Less Traveled suggests that we consider taking the alternative route – the metaphorical road that's filled with bumps, potholes, and possibilities for getting lost. By taking these roads instead of the easier ones, we'll become more spiritually enlightened and will grow in ways that we can't imagine. I can say that is very true for me. Caring for Cat has not been easy by any stretch of the imagination. There were much easier paths on this journey with her I could have taken.

I could have continued working until the usual retirement age of 65 for pilots, or as the disease progressed, I could have found a very nice memory care facility for her. Neither of those options seemed like viable options to me. I have always looked at Alzheimer's disease as one that requires a team effort since the outcomes can vary widely from patient to patient. For me, that meant that we both needed to have a fulfilling life for as long as possible.

If that means chasing our goals and dreams, so be it. As long as we do it together. With winter right around the corner, it is now time for me to look for warm destinations about once a month till spring race season is in full bloom.

Laughlin Nevada
November 9, 2023

CHAPTER 39

Good Grief

♦ ♦ ♦

"Good grief, Charlie Brown" ~Charles Shultz

The term good grief is often used when someone is surprised, stunned, amazed, annoyed, or perplexed by lots of situations. Grief itself isn't good or bad, or right or wrong. Grief just is. Grief is the array of emotions we feel in response to losing someone or something we love or value in our lives. The important part to focus on is how we handle grief. Many times I have been surprised, stunned, amazed, annoyed, and perplexed by lots of situations while caring for Cat. Grief involves painful emotions such as sadness, anger, and guilt. It can be tempting to avoid these feelings, burying them rather than facing them. However, working through grief means confronting, naming, and making sense of these emotions.

I would like to first talk about grief from my perspective. In two earlier chapters, I presented the stages of grief and some valuable information concerning grief. As opposed to other life-threatening illnesses where grief before death is usually short, with Alzheimer's in general, grief can start many years prior. Earlier I also talked about ambiguous loss. Here is a definition for reference.

Ambiguous loss is a loss that occurs without a significant likelihood of reaching emotional closure or a clear understanding. This kind of loss leaves a person searching for answers, and thus complicates and delays the process of grieving, and often results in unresolved grief. An example for our discussion a family member or partner being physically alive but in a state of cognitive decline due to Alzheimer's disease or dementia. An ambiguous loss can be categorized into two types of loss: physical or psychological. Physical loss and psychological loss differ in terms of what is being grieved for, the loss of the physical body, or the psychological mind. Experiencing an ambiguous loss can lead to personal questions, such as, "Am I still married to my missing spouse?," or "Am I still a child to a parent who no longer remembers me?" Since the grief process in an ambiguous loss is halted, it is harder to cope or move on to acceptance of the type of loss experienced. Various types of grief can occur due to the type of ambiguity experienced and corresponding therapy techniques to address certain types of grief. The overall goal of therapy to cope with ambiguous loss is to overcome the trauma associated with it and restore resilience.

Over the last ten years since Cat's diagnosis I have, lost parts of her over the years. Some are not that significant but others in retrospect were devastating. For example the last time she said, "I love you," or responded in any way shape, or form when I said the same to her. I have no way of knowing how this will influence my grieving process when she passes. I do know that I will continue to focus on what we can still do together and put the things she can no longer do in the rear view mirror. Later I will have Tammy, who helps me care for Cat give her perspective since she cared for her husband for many years before he passed from Frontotemporal dementia three years ago.

In one respect our journey has been much easier than most since we became nomads and traveled the world for 8 years. The sights sounds and numerous races in far-flung destinations were very healthy distractions from the continual loss we both experienced over the years. Not only our transition to our current living arrangements but also the outstanding help we have has kept us from having to make that tough decision to separate from each other by having her in a Memory Care Facility or Nursing Home. Even though early onset Alzheimer's might be a more aggressive form of Alzheimer's since the diagnosis was early on I am still fit enough along with excellent help to care for her as we continue to battle this disease as a team effort.

Here is Tammy's unique perspective on grief since she experienced it both before and after the passing of her husband.

My husband, Mat, was diagnosed with Frontotemporal dementia (FTD) at the age of 51. Our son was one, and our daughter was sixteen. In addition to my husband's illness, I belonged to what they refer to as the "sandwich generation," a rapidly growing group of middle-aged people who care for their aging parents, plus their children, at the same time. I was also caring for both of Mat's parents, who in addition to other ailments, had two other common forms of dementia, Alzheimer's and Vascular dementia. My husband was still working when his symptoms began. The problem showed up at work before us being aware of it at home. A year prior, he began having problems completing his work assignments on time. He was fired. Circumstances were such with taking on a new role and a new boss that we had no way of knowing it wasn't performance related. Mat was either in denial or, because of the nature of the disease, unable to comprehend what was happening.

I tell you this to help you understand the enormous amount of stress one can be under while managing grief. Perhaps my situation was extreme. Years have passed. My husband passed away over 3 years ago now. I have been working in the field of dementia care for over 12 years. I started my own non-profit and small business while he was ill and have seen scores of families navigate a dementia diagnosis. I have yet to see one that is easy.

I have been told by several people that they would rather have their loved one die of almost any other disease. They have shared their stories with me of losing one parent to cancer and another to dementia, and how much harder dementia is to handle. The care for your loved one will progress from intense, to almost impossible for one person to handle alone. They will eventually need 24x7 care as they develop cognitive and physical problems that make it difficult for you to easily help them. Maybe they can no longer sit down on command or become aggressive when you try to groom them. They are just two examples of a myriad of problems you will have to navigate daily. Frequently, additional medical issues arise, as they lose the ability to walk or swallow well. They are unable to communicate to you what is bothering them. Responding to physical and behavioral issues becomes a trial-and-error approach. Just as you resolve one issue, the next one rears its head. This is a progressive, degenerating disease so nothing is easy or static.

Grief while losing a loved one to dementia is intense. It follows no normal pattern. You struggle to go through the cycle of grief, which usually includes denial, bargaining, depression, anger, and acceptance. It's like you're stuck in the movie Groundhog Day living the same day over and over again. You grieve the ancillary losses. You feel like you are losing them in pieces. It is very common to lose friends in the process. You become isolated, as taking them out becomes more and more difficult and the people you once socialized with, and the things you routinely used to do are no longer available to you. If you're not careful you can become very angry and bitter at those that you feel have abandoned, you. This is all happening while trying to cherish the days and moments with your loved one because they have a terminal illness. This illness does not currently have a cure or any treatment options that slow the progression. There is no treatment to throw your energy into, hoping and praying for a good outcome. You are heavily anticipating the loss to come.

If I had to go back and describe a given day, it could vary greatly. My husband and I still traveled, had a supportive family, though they were not all local, and enjoyed many aspects of life, especially in the beginning and middle stages of the disease. However, I also remember crying almost every night, overwhelmed with feelings of grief. In one moment, I was grieving that he was going to be taken from me, angry at a group of friends for not visiting, intensely sad he could no longer enjoy the things that used to bring him joy, work, help with his children, and stressed because he could not drive and help with anything around the house. I was managing everything, frustrated with his behavior, and so overwhelmed it was hard to get ahead of the process. I was intensely grieving alone because I could not talk to him about missing him already. The ability to communicate or understand what is going on happened early. I would work hard to overcome and process my feelings, believing I was getting a grip on it, only to have it start anew with the next wave of losses.

Towards the end, I felt I had grieved almost all that I could. He was a shell of himself, suffering. I had reached a stage where we had done all we could do and when he was ready, I was ready to say goodbye. The end was a partial relief, knowing his pain was over, but it started another round of immense grief. Then, I also grieved the loss of my dreams of what I thought my future would look like. I was upended. I was no longer working and spent all of my time taking care of him, so in a way, I felt I also lost my "job."

I lost my spouse, my planned future, my focus in life, a good number of friends, and support with my kids, all because of this horrible disease.

Initially, I felt like I had PTSD. I was triggered by so many things. I couldn't handle large crowds without getting anxious. Sitting at restaurants and in public places where others were out, enjoying themselves would trigger sadness. The memories of his suffering were foremost in my mind.

Fast forward three years, and I have worked through the majority of my grief. When I think of Mat now, it's usually happy memories and gratitude for the good times we had together. I have let go of the anger I had towards any perceived abandonment. Some friendships I resumed, but most I did not. I have made new friends and found a new job, with ways to spend my days that bring me joy. I have found meaning in my losses and I use my experiences to help others. I have a new appreciation for living and loving in the moment. I have tried to learn what I can grow where I can, and let go of the rest. I do not beat myself up over what I could have done differently. I did the best I could. Not all can do this or do this as quickly as I have done.

I write this not to overwhelm you, but to encourage you to start early and get help. Don't make some of the same mistakes I did of trying to go it alone or to think that you have it covered when you may not. I made a list of things you must do, hoping to help you on your grief journey.

1. Get caregiving help early and increase it as your loved one's needs increase. Do not wait until you are overwhelmed. You may tend to want to save money because you don't know what the future may hold. Maybe you are holding on too tightly to providing the perfect care and won't let others help, or maybe you don't like asking others for help. Whatever is holding you back, work on overcoming it.

Even getting help once a week for a few hours, but recurring will be a huge help. Not doing so will be devastating. It is no exaggeration that the majority of healthy caregivers do not outlive their loved ones with dementia. My father-in-law, who was otherwise healthy before my mother-in-law's diagnosis, ended up on dialysis, living in a nursing home, and with vascular dementia within a year of her death. He almost passed away twice before her death. My intervention and getting him to a hospital was all that saved him or he would have been part of that statistic.

2. Find a good grief counselor AND a good support group (or someone who has been through this that you can talk to regularly). The number of people I have found who are not receptive to this is staggering. Finding a good counselor/group takes time. I had to go through several attempts before I eventually formed my group. It was worth the effort. In addition to emotional support, sharing tips and resources made it well worth the effort.

3. For heaven's sake be open to taking advice and trying new things with your loved one. They can not change their behavior. You can change the way you respond to them, or change things in your environment. Don't give up just because you don't see immediate relief. Keep making one change after another.

4. Put on your own oxygen mask first. Find a way to recharge your batteries. Schedule it and make it the first priority in scheduling your time. Don't neglect getting exercise and eating well. Find other outlets, be it a hobby, a girl's or boy's night out, a spa day, etc. When you are stressed you will respond negatively to your frustrations, causing a downward spiral in your loved one that will just intensify the complexity of caring for them well.

5. Watch out for ways in which you are bandaging your grief alcohol, sleeping too much, or shutting down emotionally for example. Even good things like exercising, or travel, can be used to numb the pain. Don't stop doing those good things but make sure you're being honest with yourself about what you're feeling so you can work through it with your counselor and support group.

6. Watch out for depression. It very likely will rear its ugly head and at least for me, it wasn't what I thought so I did not know I was depressed. It's not just being tired, or crying a lot. I was high functioning. It starts slowly and so much is changing that you are not aware that you aren't behaving like you used to. Depression can also be a foggy brain, inability to focus, and other ADD-like symptoms. See your doctor regularly and make sure to tell them how you are feeling and what your struggles are like so they can be on the lookout and prescribe medication if needed. Please get over your stigma of depression medication, if you have one. We take Tylenol when we have a headache and treatment for cancer and other illnesses. The brain is no different. There are plenty of non-addictive, mild medications that can help you dramatically. By all means you should exercise and do the non-medical things that will help you but we can not always pull ourselves up by our bootstraps. Medication may be what you need to be able to start doing these healthy things.

7. Try to find something to live for, that motivates and inspires you to get up each day. Maybe it's spending time with your grandchildren, or travel, or throwing yourself into volunteer work for the Alzheimer's Association. Yes, you're busy and overwhelmed but if you do not, you will find your desire to fight a new each day will become more

and more difficult. Tony has done an amazing thing. He sold his house and car. Now lives in an Independent Living Facility and uses the funds that he freed up to be able to hire help and continue to travel. He and I are running two half marathons, pushing his partner, Cat, as we go. It will be an adventure. I am sure I will be questioning my sanity as we run but also enjoying every moment of it. Let him and I inspire you to think outside of the box. I started a non-profit and threw myself into helping others. Tony has written two books now and routinely does podcasts. Yes, this disease brings so much sadness but every day you have an opportunity to get up and redefine what brings you joy, with whatever capabilities and assets your own story brings to the table.

8. Finally, be careful of bandaids that allow you to suppress what you are feeling, lulling you into a false sense of security. While sometimes we do need to push down our feelings to function, doing so over a prolonged period is problematic. Unfortunately, it's not over until you can one day look back on everything and truly see that you have processed and moved on from all the traumas that your loved one's illness, prolonged care, and death have thrown at you.

I wish you luck on your grief journey. I hope my story will inspire you that there is hope. Moving through grief is not easy and our goal is not to just "get over" the trauma but to thrive, and find life through all the phases. I pray that you can find ways to continue to live and experience life, even as you are caring for your sick loved one. Tony is quite an inspiration in that end as well. Let's throw away the mold of what caring for a loved one with dementia looks like. Find an accountability partner and start to work on making each day a better one.

I'll leave you with a favorite quote and one of Tony's that sums up our outtake on life.

"Life isn't finding shelter in the storm. It's learning to dance in the rain." "Life should NOT be a journey to the grave to arrive safely in an attractive and well-preserved body, but rather to skid in sideways, chocolate in one hand, margarita in the other, body thoroughly used up, totally worn out and screaming ~ WOO HOO what a ride!"

I pray that you will find ways to be able to say you did just these two things.

Tammy has some great suggestions which I will be sure to draw from down the road. Over the last year, she has given me some great pointers. For Cat and I, we plan to continue doing as much as we can for as long as we can.

I will close with this poem:

Do Not Stand at My Grave and Weep-Mary Elizabeth Frye

Do not stand at my grave and weep
I am not there. I do not sleep.
I am a thousand winds that blow.
I am the diamond glints on snow.
I am the sunlight on ripened grain.
I am the gentle autumn rain.
When you awaken in the morning's hush
I am the swift uplifting rush
Of quiet birds in circled flight.
I am the soft stars that shine at night.
Do not stand at my grave and cry;
I am not there. I did not die.

CHAPTER 40
Ten Years and Counting, More Goals to be Set
♦ ♦ ♦

"Expect the best. Prepare for the worst. Capitalize on what comes." ~Zig Ziglar

This final chapter will center around Cat and I's last half marathon state in Wisconsin on April 20, 2024. The other significance of this date is that she was diagnosed exactly 10 years ago. I know I have said this many times before, but this race will put Cat in a very small category of women who have done a marathon in all 50 states, all of the major world marathons, and at least a half marathon on all 7 continents. Cat also ran an Ultra Marathon in 2005 at the famous JFK 50-miler. She became an Iron Man in 2011. She was able to run 43 of the half marathon states and I in turn will have pushed her in the CatMobile for the final 7. All but this race she walked a 5K during the half marathons. More about that later. Of course, we will once again finish hand in hand.

First I needed to see if I could get another state checked off of my 10K list and Alabama seemed like the perfect place to do so. So off we were to a little town of Eufaula, AL. Once again a small park was selected by Mainly Marathons and this time the rain Gods decided to give me a break. It rained just before my start and picked up again after I was done. I planned to take it easy but the temperatures were perfect so I had a very respectful time while Cat and Tammy relaxed at the hotel.

I did indulge in some freshly made donuts at a nearby donut shop before our 3-hour drive over to Macon, GA for a practice 1/2 Marathon at Amerson River Park. Cat and I had been there once before over Christmas of 2022 just because we could. We walked the park on Christmas day as our Christmas presents to each other. Tammy had not run a half marathon in several years and thought it would be great to get a practice race under our feet while we took turns pushing Cat in the Catmobile and walking with her so she could once again get a 5K done. The race went off without a hitch and everyone there with Mainly Marathons were very supportive.

I learn something new every day. I had not heard, of "burns my biscuits" before. So while we were doing our walk breaks every 1/4 mile Tammy commented that it burns her biscuits and that she still had to jog during those walk breaks since my legs were so long. I have heard those types of complaints over the last 25 years. Early on when I walked most of our races because I was not in shape enough to run the entire race. Then again when I injured my right knee and had to race walk several races. For many years now I consistently take walk breaks. It helps to alleviate muscle fatigue. I kind of shuffle while I run but take nice long strides when I walk. Turns out the pace between the two is only 2 minutes per mile. With exactly a month between the practice race and our final half marathon, all I need to do now is nothing stupid. An injury this close in would be devastating.

I have asked a few people from Wisconsin what to expect the weather to be like and all have said it could be a beautiful spring day or it could snow. Not much I can do about the possibility of snow so I will do as this chapter title suggests and expect the best.

I have learned to be flexible and will adjust my plans accordingly if we get the worst.

We do have a couple of advantages when it comes to this race. The race does not start until 8 am and being an hour behind I should not have any problems getting Cat up ready and to the start line on time. When we travel back in time I usually keep our body clocks on East Coast time. The course looks pretty flat and since the race director knows what we are trying to accomplish doing this particular race I am sure they will be accommodating if we are a few minutes over the allotted 3 hours and 30 minutes time limit.

Simultaneously I am still putting together plans for what to do after this milestone. So far a visit to San Diego in May to see my newest grandson who made his arrival back in March. My daughter, Mariah, will be our Travel Companion for that trip. Roman was a little tyke when he came into the world but I hear he is taking after his dad, Aaron, and putting on the much-needed weight.

In June we are off to Tennessee for a 10K. State number 16. I will push Cat during this race and Heather, who also helps me care for Cat and also now travels with us is going to do her first 5K. A week later off to Cancun to celebrate.

After going back and forth in my mind I decided to check off Marathon 69 in Minnesota shortly after I turned 69. That will only leave 7 states for me to get all 50 done. I decided not to push Cat the entire race but will at least push her 6.2 miles, the distance of a 10k. I will build up over time for me to be able to push her during my last Marathon State whenever that might be. Heather and Cat can walk some amongst the Mainly Marathon family while I do a few out and backs by myself.

We then will be off to San Juan later that month to celebrate, once again. We have fond memories of getting on a Windstar Cruise ship there several times back when we were nomads.

In August we will probably go to Cincinnati to see my other son, Shawn, and his family. Of course, I have an eye on a 10k race while there. Not sure where to after that but it will be the fall race season so I am sure there is another 10k with my name on it.

Once again Tammy's heated jacket came in handy for Cat with a feels-like temperature in the 20s the entire race. The constant 15 mph wind with gusts in the 20s we flirted with the worst. Layers and plenty of them were the only way to survive. Out of respect Cat and I both wore our Antarctica T-shirts. There we also had to contend with snow flurries back in 2017. This was also reminiscent of what we had to deal with when Cat got her 50th state as a marathon in Narrassate RI back in 2020.

This was the largest field of runners for a race in many years, with 3000 runners for all 4 races. The saying misery loves company comes to mind. They warned us that the parking lots close to the start would fill up so we arrived an hour prior and stayed in the warm car until the last possible moment.

My biggest fear was that to stay warm I would forgo our planned walk breaks. I did that once before and that did not work out so well as I got into oxygen debt early on. Not a problem here since we went uphill for the first half mile. I remember the days when my parents would say they had to walk uphill both ways in the snow to and from school. No snow here but this out-and-back course mostly on the Oak Leaf paved trail system adjacent to the Milwaukee River reminded me of the often-heard comment. On the way out I was looking forward to the downhill with a tail wind but when we turned around it also seemed like we were going uphill and of course, the wind died down. Looking on the bright side at least it was a sunny day.

Cat had a great time smiling, laughing, and cheering on the runners and spectators. She was able to walk a mile of the course

1/4 mile at a time and we once again walked across the finish this time arm and arm to the cheering fans.

Many people have asked me if I have lost my mind with all the expenses and logistics of doing races like this. Airfare, rental car, hotel, travel companion, and meals do add up. On top of that the logistics of transporting the Cat Mobile keeps things interesting. My thoughts always come back to the fact that if this keeps Cat's brain talking to her body it is all worth it in the long run. Pun intended. Not only that but seeing the smile I fell in love with was icing on the cake.

As you can see I have left no stone unturned during this arduous journey with Cat as we navigated the maze of Early-onset Alzheimer's. For the first 7 or so years it was to find a cure while at the same time finding those gems of joy all over the world. I have learned a lot about myself during this process and hopefully, these lessons learned will pay benefits throughout my life.

I do have one regret. I took thousands of pictures of Cat and us throughout our travels. We watch them often on our TV via the Amazon Fire Stick and have many medals and pictures throughout our apartment and they even adorn the space outside our apartment door. The one regret is that I have very few videos that fully capture her personality. Unfortunately, ALZ is taking that bigger-than-life personality away from me day by day.

So I encourage everyone to also take videos of their loved ones now and then. I do have a professional 15-minute short film which was done back in February 2022. I still get choked up every time I watch it and sometimes Cat watches for a bit when she hears my voice since I narrate during the film. Maybe our story will one day make it to the big screen. I wish I had some videos before the diagnosis or at least early on.

We still listen to our first book on Audible during road trips by car and plan on using the Speechify application to listen to this book when it is done. With that application, you can copy and paste text, go to websites, and have the application read the article to you. It can read entire documents as files as I will do in this case.

Cat turns 63 on May 1st, 2024. When we first got the diagnosis back in 2014 I had very few reference points to draw on in terms of the time horizon before she would succumb to ALZ. Her father had vascular dementia in his early 70's and passed away 2 years later. Other experiences gave me the impression that it was a disease for the much older generation. I had only a few reference points for Early-onset Alzheimer's so we initially thought it would be 2 years.

We packed in as many races and destinations as possible for the first 2 years. After that date came and went we selected 5 years which coincided with how long my savings would last at our then-current cash burn rate per day. Early on as a stretch goal I had my eye on the Kentucky Derby on her 60th birthday seven years after diagnosis. So I started making plans to attend.

We had a great time celebrating her birthday at the derby so another goal was set. That being, 10 years since diagnosis. The average is 8 years with a life expectancy range of 2-20 years. They say Early Onset Alzheimer's is a bit more aggressive so I am unsure what exactly that means in relationship to life expectancy.

We concentrate on quality and let the quantity of life take care of itself. I feel that I have done the very best that I can to provide Cat the best life possible under these circumstances and in my humble opinion better than most on both fronts. You can see, as the title of this chapter suggests we have, so far, capitalized on what came our way.

I will now do all that is possible to be able to celebrate her 65th birthday in 2 years. I am sure I will come up with some fantastic destination or race or both on that day.

As you have read Cat's abilities decreased from running marathons all over the world to walking as much as she can when she can and the relevance to how now we are holding on to footsteps as long as we can. People are often amazed at how well Cat can still walk despite the disease's progression. Some days are much better and she can walk longer than others. The CatMobile or a version of it will always be there with me sometimes just so I can take my own footsteps as we continue to see and experience as much as we can.

I now have 4 fabulous ladies who work about 20 hours a week combined. It gives me the ability to take time for myself and thus take care of myself. Two of them are willing to invest their time towards Cat as paid Travel Companions as we continue to achieve goals and set new ones at the same time. Someone once told me that if you don't ask for help people assume that you don't need it. Over the last two years, I have managed to reframe my brain to the point that I do not hesitate to ask for help.

In an earlier chapter, I talked briefly about how I do not look at Alzheimer's as a death sentence but more of a life lesson, something that you can use for the rest of your life even after your loved one is gone.

Here are a few of the life lessons I have learned.

- Patience

  They say patience is a virtue. I have learned that in this case, it is a necessity.

- Flexibility

  Raising my three kids I learned to be flexible but caring for someone with ALZ I have learned that you have to add flexibility to the daily plan.

- How to look for gems of joy

  They are everywhere and I have learned to be more aware of their existence daily.

- That my will is stronger than I thought possible
  There have been times when I thought I was way over my head but each time I was able to find the inner strength to move forward.
- Some things you just can't do on your own.
  Early on I tried to do everything myself but realized that asking for help is not a sign of weakness.
- You are not being selfish if you take care of yourself.
  So much has been said about taking care of oneself. In actuality, for me to be there for Cat I must take care of myself.
- Do all that is necessary to keep my brain as healthy as possible
  I have learned so much about this disease through research and experience. I will use both to position myself in a way not to be affected by this dreadful disease.
- If at first, you don't succeed try and try again.
  We have heard this so many times growing up but, in this case, it rings true since things that worked before might not work today and vice versa.

I will close with this notable Quote by Eugene Bell Jr.: "Aspire to Inspire before you Expire!"

The simple meaning of this is that one should learn something and stand as an inspiration to at least one individual in life before its ends. I have modified it somewhat to add my personal touch.

I aspire to inspire till I expire.

For me, to inspire others is one of my many goals. The small change I make to this quote reflects my desire and goal to do this every day to anyone I can as long as I live. I hope this and my first book have done just that. I will continue to write to my blog, RunningwithCat.com, do podcast interviews, and as always, I am willing to talk to anyone interested in hearing about our often joyous and inspiring journey together with Early Onset Alzheimer's.

Milwaukee, Wisconsin
April 20, 2024

Milwaukee, Wisconsin
April 20, 2024

ABOUT THE AUTHOR

Anthony L. Copeland-Parker was a professional Pilot/Manager for thirty-seven years, the last twenty-seven with United Parcel Service. His last job had him managing pilots and flying B757/767-type aircraft all over the world. When he retired, he began writing his blog, RunningwithCat.com. Since then, he and his partner Catherine have traveled to eighty-two different countries. They have run at least a half-marathon in thirty-five countries and on all seven continents. This is his third book, the first being Running All Over the World, Our Race Against Early Onset Alzheimer's, published by Newman Springs Publishing. The second is an abridged version published by Morgan James Publishing.

Spring, Texas
January 2, 2021